# Education, Training and the Global Economy

# Education, Training and the Global Economy

David Ashton

*Professor of Sociology and Director*
*Centre for Labour Market Studies*
*University of Leicester, UK*

*and*

Francis Green

*Professor of Economics*
*University of Kent at Canterbury, UK*

**Edward Elgar**
Cheltenham, UK • Northampton, MA, USA

Published by
Edward Elgar Publishing Limited
Glensanda House
Montpellier Parade
Cheltenham
Glos GL50 1UA, UK

Edward Elgar Publishing, Inc.
6 Market Street
Northampton
Massachusetts 01060, USA

Paperback edition 1997
Cased edition reprinted 1997
Paperback edition reprinted 1999


**British Library Cataloguing in Publication Data**
Ashton, D. N. (David Norman), 1942–
    Education, training and the global economy
    1. Labor supply – Effect of education on  2. Education
    3. Economics
    I. Title  II. Green, Francis
    331.1'142

**Library of Congress Cataloguing in Publication Data**
Ashton, D. N.
    Education, training, and the global economy / David Ashton and
Francis Green.
    Includes bibliographical references and index.
    1. Economic development—Effect of education on. I. Green,
Francis. II. Title
    HD75.7.A84 1996
    338.9—dc20                                                95–42418
                                                               CIP
ISBN 1 85278 970 0 (cased)
     1 85278 973 5 (paperback)


Printed in Great Britain at the University Press, Cambridge

# Contents

# Tables

# Acknowledgements

Several busy people have kindly taken the time to read parts of early drafts of this book in its long period of gestation. We should specifically like to thank Peter Dolton, Christine Greenhalgh, Gerry Makepeace, Geoff Mason and Paul Ryan for their helpful comments and suggestions. A special debt of gratitude is owed to Paul Auerbach who contributed numerous points of improvement in style and substance, after being subjected by ourselves to virtually the whole manuscript at various stages. Johnny Sung is also to be thanked for his many insights into the institutions and procedures of Singapore and other Pacific Rim economies, which he has generously shared with us. Finally, John Hillard has been immensely helpful in the final stages of producing this manuscript and we are very grateful for this. Naturally, the usual disclaimers apply: we must take full responsibility for the product.

# Acronyms and Abbreviations

| | |
|---|---|
| ASEAN | Association of South East Asian Nations |
| BEST | Basic Education for Skills Training |
| DOT | Dictionary of Occupational Titles |
| EDB | Economic Development Board |
| ET | Education and Training |
| FPC | Formation Professionelle Continue |
| GED | General Educational Development |
| HRD | Human Resource Development |
| ILM | Internal Labour Market |
| ITE | Institute of Technical Education (previously VITB) |
| JAM | Job classifications, Adversarial relations, Minimal training |
| LEC | Local Enterprise Company |
| MITI | Ministry of International Trade and Industry |
| MNC | Multinational Corporation |
| MOST | Modular Skills Training Programme |
| NPB | National Productivity Board |
| NTUC | National Trades Union Congress |
| NIDL | New International Division of Labour |
| NIE | Newly Industrialised Economy |
| OECD | Organisation for Economic Cooperation and Development |
| OJT | On-The-Job Training |
| Off-JT | Off-The-Job Training |
| PIC | Private Industry Council |
| POCADS | Personnel Office Care Deployment Systems |
| SDF | Skills Development Fund |
| SET | Security, Employee involvement, Training |
| SME | Small and Medium Sized Enterprises |
| SVP | Specific Vocational Preparation |
| TEC | Training and Enterprise Council |

| | |
|---|---|
| VET | Vocational Education and Training |
| VITB | Vocational and Industrial Training Board (later re-named ITE) |
| YTS | Youth Training Scheme |

# 1  Introduction and Overview: Capitalism and Skill Formation

At no time in the history of capitalism has the education and training of the workforce assumed such widespread importance as at the present conjuncture. Whenever and wherever capitalism has made its great forward leaps in human productivity, it has done so on the basis of primitive accumulations of riches, of devastating exploitation of human labour, of revolutionary technological changes and alterations in the accepted patterns of work, or through the appropriation of vast accumulations of raw material wealth. Rarely if ever has the education of the large majority of the workforce been seen as the central lever of economic growth. Now, however, as twentieth century capitalism draws to a close, a new consensus is emerging among politicians of many different persuasions, among scholarly writers and among popular feeling, a consensus that the salience of a nation's education and training system is becoming the key item in the struggle for competitive superiority.

The concern with education and training is by no means confined to a few specially successful countries. Across the industrialised world, and in many developing countries too, the thought is paramount that the way to economic growth is via skill formation to raise labour productivity and hence average living standards. The search for better institutions for fostering skill formation preoccupies policy-makers. They scour their home-grown ideologies for solutions to the problem, and they look abroad to see what can be learned from other 'competitor nations', to borrow new policies or to provide benchmarks for their own. Often the grass is seen to be greener on the other side of the national border-fence. Curiously, nations even decide sometimes to borrow policies that do not work particularly well in the nation whence they are borrowed.

Perhaps the chief reason why education and training have penetrated the popular agenda in so many countries and to such an extent, is the expected link between improving the education and training system and raising general living standards. This is not to deny that there are far wider, and to some people more profound, outcomes of a decent education, than merely an improved chance of finding employment and a larger wage packet. Education for citizenship, or for personal self-fulfilment in this life, have

1

always been and should remain central to the objectives of any desirable skill formation system. It is possible that, with new-found affluence, there is a rising demand for the kind of liberation that education can bring to life, though to assert that would not do justice to the fervent aspirations of many earlier writers of this and the last century who have pressed education's claims. In this book, however, our canvas is not so broad: we are going to look almost exclusively at the economics of the matter. Specifically, our subject is the link between modern education and training systems and modern capitalist economies.

One might think that, since almost everyone apparently agrees that more education and training is good for the modern economy, the only question to discuss is how most efficiently to raise the standards of the education and training system. The reason for writing this book is our dissatisfaction with both the theory and the evidence which currently underpins the consensus viewpoint. On the one hand, without denying the salience of education and training in the current era, there are severe limitations in the way that their impact on economic performance is conceived. Typically, education and training are seen to improve performance in an unproblematic manner, by making people more productive workers. There is hardly scope, in much of the writing on this issue, for an understanding of how some forms of skill formation have much more impact on performance for some groups of workers than for others. Nor indeed can the somewhat simplistic consensus conceive that, in large swathes of seemingly still successful industrial capitalism, there are distinctly low limits on the demands placed on the education and training system by employers, without resorting to the saving tactic of believing that those employers must be ill-informed or irrational. Commonly, training systems are seen as institutions designed to improve the lot of all parties, be they workers or companies of whatever kind; but little notice is taken of the fact that such systems are frequently the object of intense conflict.

On the other hand, despite an increasing effort on the part of empirical researchers, there remain enormous gaps in the knowledge of the magnitude of any links between skill formation and economic performance. If, for instance, improved skill formation is theorised to raise the long-term profits of capitalist enterprises, this remains at the level of belief rather than demonstrated fact. If an improvement in the university education systems of the advanced industrialised countries is said to be a way of raising its economic growth, there remains scant direct evidence for this proposition, despite recent improvements in long-term data on economic growth. If employers are held to be demanding ever-increasing levels of skills in their workforces, the backing for this is at best incomplete and imprecise because of fuzziness over what is actually meant by 'skill', and at worst lacking altogether.

Although there is this belief that the link between the economic system and skill formation is at its strongest in the modern day, there remains an urgent need for more understanding of the connections that make up this link, both for theoretical clarification and for more resources to be devoted to gaining adequately informed empirical knowledge. Perhaps the largest gap in our current knowledge pertains to just that area of the world where high levels of investment in education and training are now believed to be of particular significance in sustaining a historically astonishing pace of economic development, namely the newly industrialised economies of the Pacific Rim. Most analyses hitherto have concentrated on western and Japanese forms of capitalism.

## OVERVIEW OF THE ARGUMENT OF THE BOOK

At its briefest the consensus argument for education and training goes something like this. There has, it is said, been an intensification of international competition brought about by the integration of the world's economies into one global economy, and by modern forms of technology which are primarily 'knowledge-based', that is, intensive in the use of conceptual skills. This has led older forms of production, especially those based on Fordist mass production technologies and associated forms of work organisation, to become inefficient by comparison with newer forms that utilise the skills of the full range of the workforce, rather than just those of an elite managerial caste. These twin forces of global integration and technical change have rendered education and training of paramount importance in the competitive process. The central issue for discussion in each and every industrialised country is therefore taken to be the manner in which the education and training system can be improved and skills raised. More and better skills, so the argument goes, and prosperity will follow. Policy debates, and much scholarly discussion, begin from this point.

The first set of chapters, 2 to 4, constitute in effect a sustained theoretical and empirical investigation of this simplistic consensus. We argue that the consensus is deficient in four general ways. First, it is incorrect to assume a linear and automatic connection between skill formation and economic performance. In Chapter 2 we examine a range of theoretical perspectives on this connection. The most important finding is that the link between skills and performance has to be seen in its social context. The context both influences the strength of the link, and helps to determine the variables of interest, especially the nature of skill. Furthermore, it emerges that education and training have to be understood as areas of potential conflict: both political conflict at the level of national or international politics and more localised conflict in terms of industrial relations systems. These factors imply that the neoclassical economic theory of skill acquisition, which couches the argument in terms of individualistic utility functions, and going under the name of 'human capital theory', has severe limitations as to the breadth of its applicability: it only makes sense when the social parameters of the education and training situation remain constant.

For many purposes, therefore, we prefer to include also the insights of sociologists and political scientists who theorise how the institutional context can influence the salience of skill formation systems. Nevertheless, even these approaches appear to be locked into the belief that better education and training would be voted for by all parties concerned if only we could remove the institutional barriers. We question whether this is necessarily so, and argue that there may still be a strong case as far as businesses are concerned for placing strict limits on the amount spent on raising the skill levels of their workforces in certain parts of the industrialised world. We also call for a more sophisticated understanding of the role of nation states in these matters. Rather than seeing the state as some kind of resultant of the manifold interests of the populace or of multiple interest groups (the pluralist model) we take it to be an arena of political conflict. The actions of the state can sometimes best be understood as the outcome of that conflict. In particular, we develop the argument that the state in the Pacific Rim countries has been especially important in the skill formation process, and link this role to the needs of the ruling classes of those nations to legitimise their position.

The second way in which we find that the simplistic consensus is deficient concerns the 'hard' empirical evidence about links between education, training and economic performance. Chapter 3 contributes a wide-ranging review of the evidence, the conclusion of which is that, despite the accumulation of a considerable number of studies, there remain significant areas of ignorance (such as those mentioned above). Part of the reason for this ignorance concerns the complex statistical and econometric problems involved in arriving at a scientifically acceptable standard of evidence. In particular, the data requirements of an ideal investigation are almost always far beyond what is normally available, either because of prohibitive cost in terms of the resources available to researching communities, or because in the very nature of the matter the data could never be collected (for example, if the companies which might be the source of the data simply do not themselves know how much they devote to skill formation, it may be virtually impossible for researchers to find out even if they have unrestricted access to company records and personnel, which they normally would not). The empirical evidence upon which we can reasonably rely shows that there are strong and robust connections between education and training experiences and economic performance measured in certain ways. In particular, the link between education and wages is perhaps one of the most robust empirical findings in economics. But, it is also clear that not all forms of training lead to higher wages or productivity, and that the links with profitability or with economic growth are still largely in the realm of theoretical belief or just plain hope.

Third, we take issue with the simplistic notion of a globally integrated economy, and more especially with the associated notion that there is an ever greater convergence of national economies within that integrated whole. In Chapter 4 we briefly chart some of the major macroeconomic developments across the world, and consider the econometric and other evidence for convergence of national economic systems. We conclude that there remains substantial diversity, even though there have been periods, especially after the second world war, of catching up with the leading nation, the United States. There is also no evidence that convergence among countries is an accelerating trend of recent decades. In the light of this, and in the light of our theoretical arguments about the social context of skill formation, there is little alternative to beginning an empirical search to discover more about skill trends across different parts of the globe. This is the fourth area in which the simplistic consensus about the skills needed for the modern economy is inadequate. There are some key questions for investigation here: in principle it should be possible to understand the pattern of skill levels and changes in terms of the theories we have reviewed, relating those trends to the institutions of the various countries and to the changes in those institutions. But despite the obvious importance of this question, there is remarkably little evidence with which to substantiate or refute any existing theories about deskilling or up-skilling of workforces, or about the pattern of polarisation of skills. We have attempted instead, however, to review methods of measuring skill levels and trends, and provided for the first time (to our knowledge) an international overview of the findings of this relatively limited literature. We also use this part of Chapter 4 to set the stage for the ensuing chapters, where we begin to examine the process of skill formation in specific countries.

If, in the face of an increasingly internationalised economy, there persists a substantial diversity in both skill formation systems and more generally in national economic systems, how can we explain this diversity? This is too big a question to be answered here, but we attempt instead a more limited objective. We propose, in Chapter 5, a theory of skill formation systems. Building on a number of the theories that we had discussed earlier, we first consider the national institutional requirements for successfully pursuing a high-skill 'route to accumulation', that is, a period of relatively successful economic growth and development lasting at least a decade, based on the predominant usage of high-level skills in high-value-added production technologies. We hypothesise that if the institutional requirements are found not to be fulfilled, it is more likely that the nation will follow a low-skill route. The requirements are: that the ruling political elites should be firmly committed to the high-skill route, and that they effect this commitment both in their general management of the economy and in their support of the education system; that a sufficient majority of employers is also committed to both demanding high skills from their workforces and providing the means for acquisition of workplace skills on the job; that there is an adequate regulatory system to control both the quality and the quantity of workplace training; that there are sufficiently comprehensive incentives for virtually all young people and workers to acquire and to continue to acquire skills; and finally that the education and training system is sufficiently developed to allow workers to achieve a mix of on-the-job and off-the-job training. An important aspect of this approach is that it refers both to the supply side of the skills equation (i.e. the education and training institutions) and to the demand side (i.e. the factors that condition the skill demands made by employers). Another important feature is that they incorporate imperatives drawn from several disciplines, combining the recognition of the need for economic incentives, of the satisfaction of psychological premises for learning, of the political prerequisites for the successful functioning of institutions and of the necessary social framework for skill formation.

Next comes the deeper and more complex part of the question: how are these institutions formed? We concentrate in this book on the most crucial, but perhaps also the most difficult aspect of this question, namely the origins of the commitment to high skill formation. We develop an account of the routes along which high levels of commitment to skill formation are reached. We take a broad historical approach, which sees this commitment as deriving from two interdependent but relatively autonomous processes, those of state formation and industrialisation. There are very long-lasting legacies in this area of skill formation institutions, if only simply because education systems typically enjoy considerable autonomy from developments elsewhere in society. In particular, we suggest that the education and training system that is set up at the time a country becomes industrialised sets the tone for the subsequent character of the system. The motivation for developing a national education system need have nothing directly to do with economic requirements, and indeed in a number of cases it was international relations and associated military requirements that pressed the case for education. In some cases, particularly in the United Kingdom and in the United States, the need for a national education system was not based primarily on the demands of the economy at the time of industrialisation. With the exception of the managerial classes, from which at an early stage in the US there grew a significant demand for higher education, both countries industrialised on the basis of quite poorly educated working classes. We draw the contrast with Germany and Japan, two countries which we characterise as broadly on a high-skill route, where at the time of industrialisation the ruling elites saw particular merit in developing the education, including the technical skills, of the working classes. Subsequent developments of the system derive from the continuing processes of state formation and industrial development as the productive system moves to higher stages of technological development. We also point here, for the first time, to the impact of the late industrialisation of the countries of the Pacific Rim, and to the evident link to systems of high-skill formation. We argue that this is, in effect, an aspect of the programme of the 'developmental states' in this region, places where the ruling elites derive their legitimation from economic development.

The succeeding two chapters work this argument out, through an examination of the specific historical development of skill formation systems in five countries. As examples of the origins of low skill routes to accumulation we consider in Chapter 6 the origins of skill formation institutions in the UK and the US, since these two countries are most commonly considered as falling into this category. There are good grounds for accepting this premise in the case of the UK, but in the US the characterisation of that nation as on a low skills path seems less than adequate. As is discussed in Chapter 4, there is an astonishing polarisation developing in the living standards of Americans, and this is likely a reflection of polarisation of skills. While quite large numbers have access to further or higher education, many millions find themselves limited to poorly paid jobs with conditions worsening by the year, and little evidence of an increase in their work skills. In both the US and the UK we find that the historical approach has much to recommend it as a basis for understanding the present conjuncture in these countries.

Chapter 7 tackles the high-skill routes, starting first with the better-known examples of Germany and Japan. There are several references throughout this book to these countries as exemplars of particular institutional solutions to the problems of skill formation systems. In this chapter we apply the same historical method to provide the framework for understanding why these institutions have arisen. It will be apparent that they have not necessarily arisen through some brilliant far-sighted strategy on the part of the ruling classes of those nations, but have emerged as the outcome of a conflictual process, a struggle for power and wealth both within those nations and with competing nations. We also in this chapter devote space to a much less well-known exemplar, namely Singapore. In that relatively small country of about three million people, a system of skill formation has developed over the last few decades which has, we argue, provided a new model of a successful skill formation system, not the same as either the German model with all its rich institutional controls or the Japanese model based on a highly competitive education system and enterprise-based intensive training and skill formation. The Singapore model is chiefly characterised by a high level of integration of human resource planning with interventionist trade and industrial policy-making. Because this is relatively unfamiliar territory, we go into the way this system works in some detail.

## METHOD

Before proceeding with the substance we wish to clarify two aspects of the methodology we are here adopting. Most importantly, we have attempted to avoid prescriptive language, and aim for an analysis of systems interpretable in the light of theory. Thus we have tried to avoid a normative tone that implicitly assumes that the reader shares the same objectives as ourselves with respect to education and training systems and the economy. In particular, we have not advocated specific policy measures. In part this is because our scope is global and a portion of our argument is that policies would have to be interpreted in their national institutional context. But it is also because, even in considering the institutional requirements for high levels of skill formation, we find that there are generally conflicts involved, a political resolution of which is needed before any policies can have a fertile context in which to bear fruit.

Second, it will be obvious and sometimes explicit that our approach is interdisciplinary. It is perhaps unsurprising, but nevertheless disappointing, that social scientists have not hitherto come together on many issues of importance to people's welfare at work. Debates on education and training are no exception, and while economists, educationalists, historians, political scientists, psychologists and sociologists, have all contributed many insights to the role of education and training in modern society, it is comparatively rare for these insights to be woven together. We do not claim to have achieved a perfect weave, one that might include the best that every school has to offer in one all-embracing theory. But we have consciously attempted to blend insights from a number of different disciplines.[1] The reader will find, therefore, a range of concepts and techniques within the book. The central methodological approach shelters under the rubric of 'political economy', as interpreted in the Western tradition to refer to a broadly materialist analysis of social phenomena.[2] This unifying methodology should avoid the charge of mere eclecticism, picking and choosing our bits of explanations from here and there. Under the umbrella of political economy we employ the various methods of the econometrician, the economist, the historian and the sociologist, but our analysis remains guided by the signposts marked out in the institutionalist and marxist traditions. In addition, we adopt also the method of international comparisons. This is a rarely theorised but growing method, which by virtue of necessity is usually interdisciplinary, and which we believe to be of value in understanding the institutions of different countries. It is increasingly used in the field of labour market and skill formation analyses because these institutions tend to have nationally specific characteristics, and therefore provide interesting benchmarks by means of which systems may be evaluated. In that sense, the method is akin to the popular management technique of benchmarking a company's structures and performance against those of another more successful one.

Finally breaking with our previously avowedly neutral stance on the rights and wrongs of education and training systems, we might ask in conclusion whether the analysis provides any firm conclusions as to the policies that a government might adopt. Assuming that a high-skill route to accumulation is to be the strategy, what is it possible for governments to do? We tackle this question in the final chapter of the book. This policy analysis is of necessity brief since it is an outcome of our theory that all policies must be evaluated in specific national contexts. But two points are worth stating, even here before the analysis begins. First, it is not impossible for countries to consider borrowing or mimicking the policy solutions of other countries, for example by devising similar regulatory institutions, but it is absolutely necessary to consider these policies in their new context, and if necessary adapt them to suit that context. Second, it does seem worthwhile for policy analysts to consider the alternative solutions to the problems of skill formation now being forged in the Pacific Rim, rather than the perpetual inward-looking search for traditional Western solutions. In particular, the East Asian solutions may be showing a model which is superior in economic terms for the current era. Even if that remains unproven, it remains the best available model for the rapid transformation of agrarian into industrialised economies and then to relatively high-skill economies, which makes it of special potential for developing countries still approaching these stages.

## NOTES

1. No doubt our own subject disciplines – respectively, sociology and economics – colour the mix that we have come up with.
2. To be specific, we do not mean the sort of political economy practised in Eastern Europe before the fall of communism, being identified with Stalinism.  Nor, on the other hand, do we mean the more restricted sort of Western political economy which defines its scope as understanding the actions of the state from an economic point of view, usually a neoclassical economic angle.

# 2 Education, Training and Industrialised Economies

The world's most successful economies over the past two decades have given a high priority to education, skills and training as vital factors in their economic success. (The Australian Minister for Employment, Education and Training, quoted in OECD, 1989)

The future now belongs to societies that organize themselves for learning. What we know and can do holds the key to economic progress just as command of natural resources once did ... The prize will go to those countries that are organized as national learning systems, and where all institutions are organized to learn and to act on what they learn. (Marshall and Tucker, 1992: xiii)

Economists, educationalists, sociologists and political scientists have all, in recent times, recognised the importance of different countries' education and training systems. They have brought to bear a range of analytical perspectives on education and training systems and on their links with economic systems in the advanced industrialised world. In some cases this link is conceived in quite simple terms: conventional wisdom has emerged, wherein 'better' education or training is assumed to lead automatically to improved economic performance. There is, however, a danger that any perspective drawn from within a closed disciplinary boundary is liable to be misconceived, and hence to convey flawed policy conclusions. This danger is heightened when the diversity of commentary makes it likely that many writers are unaware of the perspectives taken on the same problem by other writers in different fields.

We shall examine in this chapter a range of prominent perspectives on the education and training system and its relation to the economic system. We shall show that, despite the respective strengths of these approaches, each leads to an oversimplified and, in some cases, unduly linear conception of the relation. This will pave the way for a presentation of our own preferred approach, which builds on the strengths of the existing multidisciplinary perspectives, but which adopts a dialectical and a dynamic approach. We argue that only with this more complex approach is it possible to begin to understand developments in education and training policy across the world.

11

# THE LIBERAL APPROACH TO EDUCATION AND TRAINING SYSTEMS

We begin with what we will term the liberal approach, since this is the most widely held.  By 'liberal' we refer here to the large range of commentators driven by the philosophy that, while individuals are normally best left to their own devices in the market place, the state has an important role to play in ensuring that the market works and that there is equal opportunity for all people to participate in the market – and hence that there is an efficient and productive education and training system. President Clinton's programme to boost education and training in the United States is an apt example.  The programme built on an influential body of analysis linking productivity problems in the US economy to shortcomings in the US education system (Commission on the Skills of the American Workforce, 1990; Dertouzos *et al.*, 1989; Johnston and Packer, 1987; Marshall, 1990; Marshall and Tucker, 1992; Reich, 1988; Thurow, 1993).  The conclusions of this analysis were entirely in tune with the liberal establishment.[1] As *Business Week* (17 December 1990) reported:

> Workers must get as much schooling as possible, demand broader duties on the job, and take on more responsibility for the company's success.  Americans, in short, must revolutionize the way they organize, manage, and carry out work, or their jobs will disappear in the fast-paced global economy.  But this new industrial America may not outlast its infancy unless the US vastly improves public education and creates a national apprenticeship system.

Fitting within this general liberal perspective lie two important distinct approaches to the education and training system: that of the educationalist and that of the mainstream economist (that is, the human capital theorist).

## The Institutional Architecture of Education and Training Systems

Underlying much of the recent educational debate in many countries has been an assumption about the economic importance of improving education and training provision, even if many issues do not appear to have an obvious direct bearing on economic performance.[2]  Most prominent in this regard has been the issue of what is an effective institutional architecture for the vocational education and training system, and how it is articulated with the labour market.  Attention is drawn to the various ways in which vocational education and training is delivered in various countries (Cantor, 1989; OECD, 1985; Caillods, 1994; CEDEFOP, 1984).  As regards initial vocational education and training, three models can be identified. In the 'dual' model, exemplified in Germany but found also in Switzerland and Austria, young people leave school but enrol in apprenticeships that involve continued general and vocational education away from the job. In the 'schooling' model, found ideally in such places as Belgium, Sweden, Japan or North America, vocational education is provided in schools up to age 18. And in the 'mixed' model, exemplified by Britain, vocational education is provided for youths outside the schools in a non-formal sector (Furth, 1985). Within the schooling model it is possible to distinguish further between the separatist approach exemplified in France, with its distinct vocational schools, and the integrated model found in Sweden, where academic and vocational education are combined within one institution, (the two types are however separately streamed, and pupils are largely confined to one or another stream) (Green, 1991).

The purpose of such cross-country institutional comparisons is to identify common problems and issues for policy. It is evident that some models are more successful than others in attracting higher participation of young people in education or training. Low participation rates in the UK and New Zealand, for example, are linked with the confinement of their schools largely to academic education. And the differences in participation between males and females are more pronounced in systems that rely more on post-school training, such as apprenticeships, rather than on vocational education within schools (Furth, 1985).[3]

There can be little quarrel here with the general importance that the liberal educationalist attaches to education and training in today's economies. However, the theory which informs this analysis is thin. It does not examine the underlying principles for organising a training system, for example market or planning principles. Caillods (1994), for example, provides a useful description of vocational education and training (VET) systems in many parts of the globe, but finds it hard to identify converging trends (apart from an expansion of education), or any link between VET architectures and levels of economic development. On its own the description of education and training institutions tells us nothing about the salience of the different forms that training programmes take. For this we must look to some conventional economic techniques for empirical enlightenment. Moreover the analysis is 'institution free', in that it assumes that the economy and society can benefit from good skill formation programmes no matter what kind of industrial relations and other socioeconomic contexts prevail. There is nothing to embed the organisational description in an adequate social or economic theory.[4]

## The Theory of Human Capital or of Capital Humans[5]

Mainstream economics has provided us with both the techniques and a theoretical framework with which to resolve the issue of the economic effectiveness of various skill formation programmes and institutions. Thus, the theory of human capital constitutes the economists' complement to the liberal educationalist approach.

At its simplest, human capital theory amounts to the proposition that education or training can be regarded as investments with future material pay-offs, analogously to investments in physical capital. It is common to refer to the authority of that most famous of liberals, Adam Smith:

> When any expensive machine is erected, the extraordinary work to be performed by it ... will replace the capital laid out upon it, with at least the ordinary profits. A man educated at the expense of much labour and time to any of those employments which require extraordinary dexterity and skill may be compared to one of those expensive machines. The work which he learns to perform, it must be expected, over and above the usual wages of common labour, will replace to him the whole expense of his education, with at least the ordinary profits of an equally valuable capital ... The difference between the wages of skilled labour and those of common labour, is founded upon this principle. (Smith, 1888: 46)

Such a citation is, however, tinged with irony for a distinctive aspect of Smith's theory of economic growth was that education and training played little or no part in it.[6] The detailed in-plant division of labour, which he so eloquently advocated, rendered most jobs unskilled and cheap, while apprenticeships he viewed as outdated hindrances to trade. Smith remained a firm supporter of state education aimed at minimising the costs of economic growth, as a compensation for the social degradation that accompanied a manufacturing society (Smith, 1888: 350–53) – an apt reminder that any link between the economy and the education and training system is contingent on prevailing institutions and technologies. It was only much later in the development of economic thought, in changed circumstances, that a broad economic purpose for widespread education and training was recognised through the work of J.S. Mill and later Alfred Marshall (Bowman, 1990). Later still, and into modern times, it fell to Becker (1964) to systematise the theory within the individualistic framework of neoclassical economics. He thereby made education economics respectable by transforming it from the sidelines into a key aspect of capital theory.

Human capital theory proposes an unproblematic link between the stock of skills and the outputs of a productive system, wherein the human capital input has equal status with the physical capital input, with the only proviso that human capital cannot be sold by its owner (except in a slave society). Individuals and firms are then said to respond to the incentives engendered by this relationship.   This response is driven by the calculus of a conventional individualistic optimisation process, with appropriate discounting of future income benefits.   The division of the costs and benefits of training between firms and employees depends, in a world of full information,[7] on how general or how job-specific are the skills being produced: general training is likely to be funded by employees but specific training costs may be shared.

Human capital theory provides a theory of the individual's demand for education and training.   Aggregating to the whole of society, an independent but similar framework has developed within sociology to explain society's demand for increased education and training, both for investment and for consumption purposes.   This theory is part of the 'convergence' thesis, proposed to explain the institutions found in modern industrial societies.   The *locus classicus* is Kerr *et al.* (1962).   Originally formulated as an alternative to Marxism, the authors argued that there is an inherent logic to the process of industrialisation.   Once industrialisation is under way then the establishment of modern forms of production necessitate a number of other structural changes which follow as an inevitable consequence.

These changes include the establishment of a workforce committed to the imperatives of industrial production.   Such a workforce must be educated, in order to receive instructions, follow directions and keep records.   In addition, managers must be trained to operate the new productive system. Hence the need for an education system 'functionally related to the skills and professional imperatives of its technology' (Kerr *et al.*, 1962: 36).   As the technological basis of production is constantly changing, so the educational level of the labour force has to be increased.[8] The numerous skills required for industrial production have to be organised, and this is said to increase the need for hierarchy in the management of organisations.   Control over the workforce is achieved through the introduction of a web of rules, governing hirings, layoffs, promotions and so on. The emergence of these rules is associated with the growth of unions and a separate industrial relations system. The spread of large-scale enterprises stimulates the process of urbanisation. The scale of production and the need for an elaborate economic and social infrastructure means that the government has to become more involved in the organisation of society.   These processes do not necessarily imply uniformity, because they interact with the society's cultural background, economic constraints and the strategies of the industrialising elites.   This gives rise to diversity and peculiarities in, for example, the relationship between managers and managed. Nevertheless, in the longer term it is argued that the complexity of production, the enhanced education and skill levels required for production and the impact of universal education, will result in industrial pluralism becoming the dominant mode of social and political organisation. Later, the authors modified their original position, arguing that there was no trend towards uniformity but that countries will converge towards a range of alternatives (Kerr *et al.*, 1971).

The thesis has given rise to endless debates about whether or not industrial societies are converging, and, if they are, whether they are converging around what many see as a distinctively American form of industrial pluralism. Our concern is with the relationship it posits between the development of the modern forms of production and the level of skill of the labour force. Kerr *et al.* propose that the imperative of technological change requires a constant increase in the level of skill of the labour force. They are confident that:

> The industrial society tends to create an increasing level of general education for all citizens, not only because it facilitates training and flexibility in the workforce, but also because as incomes rise natural curiosity increases the demand for formal education, and education becomes one of the principal means of vertical social mobility in a technical world. (Kerr *et al.*, 1962: 37)

Given this individual and aggregate demand for skill acquisition, human capital theory nevertheless gives grounds for substantive concern that insufficient investment in education or training will be forthcoming in a free-market environment. Certain contingent factors intervene in the operation of the market for human capital acquisition. First, the imperfection of capital markets leads to under provision of loans to individuals to fund the investment. Second, even if loans were provided at market rates, much training is not *general*, in the sense of being equally valuable to any of a large number of employers, but is nevertheless *transferable*, of some variable value to some employers other than that providing the training. In such circumstances, individuals will face a reduced incentive to fund their own training when there is some chance that they will have to part company with their employers and if labour markets are imperfect (Stevens, 1994). Moreover, where training is complementary with the investments linked to innovations, there arises also an externality leading to sub-optimal investment and innovation (Acemoglu, 1993). There can also be a simple and direct externality with both education and training. One person's education is to the benefit of others (for a host of reasons) and so, too, one person's training could raise the productivity of fellow workers.[9] Where the training benefits other firms, the externality constitutes a source of suboptimal growth rates

(Lucas, 1988).[10]

Finally there has, it is often alleged, been an acceleration of technical change in recent decades. The new technology, and the greater pace of change itself, requires higher-skilled workers, but this need invokes only a belated response in individuals and firms who underestimate the benefits to training.

For all these reasons, within the framework of neoclassical economics, there is a case for state intervention to regulate, stimulate and subsidise as necessary the provision of vocational education and training. This case is strengthened where the intervening institutions are capable of adapting quickly to change, but weakened if political processes inhibit that adaptability.

Human capital theory has also given rise to a voluminous supporting empirical literature aimed at measuring the effectiveness of acquiring human capital as an investment. The techniques engendered for estimating the rate of return to education or training do not in fact depend on the theory, but they serve to provide an empirical context and a basis for policy analysis. In the developed world these techniques have been widely used to measure the returns to individuals and firms of education and training programmes. In the third world the human capital approach has been influential in evaluating the effectiveness of vocational education compared to more general education. There have also been attempts to identify and quantify the impact of education and training on economic growth across the world (see next chapter).

Yet for all its usefulness as a technique for estimating the effectiveness of training in given social and economic situations, human capital theory portrays the link between training and the economy in a simplistic and misleading manner. The fundamental weakness of the theory, and accordingly of much public discussion within the liberal approach, is that in regarding human capital as a 'thing', to be acquired and utilised alongside other factor inputs, it misses the social context of skill and of technology. Human capital theory gives precisely the same level of understanding of skill acquisition as does neoclassical exchange theory of the economy generally. It is a familiar Marxist argument that the theory of exchange is an aspect of the fetishism of commodities, wherein relations between producers are reified, appearing as objective external processes which deceive agents as to the import of their activities. This critique declares that the theory of exchange is not 'false', since commodities really do appear in this manner for economic agents, workers and capitalists, but asserts that it is ideological, since it gives a one-sided and incomplete and, hence, 'delusory' perspective on the economy (Mohun, 1979). The concept of 'human capital' is a particular example of commodity fetishism.

The theory is not false, since there really are incentives to skill acquisition and these skills really do become marketable: relations between the 'qualified' worker and other commodities are objectively perceived in the wage relativity attached to that qualification in the labour market. It is, however, an ideological as opposed to a scientific approach in that it obscures the nature of the social relations under which both commodities and human capital are produced – that is, capitalist relations in the economy, and an education and training system that indirectly reflects its capitalist context. The power of human capital as ideology is reflected in everyday language: one speaks of an unemployed individual's 'portfolio of skills' which has to be identified and marketed like the samples in the sales rep's case. Local governments perform 'skill inventories' to attract business to their areas and, of course, training is seen, precisely, as 'investment'. It might have been more accurate to speak instead of the 'theory of capital humans' as this would capture the fact that it is humans whose skills are being objectified, rather than physical capital which is being dignified with humanity.

Human capital theory treats the education and training process as a 'black box', in which skills are produced. What goes on inside that box is the educationalist's, not the economist's, business. This approach is evident in recent 'endogenous growth' models, in which human capital formation and training externalities play a prominent part in explaining divergence of national growth rates (Lucas, 1988). These models treat skill acquisition as just another (fetishised) production process and skill itself as if it were a form of physical capital.

Moreover, the decision process is infused with an assumption of instrumental rationality which to many writers would seem hardly credible. On the one hand, individuals are expected to make instrumentally rational calculations about their optimal training and education, taking into account their knowledge both of the effectiveness of the training and of the value of future economic variables, as far as the end of their working life. Quite fantastically complex calculations are called upon from individuals, even assuming they have a reasonable basis for forming future expectations. The sheer complexity suggests, at the least, a satisficing mode of behaviour as envisaged by Herbert Simon, owing to the inevitable boundedness of rationality. It might be more credible, indeed, to locate education and training decisions in the realm of 'procedural' or of 'expressive' rationality, forms of rationality which call on social convention to resolve otherwise insoluble economic decision processes (Hargreaves Heap, 1989). Research findings which add weight to this have recently been produced by Hodkinson and Sparkes (1994) who studied the decision-making process among young people spending their Youth Credits on purchasing training. They refer to the process they observed among these young adults as one of pragmatic rationality.

The recognition that education's function in providing human capital is socially constructed arises in a variety of traditions outside mainstream neoclassical economics. First, for many economists the assumption of perfect information has come to be rejected in recent years and one aspect of this is the theory of 'signalling', wherein achievement in education is taken as a signal of abilities useful for employers. In its extreme form this theory asserts that education is not productive for the economy, since nothing of relevance to work is learned in education. Nevertheless, education serves an informational function for employers, and hence can still raise overall production via an improved allocation of resources (Arrow, 1973). This process may be thought of as socially loaded. The acceptability of educational qualifications and experiences in the workplace depends on social norms, and in general information flows should be seen as carrying socially determined meanings.

A more direct way in which it is seen that skills and skill acquisition have social content arises from the influential critique of US education by Bowles and Gintis (1976). In taking a neo-Marxist viewpoint of the economy, economic relations are seen as capitalist and skills are constructed according to the material conditions of each particular capitalist era: in the post-war US, a segmented and subordinated labour force with a range of control-types, market-types and associated forms of skill. There is, then, argued to be a long-run tendency for a 'correspondence' to develop between the social relations of education and economic life. Not only is there an 'accommodation of educational structures to the economic division of labour' (Bowles and Gintis, 1988: 238), in particular to its hierarchical structure, there is also a correspondence between the forms of relationship nurtured in formal education and those necessary for effective performance in the capitalist labour market. Virtues such as submissiveness to authority, punctuality, passivity and loyalty are rewarded in education, as in work, while creativity, aggressiveness and independence are penalised. This correspondence principle does not in general preclude a relative autonomy for educational systems, and allows for temporal disjuncture between educational and economic change, and for a conflict-laden path of educational development. The theory amounts, in effect, not so much to a theory of education as to a framework for analysing the relation between education and the economy: as such it constitutes a more fundamental and far-ranging critique of the linear, individualistic human capital theory than the screening critique.[11]

At the same time that Bowles and Gintis were publishing their work in the US, Ashton and Field (1976) and Willis (1977) were dealing with the same issue in the UK. They, too, argued that there was a correspondence between the output of the schools and the demands of the workplace. For some groups this was the result of deliberate policy on the part of the schools, for example the Grammar schools socialising young people for careers in the professions and management. However, for the unskilled working class, the correspondence was an unintended consequence of the clash between working-class culture and the demands of a middle-class education system.

The correspondence principle has found a wide resonance among analysts confronted by the failures of the liberal reform programme for schooling in the US and elsewhere, and it may be applied as well to many forms of training. In the UK one may point to the role of the Youth Training Scheme (later named YT) in supplementing formal education with an inculcation of 'low-level skills', by which are meant the necessary social skills needed for participating in the labour market. These have been the findings of a number of research studies of the youth training schemes (Lee *et al.,* 1989; Finn, 1987). In New Zealand, Higgins (1994) has shown how the youth training scheme introduced there was instrumental in preparing young people for deskilled work. Note also, for example, the study of Oliver and Turton (1982) which showed that the meaning frequently attached by British employers to 'skills' was the idea of 'the good bloke', i.e. a worker (male) with appropriate social skills, including reliability and submissiveness, for fitting into the workplace.

Bowles and Gintis's framework leaves room for a variety of processes of social determination, any of which essentially undermines the fetishistic human capital tradition. One such process, though not developed by the authors themselves, is central to the analysis of modern labour markets: the relationship of gender. It is well-known that, despite the numerical expansion of women's role in the labour markets of the advanced capitalist countries, women remain horizontally segregated in certain occupations and industries, and vertically segregated at relatively low levels in workplace hierarchies. Reflecting the gendered relations of work, skills acquire specific features associated with males and females. The skills at which males shine differ from those regarded as the provenance of females, both in people's perceptions and in actuality (Horrell, Rubery and Burchell, 1990). These skills need not be formal, or attached to appropriate qualifications, but may be 'tacitly' recognised by employers (Curran, 1988). Meanwhile the label 'skilled' has been utilised by males as an aid to sustaining their higher status and earnings (Cockburn, 1983; Coyle, 1982). That such labels are not objective is revealed in the re-evaluations of skill (and pay) brought about in the US by the comparable worth political strategy. Thus the market valuation of skills acquires a gendered dimension consistent with patriarchal valuations, expressed in economic terms as sex discrimination on pay.

The social nature of skills also reflects the technological and organisational context in which skills are going to be used. Thus, the spread of Taylorist methods of scientific management in the twentieth century brought with it the systematic, though often contested, deskilling of workers as a means of reinforcing capitalist control of the labour process (Braverman, 1974; Hill, 1981; Littler, 1982; Wood, 1983). In parallel, Fordist mass production methods reasserted the technological control over the pace of work (Edwards, 1979). The demand for, and the return to, the acquisition of a variety of technical skills, reflects not an exogenous technical change but one which is subject to managerial strategy and conflict. More generally, it is the institutional context which shapes the skills acquired (Higgins, 1993). On the demand side, an institutional culture of, for example, short-termism, or of conflictual industrial relations, influences the types of skills required. On the supply side, skills are transmitted through institutional routines (Hodgson, 1988: 142–4).

The fact that skill acquisition is a social process implies that studies in the human capital theory mould are only valid where they inhabit a limited domain where, for the purposes of the investigation, it is reasonable to assume given social parameters. This qualification allows a useful role for evaluation studies that investigate, for example, the effectiveness of public programmes in promoting employment or higher pay. But the theory can contribute little in an era when skills themselves are being defined, changed and struggled over, and does not provide a means for analysing the variable links between education and training systems and their wider context.

## THE INTERNAL LABOUR MARKETS APPROACH

Shunning the individualistic methodology that underlies human capital theory, a number of other approaches have in common an analysis of the institutional context of training. Of particular interest is the link between training and economic performance demonstrated by large Japanese companies. From this is derived what we term the 'internal labour markets' (ILM) approach, since it premisses the effectiveness of training on the existence and nature of internal labour markets (Koike and Inoki (eds), 1990).[12]

Koike and Inoki have shown that a major source of the superior productivity of large plants in Japan, compared with similar Japanese-owned plants in Thailand and Malaysia, is the greater skill formation of the Japanese workforce, and not some mysterious cultural difference. Two important facets of skill necessary for high productivity performance are the 'breadth' and 'depth' of skill. 'Breadth' of skill refers to the ability to perform a range of regular tasks; 'depth' means having also the intellectual ability to deal with 'unusual jobs', either dealing with unforeseen hitches in the production process, or introducing variations in the technology.

To acquire these kinds of skill, there are four prerequisites. First, there must be a sufficiently high level of general education among the workforce, that is, not just within an elite but among the vast majority of the population. Second, the skills can only be acquired through on-the-job training (OJT). This is because the knowledge-content of these skills cannot be precisely defined or communicated through words via off-the-job training (Off-JT) and because OJT is less costly and more concrete than Off-JT. Third, careers must be enterprise-specific, in order to keep down the costs of acquiring enterprise-specific skills, but at the same time broad within the enterprise, with OJT being supplemented every so often by short spells of Off-JT which enable workers to systemise their job experiences and develop their intellectual skills. Finally, Koike and Inoki argue that the skills are best developed in 'integrated systems' of management, that is, where there is no strict division of labour whereby ordinary workers do the usual tasks and technicians are brought in to do the unusual tasks.

The other side of the same coin is that where these features are absent in companies it is hard to move to a high-skill production system. Brown, Reich and Stern (1993) investigate the barriers to moving from a low-skill company system of employee relations called JAM (Job classifications, Adversarial relations, Minimal training) to the SET system (Security, Employee involvement, Training). This transition is impeded by the interrelated nature of the transformations that are required, which all too often in US firms proved to be an insuperable barrier.

The advantage of this internal labour markets approach is that it shows how and why the provision of a higher-level skills training system is intimately linked to the structure of enterprises. The approach suggests a number of indicators to look for in examining *any* skill acquisition system, not just in the Pacific Rim. Although in agreement with the liberal approach about some issues, particularly about the salience of a high general level of education, the internal labour markets approach goes further in delineating important characteristics to look for in the system of industrial organisation. These are: the amount of usage of OJT complemented by spells of Off-JT, the stability of enterprises providing career-long opportunities for skill formation, and the degree of integration of work organisation. To the extent that all these indicators are present, one could conclude that a production system is appropriate for a highly competitive and powerful economy.

There are, however, drawbacks to this approach. It is questionable how far its conclusions are generalisable to other economies because, apart from the contribution of the central state in providing general education and in certifying qualifications (Dore and Sako, 1989), it makes no room for occupational labour markets which are supported by corporatist-type institutions that are found often to work well in Europe. At the same time, the stability of the internal labour market system itself is not beyond question: those within the system may become frustrated, for example, with excessive reliance on seniority as the route to personal progress (Levine and Kawada, 1980). Positive evaluation of the system is based on an experience of enterprises that have never really experienced serious contraction. Moreover, the very exclusiveness of internal labour markets ensures that those excluded (in Japan those in the small firm sector, and women generally) are not provided with the same fine routes to skill acquisition. The result could be chronic low productivity outside the core sectors of the economy (Berggren,1995), depending on the available external structures of the training system. The analysis of the overall link between training and the economy should therefore go wider than just the enterprise.

## THE CORPORATIST APPROACH

Such an approach has been developed in order to explain the peculiar effectiveness of training practices within some European corporatist systems of industrial relations. In these systems, occupational labour markets are supported either separately or alongside internal labour markets (Soskice, 1994), despite the potential instabilities associated with them (Marsden, 1986). Each type of labour market is enabled by a system of regulation[13] that involves both the state, and more widely the 'social partners' (Rainbird, 1990; CEDEFOP, 1987a, 1987b; Mahnkopf, 1992).

Most influential in this approach is the work of Streeck (1989, 1991), who identifies the key to economic competitiveness in modern capitalism as a system of 'diversified quality production', a system wherein producers are able to supply with great efficiency high-quality diversified products in large volumes. Streeck notes that such a productive system can be nurtured only in 'institutionally-rich societies'. Thus, societies which embed markets in a 'thick' array of regulatory, co-operative and redistributive institutions are likely, according to the evidence from comparative analysis, to be more productive than *laissez-faire* societies. These arguments apply across a range of areas, but they are nowhere more apposite than in the link between the training system and the economic system.   Beyond the standard human capital argument that with transferable training externalities lead to suboptimal training levels (see above), Streeck proposes that there are limits to how far these could be resolved by central state intervention of vocational education.  Schools, separated from industry, fail to motivate workers to acquire work skills. Moreover, workers need socialisation in the world of work, and benefit from learning-by-doing.   Hence, enterprises must become places of learning themselves.  Yet Streeck doubts whether the state can get involved efficiently in the regulation or subsidy of enterprise learning.[14]

Apart from the need to surmount the externality problem, the characteristics of enterprise-based learning make it virtually impossible to make rational calculations about the benefits and rate of return to training. An inherent 'fuzziness' could also lead to 'under-investment' in training if the only training that took place was that for which the benefits were attributable and calculated to exceed the costs.  Systems which foster an accounting approach to justifying training expenditures in terms of identifiable benefits will therefore lose out to systems which take a productivist slant and justify training in terms of long-term productive benefits.  The latter type of system will produce an (apparent) redundancy of capabilities, in that in a polyvalent or multi-skilled context one often finds workers with ranges of skills some of which are rarely called upon.

Streeck thus widens the argument beyond the ILM theorists Koike and Inoke, by concluding from the above that for a skill formation system 'only firms will do, *but not deregulated firms*'.  In other words, some form of regulation is necessary, but it need not take place in large-scale internal labour markets.  The corporatist arrangements to be found in Germany and elsewhere in Europe could be the ingredients of a successful training strategy.  As with the internal labour markets approach, the corporatist approach directs us, when examining any country's training system, to look both at the level of general education, and at the primary location for the acquisition of work skills, that is, how much is being supplied by firms. But in addition it also directs us to focus on the mechanisms and the intermediate institutions by which training in firms is regulated.   Less emphasis, however, is placed on the stability of enterprises, and associated career-long tenure patterns within those enterprises.  This difference from Koike and Inoke is perhaps not surprising, given the difference between the German and Japanese labour market.

The corporatist approach is normally also attached to a normative concern with distributive justice.  On the one hand, it is held that political stability in many advanced industrialised countries is likely to require the maintenance of a high-wage and relatively equal-wage economy. Since this implies a high-skills economy, high-skills production methods are necessary in order to remain competitive in the current period of restructuring. On the other hand, the allocation of expenditures to training on the basis of a political commitment to equality circumvents the suboptimal outcome that would arise in the event of a strict 'economising' rationality.

Two problems, it may be suggested, attach to Streeck's analysis of skill formation systems. First that the bulk of examples and basis for empirical proof tends to be taken from just one country, Germany, leading one to doubt the extent to which generalised arguments may be correctly inferred. Streeck may have been too quick, for example, to discount the possibilities of state-supported work-related training. As we shall later see, these suspicions are justified when it comes to analysis of many countries in the Pacific Rim, which have achieved their competitive success on the back of a 'developmental state' directing enterprises: with relatively few if any intermediate institutions, these are precisely not 'institutionally-rich' economies. There, state intervention has been successful in constraining enterprises to take up the baton of skill formation. The second problem is that the least solid aspect of the evidence quoted is the view that 'diversified quality production' systems are *necessarily* more competitive than others. In fact, nowhere do Streeck, or others writing in the same vein, establish with empirical evidence that capitalist enterprises cannot act with equal or greater profitability in low-skilled economies, even in the advanced industrialised world. This is because Streeck fails to develop a comprehensive framework which deals with skill formation at different stages in the development of the productive system – an error which leads him to conflate one form of skill formation (that required for high-value-added production) with the process of skill formation *per se*. We examine this argument further below.

## SOCIOLOGICAL THEORIES: THE 'BUSINESS SYSTEMS' AND THE 'SOCIETAL' APPROACHES

Long before present-day calls for more participation and collaboration Kerr *et al.* (1962: 289) asserted that

> As the skill level rises and jobs become more responsible, any regime must be more interested in consent, in drawing forth relatively full co-operation. For the sake of real efficiency, this must be freely given. The discipline of the labor gang no longer

suffices. ... With skill and responsibilities goes the need for consent, and with consent goes influence and even authority.

Such a prognosis, if valid, would in addition to the technological imperatives have implications for the sorts of skills demanded. It is not hard to find situations where participation and co-operation between workers and firms is efficient (Mishel and Voos (eds), 1992). Yet it is equally clear that naked capitalist authority is frequently the profit-maximising form of production organisation for many firms.

A recent comparative study from the newly industrialised economies (NIEs) throws some light on this relationship (Redding and Richardson, 1986). It links the levels of productivity with the existence of participative/authoritarian management styles in Hong Kong and Singapore. The Singaporean economy is dominated by multinational companies from the older industrial countries, which have pioneered the more participative forms of management style. In contrast, Hong Kong has relatively few multinational companies. There, the economy is dominated by Chinese businesses, with their non-bureaucratic, more authoritarian style of management. The convergence thesis would predict that the more participative style of management in Singapore would give rise to higher levels of productivity. The study found a relationship between an increase in productivity in Singaporean companies and an increase in the use of more participative management styles. But this was not the case in Hong Kong. There, the increase in productivity had been higher than that achieved in Singapore, but had been achieved through the use of traditional, more authoritarian management styles. Thus, while there may be some form of link between modern forms of production and functional literacy, there does not appear to be any necessary link between modern forms of production and participative forms of management. Research findings such as these raise profound questions about both the convergence thesis and other forms of economic rationalism. Such theories assume, with little supporting evidence, that competitive market forces ensure the selection of those firms which best fit the imperatives of the market and the technology. Such arguments deny that there may be different ways of organising business, in terms of management styles and decision-making processes, as well as different ways of organising the management–worker relationship.

Recent work by Granovetter (1985), and Whitley (1992a (ed.); 1992b), among others, has presented an alternative case, namely that firms and markets are socially constructed. Work, such as that by Whitley in South East Asia, has shown how the structure of organisations and form of business practice vary between societies and can only be understood as the outcome of the different institutional, historical and cultural contexts within which they originated. Moreover, all are capable of being viable institutions for the accumulation of capital, albeit being more effective in some institutional contexts than others. Whitley ((ed.))1992b) in particular has pointed to some of the distinctive features of the South East Asian business systems, showing how what is 'rational' behaviour in one context may not be rational in another, and how different institutional contexts encourage different forms of business and market organisation to become established.

Whitley distinguishes three different types of business system in South East Asia, the Japanese, Korean and Chinese family business systems. These systems differ in terms of their 'system of authoritative co-ordination and control', 'enterprise domain and development' and 'the nature of enterprise co-ordination and market organisation' (1992: 2). In the Chinese family business, managerial authority is closely associated with personal ownership and informal co-ordination and control procedures when compared with the Japanese system. Chinese managers conceive of their role as more directive than their Japanese counterparts. In terms of the enterprise domain and development, Chinese firms tend to restrict the range of activities they co-ordinate through authority hierarchies to those involving a narrow range of skills, and organise complementary but dissimilar activities through quasi-market mechanisms. In contrast Korean companies are characterised by greater vertical integration, co-ordinating and controlling a more diverse range of activities through a common authority hierarchy, being much more vertically integrated. Inter-enterprise co-ordination and control in Chinese firms is through a series of sub-contract arrangements which tend to be loose and temporary whereas those of the Japanese are more permanent, involving a sharing of information and technology. In Korea the higher level of vertical integration means that companies are less dependent on intra-firm links. Historical differences in the political and financial systems and authority relations comprise the main reasons for the emergence of these distinctive business systems.

Whitley's work serves to illustrate how capital can be accumulated, and productivity enhanced, by different combinations of skills and different types and level of skill. In so doing, it serves as a warning to guard against attempts to read off levels of skill or types of skill from an economy at a given level of development or a particular type of technology. It also suggests that the skills required in business at all levels, from the managing director to the office or shop floor, may be culturally specific in some important respects. Given that business systems differ in significant ways between societies, we would also expect the social formation of skills to differ.   Just as historical and cultural differences in the political and financial institutions affect the character of business systems, so they also affect the ways in which skills are structured in each society.   This conclusion exemplifies again one of the weaknesses in the ILM and corporatist approaches which we identified above, namely that each generalise too readily from the experience of one historical and cultural context.

The point is illustrated also by a West/East contrast in the importance of occupation-defined skills.   The prior spread of commercialisation in Western Europe which facilitated the development of occupational groupings through the medieval guild and apprenticeship system, provided the basis for the transmission of skills through occupational associations and therefore the personal ownership of skills.   When industry developed, these were utilised by capitalists who developed mechanisms necessary for their co-ordination within the enterprise.   But, with the growth of capitalism in East Asia, the existence of strong traditional familial and personal loyalties have combined with the rapid development of industry from an agrarian base to produce different outcomes to the process of skill formation.   The relative absence of traditional crafts meant that management did not have to co-ordinate pre-existing skills.   Instead, they used the principle of familial and personal loyalty as the basis for organising the production process and structuring the process of skill formation.   For example, training in the Chinese businesses is less formal and rewards are linked directly to performance.   In Japan, the training is often formally structured but rewards are linked closely to personal loyalty to the firm in the form of length of service.   In both instances the process of skill formation is geared more to the requirements of the organisation, and less emphasis than in the West is attached to occupational skills as the basis of skill formation.

Such factors preclude any simplistic attempt to read off training needs from the technology or even the production system at different stages of its development.   Business systems organise the production process in different ways and may establish different relationships between the process of skill formation and the level of overall economic performance. This means that it may be possible for a wide range of variations within any national education and training system to satisfy the requirement of the system of production at a given stage in its development.   Thus the skills demanded from industries established in the first wave of industrialisation were relatively low.   They could be satisfied, as they were in the UK, by an uneducated labour force.   In the early phase of industrial development in the UK the skills demand was not so much for a literate labour force as for a disciplined labour force (Pollard, 1965), a lesson that was not lost on the leaders of the new industrialised economies as they started the process of industrialisation with labour-intensive, low-value-added industries (Ashton and Sung, 1994). Further evidence of employer skill demands for labour-intensive industries can be found in the work of Bowles and Gintis, Ashton and Field and Willis discussed earlier.

In those industries which emerged in the second wave of industrialisation, chemicals, petro-chemicals, steel and electrical and precision engineering, the production process rested more on scientific knowledge. There, the skills demands were higher, requiring fairly sophisticated technical and scientific knowledge on the part of the managers and a part of the labour force. The most recent wave of industries, for example, aero-space, computing, financial services and communications are all knowledge-intensive industries requiring higher levels of skill formation among a large proportion of those involved in the process of production.

While there are clear differences in the skills demand from industries which emerged at different stages in the development of the productive system, it is also clear that there are substantial variations in how these skill needs can be met. The Japanese and Germans have both developed different systems for creating the necessary skills. The Americans have been able to modify aspects of their system of production and skill formation to continue to compete in these industries (Berggren, 1995). Moreover, it may prove possible to provide the necessary skills for industries at this latest stage in the development of the productive system in countries where labour costs are lower.

Similar to the 'business systems' approach, and just as wide in its remit of institutions relevant to skill acquisition, is the 'societal' approach to the link between training and the economy originating from a research team based in Aix-en-Provence (Maurice, Sellier and Silvester, 1986).[15] Rather like the ILM approach in its emphasis on the required combination of both 'breadth' and 'depth' of skill, the societal approach identifies 'polyvalence' as a key attribute, defined as 'the capability of a worker to shift from position to position within a given productive organization'. The researchers found that this was achieved in different ways and to different extents in Germany and France. The polyvalence achieved in Germany was linked to the high level of initial general skills attained via the dual system, and to the less hierarchical nature of German workplaces. The researchers also found, however, that no single causal factor, such as a better education or training system could account for the higher productivity of German workers compared to their French counterparts. Indeed, they argued that training could only be understood in terms of its relationship with the organisation of educational provision, with the structure of production organisations, with the system of industrial relations and with the wider class structure of society. Together, these 'institutional domains' interact to produce a given outcome, perhaps in the form of higher productivity, but the result cannot be attributed to any one of these institutional structures seen in isolation. It is a fundamental premise of the societal approach that these institutional domains only take on their present form and structure by virtue of their relationship to each other. As a result, a satisfactory account of a country's training activities needs to include all the educational and organisational relationships of which they are a constituent part. This is evidently quite different from the linear conceptions of much of the literature within the liberal and human capital approach.

While this represents a step forward in our understanding of education and training systems, the societal approach does run into its own problems. In arguing that we must consider the authority structure of the firms, the industrial relations systems, the education system and so on, this approach tends to give equal weight to each of these factors. Thus, when it comes to explaining why some national systems are more efficient than others in international competition the answer is 'the system as a whole'. It lacks a dynamic historical analysis which would enable it to identify whether any of these institutions take on a greater significance at different stages in the development of the productive system.

## THE POLITICAL SCIENCE APPROACH

One common thread in all the above frameworks is the assumption that a high-skills production system would be good for competitiveness, and hence for companies' profits. Since it would also go with high wages and therefore be desirable for workers too, there is an uneasy question underlying them all, namely why are not appropriate policies adopted and institutions set in place in *all* the industrialised countries in order to reap the benefits of a high-skills system? Typical answers lie either in the predominance of misguided ideologies (e.g. the ideology of unbridled free-market capitalism) or in entrenched institutions and cultures deriving from long hard-to-shift historical processes.

Unhappy with simplistic references to history or to culture Finegold (1991, 1992a, 1992b) has attempted to build on the above approaches by asking why modern policy-makers and other economic actors are not moved to improve matters where a situation of low skills prevails. His answer draws on the metaphor of a 'game', to explain why, when alternative outcomes are possible, rational actors may behave so as to preserve an outcome which is suboptimal from the point of view of society in the country as a whole. Thus, under certain conditions it can be perfectly rational for a company manager to pursue a low-skills strategy. Under market pressure to produce short-term results, unable to find the means to cooperate productively with other businesses or with workers, experiencing difficulty in recruiting well-educated young workers, managers are likely to opt for low levels of training. At the same time individuals hemmed in by short-term constraints, lack of security and limited marginal returns to studying hard at school, rationally opt for low levels of participation in education and training. The outcome of the game played by the company and its actual or prospective workforce is a low-skill equilibrium. An alternative, high-skill, equilibrium can, however, be found where it is in the interests of the company to make use of productive techniques that require high skills, to provide the necessary training and rewards for workers with the right attitudes and education, and it is in the interests of the workers to undertake the necessary investments in themselves. Though initially applied to analysis of the interaction between two parties, firm and workforce, the concepts of high-skills or low-skills equilibria are applied by simple aggregation to the whole economy: where a majority of firms are following the high- or low-skills route, the economy is said to be in a high- or low-skills equilibrium.

Finegold also uses the game theory metaphor to characterise the possibilities facing whole classes within the economy, here including the state in a three-way interaction with firms and workers. When governments, too, feel constrained to take short-term perspectives, the outcome is a low-skills equilibrium. Finegold suggests three main conditions for a high-skills equilibrium to be the outcome. First, there should be an environment in which long-term planning is facilitated and short-termist attitudes discouraged. Second, there needs to be an atmosphere conducive to elements of co-operation and consensus among employers and between employers and workers even in the context of overall competition. Such an atmosphere could be fostered by corporatist institutions with reasonably centralised bargaining arrangements. Third, industry must have an export orientation, so that exposure to very low-wage competition from other countries rules out low-wage forms of competition at home.

Short-termism or long-termism and the degree of co-operation in economic and political life are both implicit in the features referred to in the ILM, the corporatist and the sociological frameworks discussed above. What Finegold adds, therefore, from the political science perspective, is an emphasis on these facets that helps us avoid abstract references to history or culture, and helps to explain the problems faced in countries where there is a genuine desire on the part of some to upgrade the productive system, but where the institutional mechanisms are absent.[16]   The attraction of the equilibrium concept, as used in the game theory framework, is its ability to shed light on the persistence of social outcomes, held in place by the 'mutually-reinforcing' incentives facing individuals and by the 'self-reinforcing' social institutions.

Thereby, however, lies also the disadvantage of tying one's analysis so effectively to the tree of equilibrium.  For in explaining the persistence of a social configuration it becomes more difficult to theorise the process of change except as the difference between equilibria enforced by exogenous factors.  This provides no handle for analysing the process of transition between equilibria, and rules out a proper dialectical analysis of the inherent tensions within the interactions between firms, the government and the workers.  Such an approach may be particularly important for the study of training, an area where, as we shall argue below, conflict is inherent.

## CONCLUSION: TOWARDS A MATERIALIST[17] THEORY OF EDUCATION AND TRAINING SYSTEMS

This chapter has so far shown a number of ways in which writers from varying academic disciplines and political commentators have approached the issue of the relationship of the education and training system in a country to its economic system.  Common to all is an agreement on the importance of education and training in the current era of international competition.  We agree with this perception in general, but only in so far as the competition is for high-value-added goods.  To compete in these markets we believe the evidence for the importance of high levels of education and training is overwhelming.  However, as we argued above, high levels of education and training are not required for the production of low-value-added goods and services.

We have, however, drawn attention to some criticisms of these perspectives.  While the liberal educationalist position has focused on differences in the organisation of vocational education across countries, we have found that this approach lacks the theory to conceptualise why these organisational differences should matter.  Analyses using this approach typically provide us with useful descriptions but no more.  These descriptions may be bolstered by the techniques of mainstream economics which can, within given social and economic parameters, tell us which education or training programmes are most effective in affecting wages, productivity, or other economic outcomes. Nevertheless, as theory the human capital approach feeds us only a limited, 'black-box', perspective of the effect of training on economic performance, and we have criticised this at length by examining the consequences of neglecting the social and economic context in which skills are acquired.

The internal labour markets approach goes beyond human capital theory by giving us a fruitful account of the conditions within enterprises that can foster effective skill acquisition and hence good economic performance. Its exclusive emphasis on the enterprise, however, means that it neglects to consider the effectiveness of other forms of regulation. The more general theories arising out of the corporatist and the sociological approaches have been successful in identifying important links between training systems and other societal institutions, especially the industrial relations system. This avoids the over-simplified abstractions of the other approaches, in that it cannot simply be said that 'more' training is better, since it all depends on how that training is embedded in other systems which are highly pertinent determinants of economic performance. They have also shown how the education and training systems have a degree of autonomy in relation to the productive system. Education and training systems based on different principles, the corporatist and ILM, can both produce the high level of skill required for effective competition in the production of high-value-added goods and services. Finally, ideas from the political sciences have been successfully drawn on to help understand why the various political actors may become locked into supporting an institutional equilibrium, implying a particular high or low level of skills.

Among these various approaches, even the more sophisticated institutional analyses, there remains nevertheless a key unquestioned assumption: that a widely and highly skilled labour force, with high-value-added production processes, is a necessary ingredient of economic success in the modern era. The assumption was made explicit some time ago in the convergence thesis of Kerr *et al.* (1962) – the more highly developed the economy, the more skills were used and the more education and training was demanded. And now the assumption is bolstered by the increased internationalisation of the world's economies. A thesis originally expounded by marxists came to express the nature of this new compulsion – the theory of the 'New International Division of Labour' (NIDL) (Froebel, Hendricks and Kreye, 1980). NIDL theories characterise the modern era as one where transport costs and technology allow the re-location of manufacturing for the first time ever to the third world, thereby replacing the traditional imperialist division of labour which involved undeveloped countries participating in the world economy only through the provision of raw materials. By extension, that old division of labour had led to the underdevelopment of many parts of the third world, at least according to many leading theories of development. However, the new division of global production changed the terms under which the less-developed countries are integrated with the North, implying an intensification of competition. Given the huge wage differences between the industrialised world and the third world there remains, in this conception, only one route to maintain the competitiveness of the North: to situate its industry at the high-skill, high-value-added end of the market. There arises a yet greater emphasis on the importance of new technology in the North.[18] The best strategy for northern governments is to woo the multinational corporations (the chief instruments for the re-division of labour) with the high productivity of the local workforce, and similarly to upgrade the skill levels of smaller businesses trading on the world market so as to enable them to compete.

Our objection to this assumption is one of the themes of this book. It is not *just* that skills, the training system and the businesses themselves are socially constructed and that different types of education or training can provide the necessary skills for the production of high-value-added goods and services. Our objection is that there can be quite viable routes to economic success which involve low levels of skill in the advanced industrialised world. Even in the older industrial countries capitalists can still opt to compete in markets for low-value-added goods and services, such as textiles, footwear and personal services.

We do not subscribe to the simplistic universal perspective of Braverman's monopoly capitalism wherein deskilling is an unchecked and universal tendency of capitalism. There are many critiques of this thesis.[19] But it is nevertheless evident that many forms of deskilling technology continue to flourish in the advanced industrialised world. The chief reason is that labour costs are only one, albeit important, factor determining the location of industry. Others include proximity to markets (a necessity for most services), access to those markets without encountering tariff barriers or other impediments to trade, and the stability of the government and of the workforce itself. Add to this the possibility of high degrees of automation in many lines of industry, and the impact of labour costs alone do not necessarily determine in favour of third world location. Within the industrialised world, therefore, there remains and even develops further a low-wage sector, where neo-Taylorist and neo-Fordist forms of production continue to flourish, worked by relatively insecure low-paid employees. The pay is low in relation to other sectors in the industrialised countries. The work remains largely unskilled, and tends to require only minimal levels of numeracy and literacy, and more importantly a reliable and submissive attitude to work. Apart from having higher absolute levels of pay than are found in the third world, the nature of the work is potentially similar.   Mitter (1986) has noted, in particular, the affinity between women's work for multinational corporations in different parts of the globe: the main characteristic being relatively low pay on neo-Fordist production lines.

A new general framework is needed to enable a proper understanding of education and training systems in the world economy.   Our approach has notable affinities with the theory of 'productive systems' developed by Wilkinson (1983), which focuses attention on the organisation of production as an essentially conflictual process.   Economic, social and political forces are seen to combine in determining how economies develop in 'a dynamic non-equilibrium process'.   It recognises that major differences can and do exist between different forms of productive system and that systems with different characteristic features can co-exist through international trade.   Productive systems can secure comparative advantage through changes in any one  or any group of its constituent parts:

> The costs of production of the productive system are determined by the costs of labour and the means of production, the level of technology, the skills of the work force, the effectiveness of management in both extracting labour power and running the system efficiently, and the rules and laws which impinge on the operation of the system and on the degree of responsibility of the productive system for social provision. (*ibid.*: 422).

Some forms of distributing the national product may be more effective than others in securing the compliance and commitment of the workforce. These institutional forms (industrial relations systems, ownership patterns, financial institutions and education and training practices, to name a few), can exert a powerful influence on the efficiency of the overall system. Moreover, once in existence these institutional structures are very difficult to change.   Thus, as the means of production and the characteristics of product markets change, the institutional structures may act as fetters reducing the efficiency of the productive system and intensifying conflict within the system.   In this way the relative efficiency of different systems change over time (Wilkinson, 1983).

The study of education and training systems in their economic context is still comparatively fresh, and in respect of certain parts of the world, notably the NIEs, is still in its infancy.   Here we propose, rather than a fully worked out theory,  a list of ingredients of a comprehensive theory, most of which are not found in the approaches we have reviewed.   These ingredients arise from our own fundamental approach to understanding capitalist societies, which draws on a range of traditions in political economy.

*1. What is success?*

As a preliminary it is necessary to clarify the basics of the capitalist economic system. In the nature of this system, 'economic success', for the individual capitalist, is determined primarily by profitability. Hence, in evaluating the effect of any training system on economic performance, the ultimate criterion is whether it supports the profitable accumulation of capital. In many instances researchers do not have adequate measures of profitability, and instead utilise measures such as labour productivity, investment, or the growth of gross domestic product. But these should be interpreted as intermediate measures, less-than-perfect proxies for economic success. For example, it would not be inconsistent for higher productivity to be associated sometimes with lower profits.

This definition of economic success contrasts with one couched in terms of the economic prosperity of the country's citizens – as given, say, by average wages, the rate of employment, or the distribution of income. It is of course perfectly feasible to have an economic regime that provides a profitable location for capitalist businesses but a less than congenial environment for the workers and citizens.

*2. Conflict in the education and training system*

It follows that there is always a potential for conflict in economic and related systems, and the education or training system is no exception. The approaches we have hitherto examined tend to see an improvement in the system as in everyone's interests.[20] While we would agree that better education and training is in the interests of the majority of a nation's citizenry, it is not necessarily so for the businesses that operate there. The conflict inherent in world competitiveness is expressed in conflict both between and within nations.

Between nations, there is conflict and competition over the skills and consent of the respective workforces. For example, workforces may be presented as more skilful, or more amenable, or cheaper (after taxation) or some combination of these, in order to compete. Or sometimes less trained workers are debarred from immigration while highly qualified migrants are welcomed.

The conflict within nations may be between those that strive for higher skills of the local workforce and those internationally-oriented sectors of capital whose concerns may require that local industry becomes competitive through cost-cutting and lower wages. One example of a fairly open conflict of interests was the difference between the British Conservative government's stance on education and training and on cutting taxation, in comparison with that of the opposition parties which proposed expanding expenditure on the education and training system (the Liberal Democratic Party explicitly costed the necessary increases in taxation it asked electors to vote for in 1992).

Dispute over wages constitutes perhaps the central aspect of conflict in any capitalist society, and historically this has frequently taken the form of disputes over the access to, the regulation of, and more generally the definition of skills. The social construction of skill is a conflictual process concerning the distribution of the product between workers and businesses, even if it is also a process of social division among workers. Disputes about training are typically an aspect of wider disputes about industrial relations, and about the direction of the economy. Ryan (1993a), for example, sets out the theory of how conflict over the quality of training provided by employers translates into conflict over wages. The institutional resolution of conflict over training is exemplified in France, where a system of continuing training has grown up on the basis of the Act of 16 July 1971 which compels firms to spend a minimum proportion of the payroll on training. The law (and subsequent expansions) was the product of inter-sectoral agreements among the social partners, and, no doubt because of the relatively strong employees' side, carried with it the objective of lifelong education for all as well as the objective of improved economic efficiency (Verdier, 1994). Elsewhere, Edwards and Garonna (1991) trace the changes in public training programmes in Italy and the US over three decades, and link these changes to the evolution and eventual break-down of the 'labour accord', that system of industrial relations that was so successful during the golden age period of capitalism. Their analysis is informed by the proposition that:

> Training is not a neutral activity involving simply the augmentation of labour's technical quality, but rather a vital and strategic node within the larger industrial relations system. This means, on the one side, that the articulation of training with the larger industrial relations system strongly shapes the efficacy of, and even the meaning of, training. On the other side, training often acts as a weapon in wider struggles: training controversies concern not just training but also the shaping of the industrial relations system. (*ibid.*: 151)

In general the protagonists of such conflict may be different sections of capital, or workers and capitalists in a classical class struggle, or male and female workers, or some combination of these, with the state involved at every point, sometimes with its own distinctive interests at stake, as we shall see in our discussion of the new industrial economies.

*3. Economic diversity*

Even among the older advanced industrial nations there is in the current era substantive diversity in the institutional infrastructure of their economies.[21] These differences are reflected in different economic outcomes in terms of growth, productivity, the structure of industry, unemployment, inequality, and so on. We shall refer to these differences somewhat loosely as various 'routes to accumulation'. Corresponding to this heterogeneity of routes to capital accumulation, there is diversity in the appropriate or 'ideal' forms of nations' education and training systems. In some countries, or perhaps some regions of countries, the demand is for a widely and highly skilled workforce; in others it is for a greater polarisation, with an elite holding advanced skills and the large majority holding a combination of low-level technical skills and the appropriate general skills required to 'get on' and in effect consent to the normal disciplines of the workplace. One may therefore think of high-skill and low-skill routes to accumulation. These may be distinguished from the more common currency of high- and low-skills equilibria, because of our emphasis on conflict. The routes followed are not necessarily ones that would be chosen by all parties. Rather they are the outcome of struggles between the various parties.

*4. Relative autonomy of the education and training system*

These routes, however, are no more than ideal types, which may never be realised. There are only very imperfect mechanisms for translating the ideal into the actual. One mechanism might be evolution, wherein successful systems are diffused to less successful areas, for example via the location of Japanese businesses in parts of Europe. The political process can bring about transformations in education, but this is a conflictual, imprecise and normally slow process which cannot be expected to match up education systems precisely with changing economic institutions. Education and training systems are themselves relatively autonomous, their domain separate not only from economic systems but also from nation states. The quality of an education system, for example, reflects the culture of a society and its history. Societies with a history of seeing education as important for the life-potential of their young people may now have a comparative advantage in industries requiring highly skilled workers. But that, in a sense, may be a fortune of history – the reasons for the educational success may have cultural roots that have nothing to do with modern strategies for capital accumulation. And even in recent decades many changes in national education and training systems are driven by internal dynamics – by educationalists or trainers, rather than by politicians or economists. Moreover, as we shall argue later, the degree of autonomy varies between societies: in some of the newer industrial societies governments exercise a greater degree of control over the education and training system than has been the case in the older industrial societies.

National or ethnic cultures also affect education and training systems through their impact on businesses. For example, variants of Confucian culture have shaped the form taken by business organisations and have been a powerful influence in structuring the relations between businesses in East Asia. The result is that there are clearly observable differences between Japanese and Chinese organisations. These differences can only be explained if we assume that the pre-existing culture, within which the organisation developed, has a degree of autonomy from the economy and is thereby capable of exerting an independent influence on the structure of business relationships. The implications for training are that culture will also have an independent impact on the skill formation process.

There emerges a dialectical tension between the education and training and economic systems. This inherent contradiction gives the potential for some form of economic or social crisis, with economic development subverted by ill-matched skill formation institutions. These provide the moments when radical structural changes can be introduced into the education and training system.

*5. The education and training system is just one factor in economic success*

There are several other factors determining economic success apart from the nature of the education and training system. Its importance should not, therefore, be exaggerated into becoming the sole key to prosperity, or the scapegoat for economic decline (Cutler, 1992). Skill formation institutions interact with other economic institutions. On its own, without, for example, policies designed to increase the *appropriate* physical investment, simply increasing the supply of skilled workers could lead to higher unemployment rates and lower wages for both skilled and unskilled workers, assuming that skilled and unskilled workers are perfect substitutes (Saint-Paul, 1994). As we shall see later, one of the competitive advantages of the NIEs is their ability to link education and training policies to a trade and industry policy which assures the physical capacity for the production of the appropriate goods and services is in place. Partial reforms of the skill formation system may therefore not achieve their deserved ends, if not accompanied by changes in other aspects of the economy – a fact which warns against simplistic 'policy borrowing' in the field of education and training.

*6. The role of the capitalist nation state*

It is important to utilise an adequate conception of the nation state in a capitalist world. In particular the naive Keynesian view of the nation state, implicit in the liberal versions of support for education and training reform, is to be shunned. This view is reflected in statements about what 'we', the people of this nation, – 'we Americans', or 'we British' – should be doing, and culminates in typical liberal propositions about how the state should best represent 'our' collective interests – in this case, in respect of education (Reich, 1988).[22]  Yet the pluralist model of the bourgeois democratic state always was an ideological figment.  Extensive theoretical debate has largely rejected the simple notion that the capitalist state is but 'a committee for the administration of the affairs of the bourgeoisie', and even the weaker hypothesis that the state represents particular fractions of capital (e.g. financial capital) do not bear prolonged scrutiny (Jessop, 1977).  Yet nation states are not neutral bodies.  They constitute arenas where different class interests are struggled over, with capitalist interests, especially in the older industrial countries, normally dominant.  In the modern era, with extensive internationalisation of capital, the role played by nation states of the older industrial countries is affected by the way it interacts with the forces of international competition.  As a result, there is a dialectical interplay between the interests of the domestic citizenry, the largely home-based capitalist class and the international bourgeoisie represented by the trading sectors (including financial capital) and multinational corporations.  State policies cannot be thought of as simply a linear resultant of these interests.  They are, rather, the outcome of a conflict that cannot be predetermined.

State economic policy, moreover, is also liable to be mediated by international competitive forces.  Capitalist commodity relations can take on the form of competition between nation states – for example, through competitive tax breaks, and low-wage policies to attract foreign capital, or through protectionism for domestic industry.  And now, to an important extent, education and training policy is becoming an aspect of economic policy.  States aim to compete, as far as they can, in making available an attractive workforce for international capital.  Promotion of a highly skilled workforce becomes a possible, though not universal, strategy.  Promotion of an amenable literate workforce is often as important depending on the type of capital the state is hoping to attract.

The importance of the character of the state and its influence on the skill formation system can be illustrated by the contrast between West and East, and between old and new.  The first pair of industrial nations, the UK and the US, had a competitive advantage over the non-industrial societies and so did not require their governments to be actively involved in the process of entering world markets.  Once modern forms of industry were established, that in itself provided the competitive advantage.  However, the second generation of industrial countries had to break into world markets and for this reason, political elites, such as those in Germany and Japan, sought to shape the process of industrialisation.  To this end governments used the resources of the state to provide an effective system of education and hence a skilled workforce, while leaving industrialists to develop more of a co-ordinated attack on world markets.  In the case of

Japan, the state also protected domestic industries until they were deemed capable of successfully entering world markets.

It is in the NIEs, however, where the state has played in recent decades the most decisive part in influencing the development of education and training systems. Especially in Singapore, Korea and Taiwan, the governments have sought to develop close links with industry and to shape the industrial base of the economy while ensuring a steady supply of skilled labour capable of supporting the new industries. There, government policy has not merely been to rely on providing a steady flow of literate, skilled labour and leave the rest to industry. On the contrary, their education and training policies have been closely linked to an industrial and trade policy. We discuss these policies in some detail below (Chapter 7), with a particular focus on Singapore.

## 7. Nothing is permanent

Finally, just as there are potential contradictions between the extent and direction of development of the education and training and economic systems, so also there are contradictions within the economic system - in particular, a route to accumulation may appear viable over the medium term, but that does not guarantee it can remain a stable system for the indefinite future. Researchers have widely commended the 'high-skills equilibrium' path to economic success, said to be followed in countries like Germany, Japan and Sweden. But in every case there are potential contradictions to which eventually there may be no resolution other than the undermining and reconstruction of the institutional system. For example, even high-skills production processes may eventually become uncompetitive if sufficient skills are developed in relatively low-wage areas such as the NIEs or even very low-wage areas like Mexico. Similarly, while, as we argue in this book, there remain viable low-wage production strategies within the advanced industrialised nations, these too may be squeezed between third world competition and political barriers to lowering the real wage too fast in the West. A 'route to accumulation', a phrase we frequently use in this book, represents a particular mode of economic growth with a specific agglomeration of institutions, mode of distribution and so on, that can proceed unchecked for a decade or more. It therefore constitutes a useful device for understanding the present economic conjuncture in each country. But the phrase does not imply permanence.

These seven propositions constitute the starting point of our approach to understanding how the world's education and training systems relate to its economic systems. We have attempted to construct a consciously interdisciplinary framework, which is not at the same time merely eclectic. The need for interdisciplinarity should be evident in our critique of other approaches: the limitations of single-subject approaches are not only that they do not perceive aspects of the problem outside the conventional purview of the subject, but that they may even misperceive aspects within their own domain.   An example is where the 'business systems' approach is unable to rank systems and falls into a cultural relativism uncalled for by the nature of economic competition.   Equivalently, pure economic approaches can get wrong answers to questions of resource allocation when they ignore the social and economic context of skills acquisition.   It is only through interdisciplinary eyes that much of the full complexity of the relationship between the economy and the education and training system can be revealed.  By drawing on the contributions and strengths of economics, sociology and political science we have seen how it is possible not only to perceive the two-way nature of cause and effect, but also to characterise these effects in a non-linear and non-determinate framework. We believe this is an essential first step towards an adequate understanding of the reality of skill formation systems in the present day.

Below, in Chapter 5, we utilise this beginning to formulate a number of hypotheses concerning the institutional requirements of an economic system with high skill formation.   Before then, however, we proceed further with our detailed scrutiny of the widely presumed relation between education and training and the economy, by focusing on the existing empirical evidence.

## NOTES

1. There were, however, dissenting views, e.g. Heckman (1993) or Heckman, Roselius and Smith (1994).
2. An exception is the public debate in Japan in the 1980s which recognised the problems associated with the excessive reliance on rote-learning methods in Japanese schools (Schoppa, 1990).
3. Furth includes Australia in the same category as the UK and New Zealand.
4. Nevertheless, the practitioners of the approach generally recognise that there are severe problems in, for example, borrowing the ET framework of one country and simply inserting it into another in the hope of improvement in the system (A. Green, 1991).
5. This section draws on Green (1992), Part II.
6. This point is apt to be entirely missed by modern-day liberal enthusiasts for 'building up human capital' (Business Week, 19/9/1988, p.102). At the time Smith was writing, the system of production did not require the majority of the workforce to be literate.
7. The significance of this proviso is that in a world of asymmetric information (Katz and Ziderman, 1990), or where labour mobility is for divers reasons low, general training may not be perceived in the labour market as distinguishable from specific training.
8. The argument is echoed in the work of economists who see the aggregate education level as affecting either the level of national income, or its rate of growth. Greater education is seen as facilitating growth by enabling workers more easily to adopt new technologies or devise new ones (Wolff, 1993).

9. For example, a trained worker might help a workmate avoid errors. An externality occurs if there is no enforceable contract under which the workmate could pay even indirectly for this service.

10. The presence of externalities also means that one could not derive the social demand for education and training as merely the aggregation of individuals' demands.

11. Bowles and Gintis have been criticised with charges of economism and of ignoring sexism and racism in education. For a review of such charges see Cole (1988), and for their defence see Bowles and Gintis (1988).

12. Dore (1993) has challenged the idea that all internal labour markets operate through market mechanisms. He argues that companies in Japan and organisations like the US armed forces operate not through an internal market but through what he terms Personnel Office Career Deployment Systems (POCADS) where market mechanisms are not called into play. In these organisations jobs are not advertised; instead people are posted into their jobs.

13. In this book, we use the term 'regulation' in a broad sense, to refer to the process whereby individual or small-group actors are constrained by legal rules or social convention to follow certain actions. Regulation processes external to firms derive from arrays of institutions; regulation processes within firms derive both from the external context (the legal and social obligations) and from the firm's own organisational culture. A 'deregulated' firm, in this sense, should be understood as one which both faces few external regulatory constraints and where the implicit contracts, the social obligations and associated long-termist outlook are absent.

14. Marsden (1986), pp. 239-40, takes a similar line.

15. As examples of other studies employing this framework, see Campinos-Dubernet and Grando (1988) and Rainbird (1994b).

16. This argument is put to use by Finegold and Soskice (1988) and by Soskice (1993) in the British context.

17. We use the term materialist here to distinguish our approach from the liberal approach. However, it does not follow that we give explanatory primacy to changes in the system of production. As will become clear, we see changes in the system of production as one of the major drivers of change but we also perceive changes in other social and political process, such as state formation, to be of crucial importance in explaining differences in systems of skill formation.

18. See, for example, IRDAC (1991).

19. See, for example, Wood (1983; 1989).

20. This statement is even true in Finegold's account: he sees the inherent value of the capacity to innovate, and to respond to conditions of uncertain demand, in addition to the NIDL argument, as determining the superiority of a high-skills strategy from capital's viewpoint. We argue that this point is far from proven: that low-skills, low-wage production strategies may be profit maximising for some businesses in some regions or countries and not just in the short term.

21. Radical US writers use the phrase 'social structures of accumulation'; others refer to an 'industrial order' or to regimes with different 'modes of regulation'. All encompass the notion that a particular institutional constellation in any country at any time helps to determine the way in which each national capitalist economy functions.

22. In later writing Reich makes a point of the distinction between the interests of American people and those of American businesses.

# 3 Education, Training and Economic Performance: the Empirical Evidence

In the previous chapter we examined some of the conceptual issues involved in identifying a link between education and training systems and economic systems, and we found that the relationship is nothing if not complex. Though education and training have indubitable importance in the contemporary global economy, we cannot rest this importance on the simple sentiment that better skill formation systems cause better economic performance – a sentiment which may in certain circumstances be manifestly untrue, and which in any case ignores the complex interactions of modern social life. We aim in this chapter to complement the foregoing with a general overview of the empirical evidence appertaining to the relationship between the economy and the education and training system. Does the evidence bear out the existence of such a link, and if so is it straightforward, belying the supposed complexity we have urged, or does it reflect some of this complexity?

The relevant statistical evidence, most of which arises from the work of economists, concerns two general, related issues: the determinants of who receives education or training (and how much), and the impact of each on various measures of economic performance. We shall examine these in turn, below. Within econometric theory there has developed an impressive and sophisticated battery of statistical techniques for examining the links. Given the prominence of neoclassical thinking within the economics profession, it is hardly surprising that the majority of investigations have taken the human capital approach as a guiding framework. Notwithstanding our criticisms of the human capital approach as pure theory in the previous chapter, it will be helpful to begin by outlining the manner in which hypotheses about the allocation of education and training can be derived. But, as we shall see, though the empirical findings are enlightening they are not such as to prove or disprove human capital theory compared to other theories which, while viewing education and training as investments, nevertheless do not take the individualistic approach of the pure human capital theory. Indeed the findings can generally be interpreted within a range of frameworks.

# THE ECONOMIC DETERMINANTS OF TRAINING AND EDUCATION

## The Human Capital Model

The theory of human capital includes the proposition that individuals and firms invest in education or training in response to the prospect of economic gain sufficiently large at least to offset the costs of the investment. For the purposes of this chapter, since there is no formal distinction between 'education' and 'training', even though the latter is typically thought of as work-related, we shall use 'ET' as a shorthand acronym for either education or training. Formally, the choice facing an individual is modelled by the maximisation of a lifetime utility function. A principal argument of the utility function is lifetime wealth which in turn depends on the skills acquired during the lifetime. Focusing exclusively on this wealth (that is, ignoring the non-pecuniary aspects of skill acquisition) the individual's decision on how much to invest each period in post-compulsory ET derives from maximising lifetime wealth, $W_t$, given by:

$$W_t = \sum_{t=a}^{R} \left( y_t\,(h_t) - m\,S_t \right)\left(1 + \delta\right)^{a-t} \tag{3.1}$$

$$\text{subject to } y_t - mS_t \geq \psi \tag{3.1a}$$

where $y_t(h_t)$ is income in period $t$, (derived from any wages, and/or any unemployment benefits received), $h_t$ is the accumulated skills at start of period $t$, $S_t$ is the non-negative amount of post-compulsory ET received in period $t$, $m$ is the unit cost of such ET (including any opportunity costs in terms of foregone wages, and net of any state subsidies), $\delta$ is the discount rate, $a$ is the current age and $R$ is the age of retirement. Finally, $\psi$ is the minimum income, given the presence of credit constraints, needed for spending on things other than ET; the more that borrowing is limited, the greater is $\psi$. Equation (3.1) expresses wealth as the sum of income net of ET costs, for every year of working life, with future years' values being discounted to equivalent present values.

Accumulated skills are the sum total of past skills acquired. For present purposes these skills are taken to be general, and 'realisable' as income in any employment. Because we are focusing on post-compulsory ET, accumulated skills may be written as

$$h_t = \sum_{j=1}^{t-A} S_{t-j}(1+d)^{(1-j)} + h_A(1+d)^{-(t-A)} \qquad (3.2)$$

where $A$ is the period of leaving compulsory school ($a > A$), $h_A$ is the skill level at that stage, and $d$ is the rate of depreciation of skills. Equation (3.2) says that current skill arises from ET received last year and in previous years, but that the skill gained in previous years' ET has been progressively depreciated over time.

Let us suppose that the individual knows the relationship $y(h)$ between skills acquired and income, and let this be representable by a set of parameters $\theta_h$. Then maximising (3.1) with respect to $S_t$ and $h_t$ and subject to the credit constraint, to equation (3.2) and to the non-negativity of $S_t - a$ problem in dynamic programming – gives the individual's demand for ET. Implicitly, the human capital literature assumes there is in principle a general solution, and here it will take the form:

$$S_t = f_t(m, \delta, \theta_h, d, h_A, a, R, \psi) \qquad (3.3)$$

That is, the demand for ET depends on the various exogenous variables and parameters of the model. Plausible arguments are typically used in empirical work to support the following comparative statics predictions concerning the partial derivatives (where we have dropped the time subscript):

$$\frac{\partial S}{\partial m} < 0, \quad \frac{\partial S}{\partial h_A} < 0, \quad \frac{\partial S}{\partial \delta} < 0, \quad \frac{\partial S}{\partial a} < 0 \text{ and } \frac{\partial S}{\partial R} > 0$$

That is, ET intensity is greater: the lower is its cost, the lower is the initial skill level, the lower the discount rate, the lower the current age and the greater the age of retirement. In addition, it is widely argued that beyond a certain point, credit constraints will bite, so that $\partial S / \partial \psi < 0$. The rationales for all these predictions are to be discussed shortly below (see next subsection). Meanwhile, we may illustrate the first four predictions by formal derivation in a very simple model as follows. Let there be only 2 periods until retirement, to be devoted to work or to post-compulsory schooling, and let the earnings function be of the form, $y = Bh^\alpha$, with $0 < \alpha < 1$. It is trivially true that second period ET is zero and it is easily derived that, provided initial skills $h_A$ are not so high as to preclude any positive demand for further ET, the first period demand function for ET is:

$$S = \left[\frac{\alpha B}{m(1+\delta)}\right]^{\frac{1}{1-\alpha}} - h_A \qquad (3.4)$$

from which the above predictions flow directly.

Unfortunately, even the comparatively general framework suggested by (3.1) to (3.3) misses elements of the real problem facing individuals, elements that have been identified by both theorists and practitioners. Two important issues are:

a. Different types of training have different implications for future wages. For example, transferable training should lead to higher wages than job-specific training, the extent of the difference depending on labour market structure. Moreover, the costs of different types of training will also vary, both with the type of training and with the extent of prior schooling.

b. Uncertainty about future variables is pervasive. In addition to uncertainty about the path of $m_t$, individuals may be especially imprecise about their expectations of the $\theta_h$. They are likely to be uncertain both about the probability of employment in the jobs they are training for, and about the prospective wages.

Yet these are the crucial parameters of interest to the overall human capital argument. Utilising the Von Neumann method, the maximand (3.1), should therefore be replaced by an expected utility function, whose arguments include both expected wealth and its distribution. The derivation of results and implications becomes more complex, depending as they must now do on the posited distributional parameters. Such problems are often analytically intractable.

Not only individuals, but also firms have a demand for training/education services. A formal statement of the choice over how much to demand reveals the complexity also of their decisions. Firms might be viewed as maximising a dynamic profits function

$$\pi_t = \sum_{t=0}^{\infty}(1-\tau)(P_tQ_t - w_{st}L_{st} - w_{ut}K_{ut} - c_tK_t - n\rho_tL_{ut})(1+r)^{-t} \qquad (3.5)$$

where $Q_t$ is output and $P_t$ its price; $w_{st}$ and $w_{ut}$ are the wage paths of skilled and unskilled labour, $L_t$ and $L_{ut}$; $c_t$ is the cost of capital, $K_t$; $\rho_t$ is the proportion of unskilled workers being trained and n the cost to the firm of such training (net of any subsidies); $r$ is the rate at which firms discount future profits; and $\tau$ is the tax rate. Equation (3.5) expresses long-term profits as the sum of profits in each period (measured as revenue net of labour, capital and training costs), with future profits being discounted to equivalent present values.

Assume that the effect of the training is to turn unskilled into skilled workers ready for the next period. These may be added to by recruiting skilled workers from the external market. However, by the same token skilled workers may quit. Accordingly we write the amount of skilled labour used as:

$$L_{st} = \Lambda(w_{st}) + \frac{1}{1 + D(w_{st})} \left( L_{st-1} + \rho_t L_{ut-1} \right) \quad (3.6)$$

where $\Lambda(w_{st})$ is the contemporaneous supply of skilled workers from the external labour market, and where $D$ is the rate of quitting of skilled workers, also assumed to depend on their wage rate. We are assuming there is an imperfect labour market with frictions (since otherwise no general training would be profitable).

To complete the specification, the production function is then:

$$Q_t = f\{L_{st}, (1 - \rho_t) L_{ut}, K_t, TP_t\} \quad (3.7)$$

where $TP$ captures the rate of technical progress and where it is assumed that trainees do not contribute to production.

One may, then, in an analogous way to the individual's choice, conceive of the firm maximising (3.5) with respect to the range of choice variables, including $\rho$, subject to (3.6) and (3.7). A general solution to such a problem, assuming it exists, provides the firm's unit demand for training services in the form:

$$\rho_t = \rho (n, c_t, p_t, TP_t, \tau, r, \theta_f, \theta_\Lambda, \theta_D) \quad (3.8)$$

where $\theta_f$ represents the relevant parameters of the production function (3.7), $\theta_\Lambda$ those for the external supply of skilled labour $\Lambda(w_{st})$, and $\theta_D$ those for the quit function, $D(w_s)$. As with individuals, plausible rationales can be supplied to suggest various hypotheses used in the empirical literature (see below). Again, we may illustrate the derivation of some of the hypotheses with an extreme simplification of the model. Let there be two periods and let $r = 0$ and $\tau = 0$. Let there be a unit endowment of first-period skilled labour and zero external supply of second-period skilled labour, and let skilled labour, including those that have just been trained, quit at a fixed rate, $D$. The firm is assumed to use this skilled labour together with unskilled labour to produce a unit output in each period, according to a Cobb-Douglas production function such that:

$$1 = \left[(1-\rho)L_{u_1}\right]^\beta = L_{s_2}^\alpha L_{u_2}^\beta \qquad (3.9)$$

On these assumptions the firm's rate of training in period 2 is, trivially, zero, and in period 1 may be derived as:

$$\rho = 1 - \frac{(w_u\,\alpha\,/\,\beta)^{-\beta/\alpha+\beta}}{(1 + D)} \quad [w_s + (1 + D)\,(n + w_u)]^{\beta/\alpha+\beta} \qquad (3.10)$$

From this it follows straightforwardly that $\partial\rho/\partial n < 0$, that is, the higher the training cost, the less training is undertaken. Another conclusion of interest is that $\partial\rho/\partial w_s < 0$, that is, a higher-skilled wage leads to less training. This is consistent with observations from some surveys where it is reported that firms are reluctant to train if it means that the trained worker can subsequently demand a higher wage. The firm responds by choosing a less-skilled workforce. Conversely, $\partial\rho/\partial w_u > 0$. A rise in $w_u$ induces firms to choose a more skilled workforce, hence to raise the level of training. This is the simple intuition behind the oft-expressed proposition that preventing low wages is a way of stimulating skill formation, but the model makes clear that it is unskilled workers' wages that must be supported.[1]

Again, as with individuals, so with firms there are many real-world elements that tend to complicate the analysis. The $\theta_D$, for example, are likely to depend on labour market structures, as well as on labour supply considerations.[2] There is pervasive uncertainty, not only about future prices and technology, but also about the impact of the training as represented by the relative productivity of skilled and unskilled workers, and about its cost, $m$.

Despite the inherent complexity of the choices facing individuals and firms, it is part of the human capital argument that it is possible in empirical work to identify the effect of anticipated financial gain on the demand for training. Typically, it is implicitly assumed that the expected *ex ante* returns equal the *ex-post* actual returns, possibly with a random error.[3] The effect should show up in various hypotheses about the determinants of the demand for ET consistent with the models of optimising individuals and firms.

### The Determinants of Education and Training

There is now a good deal of evidence that, at least in some circumstances, economic incentives do clearly have an effect on ET choices. The evidence relates mainly to the actual distribution of ET rather than the demand as predicted by equations (3.3) and (3.8). Thus they are in effect examining choices as constrained by the availability of employers or education providers willing to supply the instruction.[4]   In particular, individual-level studies of training must also include various company or establishment-related variables, so that we must look also to the predicted demand for training services by firms as suggested by equation (3.8). In practice, studies proxy the theoretical independent variables with measurable quantities.

a. As far as education is concerned, it has been shown in a large body of US evidence, and some from elsewhere, that enrolments in college and higher education respond to the costs and discounted prospective rewards of ensuing careers, and more generally that wage elasticities of labour supply to skilled occupations can be quite substantial.[5] Similarly, there is some evidence that prospective lifetime earnings do have a significant impact on choices made about training.[6]

In a number of studies of training from a range of countries, the following findings are fairly general[7]:

b. Training participation is greater and more extensive for individuals who already have good qualifications. At first sight this appears contrary to human capital theory predictions (as derived, for example, in (3.4)), since the assumption of diminishing returns to human capital implies that greater initial human capital will lead to lower subsequent ET. However, the contrary empirical finding has been interpreted instead as ET lowering the costs of training, either $m$ in (3.3) or $n$ in (3.8). More educated workers are said to be more 'trainable', because one of the skills they have is the ability to learn efficiently. This point is also stressed by writers using the internal labour markets and the corporatist frameworks. A further reason for this association may be that further training is to some extent a desired service in itself, for the satisfaction this brings, and that the more educated worker is likely to have the greater taste for this. Whatever the cause, one consequence is that educational inequalities tend to be reinforced by unequal opportunities for training.

Over time, however, there is evidence that some craft training programmes have been decreased following a general rise in educational standards – a finding more in line with the simple theoretical prediction based on diminishing returns.

c. Training is related to age. In a number of countries participation declines steadily with age – Austria, France, Germany, Ireland, Spain and the United Kingdom. This can be interpreted in the life-time human capital framework, since where an individual is young there is a greater expected post-training period of working life: it corresponds to the influence of variable $a$ in (3.3). However, in many of these countries, that the bulk of training activity is concentrated in the first years of working life is a feature with historical origins in the apprenticeship system and typically linked to the institutional supports of occupational labour markets. Moreover, other countries exhibit instead a hump-shaped pattern with training activity peaking in the middle of the working career – including Finland, Sweden, the United States, Japan and, in respect of external training, Australia. In Japan, at least, this pattern may be clearly related to the strength of internal labour markets, which means that firms can safely pay to retrain older workers and recoup the benefits.

d. Training is more likely to be taken by individuals who have ambitions to self-improvement in their work,[8] and in some studies training has been found less prevalent for the individual who is regarded, rightly or wrongly, as less committed to paid labour (for example, because of family caring responsibilities); this can be thought of as influencing $\theta_h$ or $\theta_D$ there being less point in acquiring new skills if they are not to be put to such good use to earn wages ($\theta_h$) or if the worker is more likely to quit ($\theta_D$). The latter has a gender dimension. In particular, although in many countries it has been found that male and female participation in training do not differ greatly, it appears that females participate less than males in formal training programmes and receive less employer-sponsorship for their training. Moreover there is some evidence of overall participation differences between the sexes after controlling for other factors. Discrimination over training access, consistent with an institutional approach, is presumably likely to vary across countries according to the social context. Without a commitment to equality of opportunity, the context of an internal labour market can be an 'ideal' cradle for potential discrimination, in that opportunities are less openly competed for and superiors can more easily exercise their prejudices. This is an important part of the explanation of the relatively poor economic status of women in the Japanese economy.

e. Training participation is high for workers recently recruited to a new job. The explanation lies in the evident requirement to learn the necessary skills early on in any production task.

f. Training participation is greater in large firms and/or establishments. On one hand, these firms can reap economies of scale in training provision, that is, they have a lower value of $n$ in (3.8). On the other hand, it is thought that large firms are generally more likely to be able to retain their trainees than small firms where pay and prospects are typically not as good; that is, they have a greater $\theta_D$ in (3.8). Again this is consistent with the role of internal labour markets, more prevalent in large firms, in promoting training.

g. Training is more frequent in firms known to be implementing technological changes (the role of *TP* in (3.8)) and in occupations where the labour process is more subject to change, mainly higher-level occupations. One of the biggest areas of change over the last decades has been in organisational and management practices, hence providing the need for a great deal of management training, but also for the training of core employees in the necessary new skills (Osterman, 1995). Another widespread development giving rise to training needs is the introduction of micro-electronics at the workplace.

h. Training is usually greater in the public sector, because public sector mobility is likely to be lower, and because private profit-maximising firms are more likely than public employers to be inhibited by the fear of poaching (again, the role of $\theta_D$). It is also arguable that public organisations might take a longer view than private firms, implying a lower discount rate, $r$.

i. There is some evidence to suggest that training is greater where firms have strategic plans, and *a fortiori* training plans (Felstead and Green, 1994, 1995). These could be interpreted as indicative of the influence of a long-term perspective, as representable by a low rate of future discounting, $r$. Where management attitudes are driven more by the need for short-term financial gain, they are less likely to give attention to training.

j. Training is greater in industries with lower turnover (at least in the US and in France), and in countries with lower overall labour turnover and higher expected job tenure for workers. This is again the role of $\theta_D$ in (3.8), but this is also part of the argument of the internal labour markets approach. The median estimated job tenure at the start of the 1990s was: 8.2 years in Japan and 7.5 years in Germany, compared to just 4.4 years in the UK and only 3.0 years in the US. Even allowing for the difficulties of making international comparisons, this appears consistent with suggestions from existing statistics that training is much more prevalent in Japan and (at least for young workers) Germany than in the UK or the US (OECD, 1993). But it should be recalled that theory does not unambiguously predict a negative relation between turnover and training.

k. In all countries there is a considerable range of training intensity across industries. More often than not, the financial sector is among the high training industries, while non-durable manufacturing industries such as textiles or clothing tend to be low trainers. A general link between training and industries with high technical progress is hard to pin down. Tan and Peterson (1992) find that high technical progress industries are associated with, if anything, lower training overall but higher company-based training for better educated workers. There is also suggestive evidence from the US that it is the more high-tech firms and industries which tend to regard the availability of a sufficient pool of technically-trained workers as a serious criterion affecting choice of region to locate (Rosenfeld and Atkinson, 1990). Beyond that the pattern is complex.

l. There is evidence for Britain, the US and Australia that union membership or recognition has a positive impact on training (Green, 1993b; Green, Machin and Wilkinson, 1995; Tan and Peterson, 1992; Osterman, 1995; Frazis, Herz and Horrigan, 1995; Kennedy, Drago and Sloan, 1994). This is interpretable as unions exercising a collective voice, both improving the quality and desirability of training and reducing labour turnover, that is, $\theta_D$ in (3.8).

m. There is also limited evidence that individuals' access to training may be constrained by lack of the necessary finance, that is, confirming the effect of $\psi$ in (3.3) (Greenhalgh and Mavrotas, 1994), while access is correspondingly enhanced by having a greater family income and lower calls by siblings on family expenditures (Cameron and Heckman, 1994).

n. The possible detrimental impact on training in an industry of having a high rate of immigration of skilled workers is a salient issue in Australia. Baker and Wooden (1992) find this has a significant but small effect.

There is a plausible ring to these general conclusions, many of which are robust, holding as they do for many different data sets in a range of countries. It can hardly be pretended, however, that these results in any way establish that training decisions are taken on the basis of the rational individualistic calculus suggested by human capital theory. Other models of training and education, outlined in the previous chapter, have similar implications in a number of areas, and the importance of institutional influences is a significant feature of these findings.

Moreover, certain institutional factors are not revealed in the sorts of economy-wide statistical study on which many of the above results are based. It is frequently reported that enterprise training is a matter of 'fashion' (de Koning, 1994), or a function of organisational culture or national context.  A recent study links the extent of training in auto plants world-wide first, to the extent to which they have introduced flexible production strategies, and second, to the influence of national-level education and training infrastructures (Macduffie and Kochan, 1995).  The pervasive influence of unions and chambers of commerce on the training agenda in Germany is not necessarily something that could be discovered by econometric analysis (CEDEFOP, 1987a, 1987b).  The embeddedness of training systems within industrial relations systems (Brown, Reich and Stern, 1990; Hashimoto, 1991) makes it hard or impossible to discern the specific determinants and influence of technical training as opposed to investment in harmonious employee relations.[9]   Such influences are perhaps to be discovered more easily through historical and comparative case study analyses.  Brown, Reich and Stern (1994) show, for example, by comparing Japanese and US companies, that the differences in training intensities are linked not just to the differences in job tenure and employee security (point (j) above), but also to differences in job assignment and promotion practices.

Finally, it is virtually never the case that firms make precise calculations linking training expenditures to prospective profits in the manner suggested by the human capital approach.  Even in Japan, where investment in the developing the skills of the core labour force is a high priority, companies have not found ways of measuring the effectiveness of that investment.  In fact, training expenditures typically receive much less evaluation than companies' investments in physical capital.  The criteria for evaluation range widely, but tend to refer to immediate measurable benefits: they never (to our knowledge) refer explicitly to companies' long-term profits position.  Sometimes, firms' decisions may be based on some kind of company strategy, but this is by no means the general rule.  Similarly, at the national level decisions about training and education might be regarded as investments in the nation's future but, even if the explicit objective is to raise productivity or economic growth, governments cannot make such investments on the basis of precise calculations.

## THE ECONOMIC EFFECTS OF EDUCATION AND TRAINING

In considering the links between the ET and the economic systems, the alternative to estimating the demands for training and education services is to attempt to estimate directly the key parameters expressing the impact of training and education: in effect to examine the *ex-post* returns to ET, rather than the impact of the *ex-ante* returns on the demand for ET. This evidence comes at several levels, that of the individual, the firm, the industry and the nation.

## The Impact on Individuals

We are interested in the effect of education and training on people's incomes. These are affected both by the likelihood of getting into jobs, and by the wages and conditions received in those jobs. Also included under this general heading can be any effect on job mobility which is a potential route to increased income. It will be useful first to review the nature of the empirical investigation, in order both to reveal the connection with the evidence presented above about the determinants of ET participation, and to give some idea of the often-underestimated difficulties involved.

It is hypothesised that the income of the ith individual at time $t$, $y_{it}$, is a function of skills, which themselves are determined according to (3.2), i.e. on past education and training plus a host of exogenous variables, $X_{it}$, comprising family background, personal circumstances, ability and so on, which help to determine both employment probabilities and wages once employed. At the same time ET itself, given by $S_{it}$, is determined by income expectations plus a number of exogenous variables, $Z_{it}$. The aim at its most general is therefore to explain the distribution across individuals and over time of both incomes and ET:

$$f(y_{it}, S_{it} \mid X_{it}, Z_{it})$$

in such a way as to estimate the parameters of $y(h)$, contained in $\theta_h$, allowing for the fact that for each ET path over time we can only observe the wages and employment histories of those who actually take that path. We cannot observe directly the wages and employment histories that they would have experienced had they not taken that path.

Unfortunately this represents only an ideal econometric objective, which is unobtainable in practice. There are many data and modelling problems which beset the endeavour, which together imply that one should not be too confident of empirical conclusions in this field. To estimate the above distribution, one would ideally need full wage and employment paths over a number of years for a large number of individuals, with a rich set of measured independent variables, including variables expressing local and aggregate labour market conditions facing each individual over time. Frequently, however, researchers are equipped with no more than survey cross-sections, and there are usually considerable problems of missing variables and incomplete data sets, with special problems of sample attrition occurring in panel data sets.

The chief econometric problem arises from the joint determination of incomes and ET. It is dangerously misleading in many cases to make the simplifying assumption that ET is exogenous. Non-random participation in ET would lead to biased estimates of the impact of ET, either masking its influence altogether (for example, if those selected for a government training programme are selected on the basis of their disadvantages in the labour market) or exaggerating its effect (for example, if those with greater ability choose greater levels of ET). Considerable attention has been devoted by econometricians to resolving the problem of how to specify the processes of selection for ET, and the appropriate means to estimate and identify the coefficients of the earnings equations.[10] One of the problems encountered is that the conclusions of studies have been found to be quite sensitive to the choice of modelling procedures, or to rest on apparently arbitrary assumptions necessary to secure identification of the earnings equations. In the case of some government programmes in the US, these modelling difficulties have been partially side-stepped by the programme design which ensured random participation in the programmes, so that experimental control groups could be set up for comparison purposes. Nevertheless even these procedures have their drawbacks (Dolton, 1993), and they do not avoid the need for appropriate modelling of behaviour (Ham and Lalonde, 1994).

Further serious problems result from the fact that workers typically choose or are selected into different occupations, and the impact of the training can be confused with, even inseparable from, the impact of the occupation. One study in the US goes so far as to suggest that when properly accounted for this renders the independent impact of training insignificantly differently from zero (Hotchkiss, 1993). In addition, the status of workers as employed or unemployed, or as in or out of the workforce, is also linked to the training decision. It is normal, for example, for the impact of training on the probability of being unemployed to be examined independently of its impact on wages. A procedure which models these processes jointly would be desirable, but the estimation methods are complex and have largely proved elusive, given the normal data shortages.

Many of these problems might not have been uncovered if it were not for the proliferation of studies in recent decades looking at the impact of ET on earnings. Let us briefly survey what this evidence says.[11]

The link between schooling and earnings is one of the most frequently studied relationships in economics, typically using the earnings function as a framework (Mincer, 1974), wherein earnings are estimated as a function of schooling (measured either by number of years or by school qualifications) and sometimes also as a quadratic function of work experience. This simple formulation has been found to hold over a large range of data sets. Most studies examine only the marginal distributions:

$$f(w_{it} \mid S_{it}, X_{it})$$

that is, treating schooling as exogenous. Yet the effects hold up even after allowing for differential ability and endogenous schooling (for a survey, see Willis, 1986). Recent estimates re-confirm the existence of substantial individual returns to schooling in the US (Card and Krueger, 1992b), while Grubb (1992, 1994) establishes that there are significant, if variable, economic returns to sub-degree level education in community colleges. Moreover, Card and Krueger (1992a) have shown that states which spend more on educating children produce adult workers with higher earning power. Not only in the advanced industrial world, but also within third world countries it has been shown in countless studies that more-educated people receive higher earnings (Psacharopoulos, 1983). The robustness of this relationship between education and earnings, the world over, is impressive. Despite the econometric problems, this is generally regarded as a reliable empirical relationship. There is much less confidence on the magnitude of this relationship, and some scepticism about whether it can be used as the basis for a policy of favouring ET over physical capital investment (Weale, 1993).

Nevertheless it is also known that education often has a greater rate of return for some individuals than for others, one reason for which is that labour markets are segmented.[12] Education is of more value to workers in the primary segment of the labour market than for those in the secondary segment because, in the latter, jobs largely require only low-skill levels. A further issue concerns the extent to which extra education causes higher earnings by adding skills rather than acting as a screen for individuals of higher ability correlated with earning power.

Evidence on the impact of training on earnings is far more limited. For a long time, the impact of training was modelled indirectly: general training was proxied by work experience, and specific training by the length of tenure in particular jobs. The significance of these variables in countless earnings equations has been taken as indicating a return to training. The marked role of job tenure in earnings regressions for Japan is seen as testimony to high levels of training in that country. Nevertheless, such indirect evidence is weak as there are other explanations as to why earnings should increase with job tenure (Brunello and Ariga, 1994). Direct evidence, where the researcher has observations on training participation and intensity, is more convincing. In the US Lynch (1992), Lillard and Tan (1986), Tan and Peterson (1992), Bishop (1994), Swaim (1993) and Barron, Black and Loewenstein (1993) confirm significant positive impacts of company training on earnings. Positive impacts have also been found in Britain (Blundell, Dearden and Meghir, 1994; Booth, 1991; Green, Hoskins and Montgomery, 1994; Greenhalgh and Stewart, 1987; Blanchflower and Lynch, 1994; Tan and Peterson, 1992), in France (Laulhe, 1990), in the Netherlands (Groot, Hartog and Oosterbeek, 1994), in Finland (Asplund, 1993) and in Norway (Elias, Hernaes and Baker, 1992).[13] However, some forms of training have less impact on wages than others. A not uncommon finding is that vocational training and education prior to work, even when certificated, has little or no discernible effect on earnings (Elias, Hernaes and Baker, 1994; Green, Hoskins and Montgomery, 1994; Hotchkiss, 1993), though where the prior training is said to be 'relevant' it has a positive impact (Bishop, 1994). By contrast, the positive impact of formal company-sponsored training appears to be a fairly robust and widespread finding.

Of particular interest for policy purposes ought to be the evaluation of public training programmes, often provided for those disadvantaged in the labour market. There are many instances where such training has been found to have no or only small effects on earnings, while occasionally the programmes appear to work well. Maynard (1994) reviews this variability in the case of the US: a broad range of studies have shown little evidence of an impact of government training programmes on the earnings of disadvantaged adult male workers, but usually a positive impact for adult female workers. However, such studies have had little impact on US policy-making. In Britain, policy on government training schemes has been driven largely by political factors. Provision for formal econometric evaluation is much more limited, and results are never available before policy moves on. A possible reason is that estimates of the effectiveness of schemes in raising earnings or employment are pessimistic (Dolton, Makepeace and Treble, 1992).[14] Sweden also presents a rather pessimistic picture in this respect, in that the few existing studies show relatively weak or zero impacts on earnings (Bjorklund, 1991). It is more common to find positive evaluations of state training programmes' effects on participants' chances of subsequent employment – as, for example, in Austria (Zweimuller and Winter-Ebmer, 1991), Ireland (Breen, 1991), France (Bonnal, Fougére and Sérandon, 1995) or Britain (Dolton, Makepeace and Treble, 1992).

In all these studies, dealing with the joint determination of incomes and ET, or the implications of not dealing with it, has cast a cloud over how strongly we can rely on the conclusions.

## The Impact on Firms

In line with the model of the profit maximising firm, a general statement of the econometric problem would be to explain the distribution of profits, $\Pi_{it}$, and training inputs, $S_{it}$, in the ith firm over time,

$$f(\Pi_{it}, S_{it} \mid V_{it})$$

in such a way as to capture the relevant assumptions about training's impact on profits. $V_{it}$ includes all the exogenous factors influencing profitability and training. In the context of the model given in equation (3.5), $S_{it}$ represents the number of untrained workers getting trained in each period, $\rho_t L_{ut}$.

Putting it in this way, however, only emphasises how little is really known about the economic role of training in firms. For there is no evidence, to our knowledge, that comes anywhere near examining the issue adequately in this framework. Because of data limitations, researchers have not been able to examine the impact on profits. Evaluations by firms themselves and by professional trainers most typically cover measurable changes in the skills, attitudes or job performance of the training participants. Less often, such evaluations do relate to organisational goals such as profits or company productivity, as perceived by the evaluators.[15] Occasionally cost–benefit techniques are employed where the benefit might be some identifiable area of productivity improvement (Bushnell, 1990; Smith and Piper, 1990). Few firms regularly measure the full costs of their training activities and many businesses do not even attempt to evaluate their training at all. As we noted in Chapter 2, this reluctance to evaluate appears to be inevitable if the impact of training is 'fuzzy', that is, difficult to specify. Even though there may be good grounds for believing in the long-term salience of training, it may not be worthwhile and could be misleading to draw up a balance of the advantages and disadvantages that can actually be measured. Such an accounting mentality could itself be the cause of low training, if training programmes were obliged to demonstrate a sufficient measurable return on investment.[16]

A number of research studies have, however, been able to trace a direct link between training and labour productivity. One approach focuses on the firms' national location as a key factor providing independent variation, linked to national ET institutions, in external skills supply. By matching similar types of workplace in different countries, according to product area and where possible also to plant size, it has been shown in a series of studies by the UK's National Institute of Economic Research that the certified skills of a firm's labour force, drawn from the national labour supply, are a significant factor determining labour productivity. Moreover, these studies have attempted to open up the 'black box' of human capital theory by identifying the mechanisms through which the higher-skilled workforce can produce more efficiently. These include: the ability of shopfloor workers to perform a wider range of tasks leads to a higher quality product or service and to a reduction in downtime from machinery breakdown; the superior ability of supervisors in organising production reduces the need for senior managers to be involved in day-to-day production decisions; a higher-skilled workforce allows an early introduction of new technology and advanced machinery; and more craft-level workers enable more complex lines of product to be made, using small-batch production techniques with high value added. Initially, researchers focused on Anglo-German comparisons (Daly, Hitchens and Wagner, 1985; Prais, Jarvis and Wagner, 1989; Steedman and Wagner, 1987, 1989). Later studies brought France and the Netherlands into the picture (Mason, 1993; Mason and van Ark, 1993; Mason, van Ark and Wagner, 1994).[17] On the other side of the world, other researchers have found that, aside from any measures of formally certified skills, much of the higher productivity in factories in Japan compared to similar Japanese-owned factories in Malaysia and Thailand, is connected to the more effective enterprise training system and consequent higher skills in Japan (Koike and Inoki (eds), 1990).

A second approach is to confine the study to one country but examine a sufficiently large sample of companies to be able to draw statistical inferences. De Koning (1994) shows support in the Netherlands for the view that some forms of education and training, especially training supplied externally to the firm, contribute to firms' labour productivity, though the effect is not large.

How far these various studies are vitiated by the problem of endogeneity of training is a moot point. Yet despite the problems, there is now a body of strongly suggestive evidence that training does raise productivity in firms. The relationship needs to be explored further in empirical work, and should involve both statistical and case study methodologies. But, finally, it is worth re-stating the obvious: that even if training raises productivity this does not mean that it necessarily raises profits. Conversely, training could raise profits, not by raising labour productivity but by raising capital productivity: for example by enabling machinery to last longer.

**Industrial and National Effects**

Estimates of individual and firm effects are likely to underestimate or overestimate the social benefits in so far as ET has external effects. The externalities are positive when one individual's (or firm's) training investments benefits another's earnings (or profits). In order to examine the social effects of ET, an industry-level or country-level analysis (or some combination) is required. Unfortunately, none of the evidence at these levels is entirely convincing.

At the national level the criterion of good economic performance, analogous to productivity at the company level, is per capita national income. The most widely practised form of analysis is the 'growth accounting' framework (Denison, 1979). The essence of this procedure is to estimate the coefficients of a production function, having inputs of capital and labour, with the quality of the labour inputs captured by an index of the years of education undergone by the workforce. The index is derived by adding together the quantities of education of varying types, weighted by the associated average wage rates. In this way, researchers have arrived at a wide range of estimates of education's contribution to economic growth by adding to the stock of human capital. According to one recent survey (Pencavel, 1991), the estimates vary across countries and time periods between as much as 34 per cent and as little as 3 per cent, but most imply that there is a substantial contribution from education to economic growth.[18] There are, however, as many critiques of this approach, perhaps, as there are independent studies (Pencavel, 1991; Wolff, 1993). Apart from the difficult problems associated with any notion of an aggregate production function, critics have objected that: a) wage differences are inadequate guides to the productivity differences between education groups; b) such studies do not capture the full impact of schooling on economic welfare, effects which are not adequately measurable by national income, such as improvements in health care; c) the studies do not take account of well-known variations in the quality of schooling; d) the studies do not take account of the costs of schooling: education itself uses up labour and physical capital which has alternative uses; e) they do not take into account the possible complementarity of skills with physical capital inputs (typically their contributions are simply added together); f) they do not take account of other determinants of growth, in particular the tendency for lagging countries to catch up with productivity leaders; and, last but not least, g) they do not account for the possible endogeneity of schooling. This last point is the same one that has plagued microeconomic assessments, and it has a particular manifestation here. Richer societies are likely to spend more on education, other things equal, so the disentangling of cause and effect, as income grows while education also grows, is exceedingly difficult. Unfortunately, the simple correlation between high levels of ET and economic success is often seen, in political circles, as *prima facie* evidence for the effect of ET.  But it is potentially very misleading to make simple comparative statements, unless one can justify how one might identify the processes of cause and effect. Taken together, these criticisms lead most analysts, ourselves included, to discount the 'growth accounting' evidence altogether.

Much more credible are some recent studies that, taking advantage of recent improvements in international data, estimate the impact of education in a multivariate regression to explain the variation in long-term growth rates across countries.  These studies can be framed in a relatively open way, as far as theory is concerned, and can allow the data to 'speak for itself' as to whether education has any role at all.  They avoid dealing with the wage/productivity nexus and to some extent succeed in disentangling cause and effect.  Finally, in eschewing a static production function with exogenous technical progress, they allow a role for education in affecting technical change and innovation.  It is assumed that either the creation of new goods through R&D is affected by the level and growth of skill, or that the ability to imitate and catch up with best practice techniques from elsewhere is enhanced by a more highly skilled workforce.  Either way, the level of economic growth might be affected by the stock, as well as the growth, of skills.

Barro (1991) treats the levels of enrolment in primary and secondary education in 1960 (and also 1950) in a large range of countries as exogenous variables, and shows that these are significant determinants of economic growth in subsequent years, after controlling for other factors, in particular the initial income.  This is confirmed by Wolff and Gittleman (1993), but they also stress that educational attainments at primary and secondary levels have a much less clear-cut effect on growth.  This is disquieting, since it is arguably the level of educational attainment of the workforce which determines the rate of adoption of more efficient technology and forms of work organisation.  Moreover, it is only among undeveloped countries that primary and secondary enrolments are found to be more important.   Among advanced industrialised countries any differences in primary and secondary schooling have no significant effect on economic growth.  Some impact is found for the impact of university education, but the effect varies a lot depending on the period looked at. For the later period (1970–88), during which it has been argued that new technology was to be especially important,  the effect is minimal and insignificant.[19]   Wolff (1993) takes these findings for the advanced countries further, with an improved data set.   Though mean years of schooling do have some impact on growth, he finds no significant effect of educational attainments or enrolments, or of the changes in these, on economic growth.  That finding includes university degree attainments – a result which must seem especially disappointing for those who believe in the efficacy of higher education in the modern era. Yet in most cases, the coefficient indicating education's impact is at least positive, if insignificant. Moreover, using a different specification that stresses the role of labour force growth interacting with educational enrolments to augment workforce skills, Gemmell (1994) detects a significant impact of both the level and the growth of skills on economic growth for the period from 1960 to 1985, for both advanced and less-developed countries. One interesting avenue is the finding of Wolff and Gittleman (1993), confirmed by Gemmell (1994), that better education also raises investment levels, and that this might prove to be an important channel through which an education effect is securely founded. Nevertheless, these conclusions should at least give pause for thought for those who simply assume that education *must* be good for economic growth. The case is still far from proven. There remain serious questions as to the reliability of official enrolment data as measures of stocks and flows of skills in different countries, and as to the appropriate specification of cause and effect in these econometric studies. If it was as important as some commentators seem to suggest, one might expect education's effect to shine through the empirical fog, and robustly show us that it is there in all sorts of different specifications and different proxies for skills. It does not.

At the industry level the evidence is no more convincing. As one example, O'Mahoney (1992) uses the growth accounting framework to estimate that over half of the difference in productivity between German and British productivity levels is accounted for by differences in human capital. This is bold stuff, but the estimate is, by the author's admission, crude and, given the above-listed problems with growth accounting as a methodology, it is hard to place much faith in this estimate. In a later study, Robinson (1995) found no correlation between the intermediate skills gap and German/British productivity differences. An alternative methodology is to conduct a factor analysis of training intensities across industries. Verdier (1994) reviews one such study in France, which showed a positive correlation between training, technical progressivity, wages and various forms of work organisation characteristic of internal labour markets. Causation, however, is by the nature of such a study not established. Of special note is that there was no correlation found between the extent of training and firms' profitability. This mirrors the finding of Haskell and Kersley (1995) that, in a survey of British establishments, those employing relatively more 'skilled workers' did not gain higher profits.

Finally, it is not uncommon to find the argument that skilled workforces in a region act as a magnet for businesses deciding where to locate.

Implicit in such arguments is the notion that such decisions are motivated by profitability, and that a good local skills supply heralds greater profits, but inward investment is generally welcomed whatever the reason. The evidence that skills attract business is still, however, somewhat sparse. Marginson *et al.* (1995) have found in a survey that a considerable majority of multinational firms rated skills and qualifications as factors influencing location at greenfield sites, and as many as 9 in 10 reported that their decisions to invest in sites were affected by the local skills base. But the same multinationals could treat skills as more important in one country and labour cost as of greater concern in another. While these findings are preliminary, they are consistent with our assertions in the previous chapter, that in some cases not all sides are interested in a raising of the skills of the local workforce. Further research is awaited on this issue, since hitherto most studies on multinational location have ignored skills and training matters.

## CONCLUSIONS: WHAT THE EVIDENCE DOES AND DOES NOT SHOW

Though few if any studies come close to the ideal methodology for accurately estimating the relationship between ET and economic performance, the totality of evidence does allow some substantial general conclusions to be drawn. First, the studies of who receives what ET are consistent with the view that a motivation for the ET is improved economic performance. Second, there is a large amount of evidence from across the world that individuals who have received more and better education earn more wages, even if the rate of return is variable. Third, there is more limited evidence that training leads to higher wages. Fourth, there is also some limited direct evidence of an effect of ET on labour productivity. Finally, there is some evidence that better primary and secondary education leads to higher economic growth for national economies outside the advanced industrial countries. These are substantial and significant findings, all sufficiently robust to inform the process of ET policy formulation.

A more specific question is posed in a recent critical overview by Maglen (1990): does ET improve labour productivity? Rejecting the evidence of ET's impact on earnings, and rightly sceptical of studies claiming an impact on economic growth, Maglen accepts only the limited findings of direct impacts on productivity, and proposes that ET policies be linked only to those findings. Thus, for example, Maglen can see no empirical basis in economics for raising the numbers of graduates.[20] Though ours is a wider remit, it is nevertheless important to contrast our list of solid findings with an account of items which, despite the fact that they are frequently adduced in favour of expansionsary ET policies and of human capital theory, are not currently supported by empirical evidence.

First, none of the evidence itself proves or disproves the individualistic methodology of the theory of human capital, since all results are interpretable in a range of frameworks including those that stress the role of institutions. Second, the evidence does not support the view that more training for all workers is desirable on economic grounds. There remain many areas where jobs do not call for more training, or even for more education, where workers' prospects are unlikely to be changed by ET alone without alteration in the nature of the jobs. Third, there is no evidence for or against the proposition that more extensive training leads to higher national economic growth. The evidence of education's link to growth is, to say the least, thin, as far as the advanced industrial countries are concerned.[21] Fourth, although it is often assumed to be self-evident by some in the education field, there is not much evidence that the availability of skills really is a major factor influencing the direction of foreign investment, more, say, than other crucial factors such as political stability and market access. Fifth, there is no direct evidence whatsoever for the proposition that more training and education lead to higher profitability for businesses. Since profit is, after all, the fundamental objective of business, it is in effect the basic criterion of competitiveness in the global economy. In this sense there is, therefore, no empirically demonstrated correlation between ET and competitiveness.

This list of missing items does not, of course, necessarily imply that the various propositions in support of ET are false. The absence of reliable data could well be the simplest explanation for the fact that the evidence is missing. It might, for example, be that better training *would* lead of itself to higher economic growth or greater profits: it just has not been demonstrated. Nor have the opposites been shown – for example, that more ET has a negative or zero effect on growth.[22] A particularly difficult argument to test empirically is the plausible proposition that good ET is a necessary ingredient of economic success when considered in conjunction with other factors and institutions. A further possible argument, one which we stress later in this book in relation to the newly industrialised countries of the Pacific Rim, is that ET is especially important for societies in a transitional phase, when crossing over from a cheap labour to a high-skill/high-value-added route to accumulation. Moreover, in view of the expectation that industries characteristic of the latest phase of development make greater demands on knowledge skills, it is quite possible that ET has acquired a particular efficacy in the current era, in ways that one would not yet expect to show up in historical time-series analyses. More research is evidently needed here.

One factor deserving of more attention is international variation in the quality and effectiveness of education. Quite large international variations are typically found in the achieved educational standards, especially in maths and sciences, of school children (International Association for the Evaluation of Educational Achievement, 1988; Robitaille and Garde (eds), 1989). There are differences, too, in expectations about the mathematical skills required of vocational education students (Hawkins and Steedman, 1993). It is a reasonable bet, and there is some supporting evidence, that differences in teacher quality, and in the time and effort that school pupils devote to study, form a good part of the explanation of varied educational performance (Bishop, 1993). Differences in the quality of higher education are likely, if anything, to be greater even than the differences in school quality. Courses vary greatly in length, in access to lecturing staff afforded to students and, especially within the US, in academic standards achieved. None of these quality differences, nor *a fortiori* trends in these differences, would be picked up in the empirical analyses we have reported. So it would be far too premature to give up on education, or even higher education, as a force for growth. But it is possible that mere enrolment, or graduation, is not enough: it could be the quality that counts and its relationship to the stage of development of the productive system.

Despite these huge gaps in our knowledge, there remains enough solid positive evidence to reaffirm the importance of ET, and that it ought to be central to economic policy analyses. Moreover, our missing list bears out the variety and complexity implied by the approach we have advocated in the previous chapter. In particular, we referred to the diversity of routes to capital accumulation, and suggested that this implies a certain heterogeneity in the role played by ET within national economies. Since skills are socially constructed, the ET/economy link should depend on socioeconomic context, which will differ between nations.[23] We are a long way from explaining this heterogeneity, in the sense of comparing and explaining the estimates of the ET/economy link in different nations (if only because of the immense problems of data comparability). But the very existence of diversity suggests we would not necessarily expect to find that more training is best (in economic terms) for all, or that it necessarily leads to greater profits. It is quite likely that firms, in some areas, can make most profits at least for the medium term by following a 'low-skills' route, where both wages and skills remain relatively low for the advanced industrialised world.

The next task of this book, therefore, is to expand upon this theme by examining the extent of diversity among the economies of the advanced industrial nations. We shall argue against the somewhat fashionable viewpoint that what we are witnessing in this era is a process of simple integration and convergence, or even one of coalescence into homogeneous trading blocs. Rather, we see some important divergent features that have, according to our schema, substantive implications for the character of the 'ideal' ET systems of the current epoch.

## NOTES

1. A further result is that $dp/dD > 0$. This conclusion comes about because, in this simple model, firms need to replace some of those quitting to maintain a profitable supply of second period skilled workers. In a model with a longer horizon and an external labour supply, it is normally assumed that higher quits would induce firms to train less, and rely instead on external sources of skilled labour and/or a less-skilled workforce.
2. For a model of some of these complexities, see Stevens (1993).
3. Alternatively, one models expectations adaptively. A textbook version of the 'cobweb' model has students enrolling for courses where future wages are simply extrapolated from current wages. Since the supply of graduates is a long process, this can cause long-term fluctuations of graduates' wages. For a basic exposition, see Pencavel (1991).
4. For a textbook explanation of the problem of conflating supply-side and demand-side forces, and the inability to identify demand factors separately, see e.g. Addison and Siebert (1979: 120).
5. See Freeman (1986) and Pencavel (1991) for surveys.
6. See Makepeace (1994) for some recent UK evidence.
7. The following are *ceteris paribus* findings, after controlling in each case for other factors. Except where otherwise indicated, original source studies for these findings are given in Ishikawa (1991) and Hashimoto (1991) for Japan; Baker (1994) and Baker and Wooden (1992) for Australia; Lyach and Black (1995) for the US; Green (1993a; 1994) for Britain, Alba-Ramirez (1994) for Spain; and for these countries and a range of others in the OECD in OECD (1991a; 1991b; 1993).
8. See Greenhalgh and Mavrotas, 1994.
9. Claydon and Green (1994) examine the constrained role of unions in training in Britain. Higgins (1993) demonstrates a role for unions in shaping the skills and training requirements of employers in local labour markets in New Zealand.
10. For a recent review, see Dolton (1993).
11. In what follows the studies quoted exemplify the existing research, but are not intended to constitute an exhaustive bibliography.
12. For examples, see Dickens and Lang (1985) and Neumann and Ziderman (1986).
13. In addition other studies have picked up an effect on mobility, including that by Lynch (1991) for the US; and those by Booth and Satchell (1993) and Elias (1994) for the UK.
14. An exception to this was the Training Opportunities Scheme, which had a beneficial impact for women (Payne, 1991).
15. Researchers can in principle build on such self-evaluations. To illustrate, a survey of US establishments reported perceived gains from programmes of basic workplace education in terms, for example, of numeracy and literacy skills, communication skills, greater work effort, company loyalty, morale, ability to work independently or in a team, safety, self-confidence, or productivity (Bassi, 1995).
16. This idea illustrates the operation of the 'uncertainty principle' in economics: we are

inherently limited in how accurately we can know about something if, in the process of measuring it, we change it.

17. Cutler (1992) has questioned how far these studies have proved their case, arguing that they do not adequately account for differences in capital equipment and that they conflate the argument for more training for a minority of key workers with the argument for more training generally. In accusing the National Institute researchers of proving what they set out to prove, and in implying with little regard for the balance of evidence that there is more or less no demand for better training in UK firms, Cutler overstates his own case. The National Institute studies have acquired a somewhat misleading status, oft-quoted and caricatured without the depth and qualifications of their argument. They ought, for the sake of due scientific process, to be replicated in similar ways by researchers independent of the National Institute.

18. See also Psacharopoulos, 1983.

19. We may add the following query: if ET is supposed to have had increasing importance in the recent era, why did not West Germany, with its superior training system, pull even further ahead of its competitors in the 1980s.

20. In our view Maglen goes too far in rejecting the ET/earnings relationship altogether, for example by entirely discounting cross-occupation studies on the strange presumption that occupational earnings and productivities are quite incommensurable. How far earnings variations reflect productivity differences is a moot point, but for individuals the fundamental variable to measure economic performance is earnings, while for firms it is not productivity but profits.

21. One reason for this may be the high level of autonomy of the ET systems in the older industrial countries. The situation may be different in the NIEs where the link between the ET system and investment in physical capacity is closer.

22. A cynic might question how easy it would be to get published a study with such results.

23. To illustrate, one might expect to find systematically different gender effects on training issues between the US and Japan.

# 4 Global Economic Transformation and Skill Trends

It is a common perception that, on the eve of a new century, we live in a world of economies that are going to 'demand' ever-increasing skills from national workforces in the advanced industrial world.[1] This perception is driven primarily by a reverence for the technological innovations of the current era, especially those associated with computers and information technology, and those linked to biotechnology. We are said to be in the new 'knowledge' society, and the successful members of society are going to be those who have the fullest access to knowledge, and the best ability to manipulate it for profitable ends. The acquisition of higher-level skills, through both education and training, are thus demanded by the very nature of modern technologies.

The more perceptive writers in this school recognise that the new technologies can also be used to lower the skills of workers, and that there remain substantive unresolved empirical questions about how technologies are put to use (Finegold, 1992a). But in addition, and partly because of the new enabling technologies that have greatly reduced transportation and communication costs, the level of competition is seen to be continually increasing, through a broadening of world markets and an increasing integration of national economies through the expansion of world trade and of the scope of multinational corporations. In the advanced industrialised world, far fewer industries can hope to shelter from the winds of competition. Not only the traditional manufacturing industries, which have been under attack for several decades and which continue to be threatened by low-cost production in China and the Pacific Rim, but also many service industries are being opened up through deregulation to global competition. The free flow of financial and industrial capital, in search of the lowest costs of production, makes it increasingly difficult for high-wage companies – those operating in the North, as well as Japan and some of the NIEs – to compete. The only way to remain competitive under these circumstances is for those in the advanced industrialised world to keep ahead of rivals in the third world in terms of their ability to harness the new technologies to new products and processes. So, the argument goes, international competition also brings an ever-increasing demand for high-level skills and a poor look-out for those in the industrialised countries who remain unskilled (Campbell, 1994).

The propensity to initiate and process change has thus acquired a premium, promoting both R&D capacity, and the capacity to turn new ideas quickly into marketable products or services, to become the major weapons of competition. Attached to this same viewpoint, though wider in scope, is the theory of post-Fordism, which argues that the onset of flexible productive systems requires the advent of multi-skilled workers. A much larger proportion of the workforce is assumed to require problem-solving skills, just to deal with regular work tasks which are now less routine than on Fordist assembly lines. Continuous technical changes necessitate regular re-training of workforces, rather than simply an initial dose of training at the beginning of a working career. The greater participation and trust that it is necessary to induce in workers in order to harness the full scope of their creativeness in problem-solving means that there must be less hierarchy than hitherto in employee relations. So executives must acquire the 'social' skills to set up and manage more flexible organisational structures. The accompanying decentralisation of organisations is said to imply a need for relatively more middle- or lower-level managers and supervisors with organisational skills. Especially in the expanding service sector, 'customer-oriented' skills are required more widely. Finally, even at the bottom end of the scale, basic skills such as literacy are argued to have an increasing role in the modern workplace.

The remarkable thing about these claims is that they are typically presented with relatively little theoretical grounding and even less of a basis in solid empirical evidence. We suspect, however, that the above trends are by no means uniform, even in the advanced industrialised world. This is not merely to say that some places are proving better than others at providing the appropriate routes to skill acquisition. Rather, we take issue with the notion of any such thing as an abstract 'skills need' dictated by technology or by international integration. It is capitalist employers who are doing the demanding for skilled or unskilled labour, and it is, ultimately, the conflicting pressures on employers which may or may not result in their demanding more skilled workers in the labour marketplace.[2] Despite the above-mentioned integrating tendencies in the international economy, there remains evidence of a notable heterogeneity in the economic development of nations, with considerable divergence along several dimensions of economic performance. Concomitantly the development of the multi-dimensional skills of national workforces presents in theory a complex pattern, and the limited empirical research has so far left us with only a fuzzy picture of what this pattern actually looks like. We seek, therefore, not to deny that some at least of the above trends may be important in the modern era, but to arrive at a more solid assessment of what is happening, basing our arguments on a review of the scientific evidence rather than on creative assertion.

We begin the chapter with a re-examination of some key trends in the global economy, those trends that seem likely to have most bearing on skill trends and on the development of national ET systems. We consider how far the notion of 'integration' is an appropriate characterisation of the present economic conjuncture, and how far these global trends are bringing about a convergence of national economies. We then look at the implications for skill trends and describe how researchers have examined them. In the process we also assemble some of the evidence about skills in particular countries whose ET systems are to be more closely examined in subsequent chapters.

## THE WORLD ECONOMY IN THE CURRENT ERA[3]

There is nothing especially new about an open economy, in terms of trade and investment. The expanding British empire in the late 19th century hosted levels of trade and foreign investment which in relative terms exceed present-day amounts. What is new, in the current era, is that the whole world has been opened up to capitalist relations of production (MacEwan, 1991). Unlike in the past, the expanding trade of the current era is all with systems imbued with capitalist relations. Foreign investment consists of constructing fully-fledged production facilities with accompanying infrastructures. The deregulation of financial markets has meant that for financial capital the world is economically one place. The contradictory dynamic forces of capitalist competition have spread to hitherto unbreached parts of the globe, a process that goes hand in hand with the intensification of such competition in and among capitalism's homelands in the North. In this sense all the world's economies have been 'integrated' within capitalism.

It would be incorrect, however, to characterise this change in the world economy as an *undifferentiated* process of integration or of 'globalization' (Hirst and Thompson, 1992). Though trade has increased its importance in the post-war economic life of most countries, the largest areas of most economies are still served by national-based firms. While there is no doubt that the spread of multinational corporations and associated foreign investment makes it possible often to talk meaningfully of the 'global factory', the truly *transnational* corporation which has no national base and no concern for national specificities remains in a small minority. The world market-place is becoming more open, and with it there comes a relentless increase in competition (Auerbach, 1988), but along with these changes there is a notable unevenness in the new economic order being created, and there are no signs of any narrowing of the gap between the 'North' and the 'South'. Let us briefly review this uneven character of the modern age.

*Table 4.1   Fractions of OECD Average GDP Per Capita*

|                                                | 1950 | 1973 | 1989 |
|------------------------------------------------|------|------|------|
| Asia                                           | 15   | 16   | 28   |
| Latin America                                  | 52   | 40   | 31   |
| Sub Saharan Africa                             | 11   | 8    | 5    |
| Eastern Europe, Middle East and North Africa   | 29   | 27   | 26   |

*Source*: World Bank, 1991.

The 1980s saw OECD countries' per capita GDP growing at a paltry 2.1 per cent per annum, not much above the late 1970s and barely more than half the rates achieved in the 1960s.  With this comparative stagnation unemployment has steadily risen, from peak to peak.  Most western economies were, at the start of the 1990s, in the throes of a major recession, a continuation of the crises that have pervaded capitalist economies since the end of the 'golden age' period of capitalism (Armstrong, Glyn and Harrison, 1991).  Nevertheless, over the long term there remains a slow accretion of average income levels, and most observers expect some sort of continuation of this trend.

Given the declining living standards of substantial chunks of the globe, this has been an era also of widening gaps between first and most third world countries, as Table 4.1 shows.  Most notably, an already impoverished sub-Saharan Africa in 1950 became in relative terms less than half as well off after nearly four decades of North–South uneven growth.  Countries with such low living standards generally also have poorly developed systems for work-based training.  The Latin American countries, some of which have significant formal training systems (Middleton, Ziderman and van Adams, 1993), also experienced substantial decline.

Against this pattern, however, Asian economies have been staging a substantial catch-up in the recent two decades.  On a weighted average, their GDP per capita doubled after 1970 in a mere 16 years, and it continues to grow at rates truly astonishing by historical standards. One group of not-so-poor countries – identifiable as Asian NIEs and comprising Hong Kong, Singapore, Taiwan, Indonesia, South Korea, Malaysia and Thailand – chalked up a doubling of real GDP over the 1980s decade. We shall consider in subsequent chapters the remarkable training strategies in the first three in this group, which have already achieved living standards comparable to many countries in the West. But the fastest growing country, though starting from a very low base, is also the largest. From 1980 to 1991 China achieved an average growth rate of nearly 10 per cent per annum on the back of its reform policies (mainly the development of some free markets, and partial liberalisation of productive enterprises), and an investment ratio of 39 per cent of GDP. Its exports rose over the same period by a factor of over four. China's GDP is already not far short of half that of Britain's, and, extrapolating Britain's long-term growth rate of 2.2 per cent and China's 1980s growth rate, one reaches the forecast that China's GDP would exceed Britain's during the first decade of the new millennium. On the same basis China's GDP would be larger than the US GDP by about 2030. Such exercises in simple arithmetic are meant not as serious forecasts but as illustrations of the sheer magnitude of the transformation now seemingly under way for more than a decade. The changes make research on the economic role of ET in China an item of increasing importance.[4]

It is not only these economic transformations but some related political-economic transformations that must concern us. In Eastern Europe the band of disparate countries that emerged from the disintegration of the Soviet Bloc and the collapse of communism are struggling with the transition to capitalism. These countries have experienced substantial cuts in output (some 20 per cent over 1989 to 1991), attributable to the multitudinous costs of economic transition, and the disaster of war in the former Yugoslavia has cast a pall over the post-Cold War era. It is hard to assess current economic trends in these countries with any confidence. Nevertheless, the labour forces in many of these countries remain relatively well educated. Another transformation with an uncertain future is taking place in South Africa. If the peaceful transition to a post-Apartheid regime is successful, there emerges a large industrial economy with an aspiring workforce that has had limited access to education and training in the past.

Another political–economic transformation with potential implications for skills is the development of distinct trading blocs. The creation of the 'Single Market' in the European Community heralds changes in the field of human resource development, even if they are much more limited than the changes in product markets. The encouragement given to the formation of Europe-wide corporations, along with inter-regional mobility of managerial and technical staff, will bring some pressures for harmonisation and convergence of conditions and of models of skill development for such highly qualified workers (Marsden, 1993).[5]

Meanwhile the erection of a free trade area in North America is less far-reaching, in that it does not involve an integration of the labour market. But the conclusion of the North American Free Trade Agreement has created the largest consumers' market in the West. In the Pacific Rim the ASEAN group of countries in South East Asia have been less successful in creating an inward-looking trading bloc, but the unplanned development of interregional trade and investment between Hong Kong, Taiwan and the southern provinces of China have created a 'Chinese Economic Area' (Jones, King and Klein, 1993), which is set to become the world's fourth largest trading entity by the year 2000, trailing only after the US, the EC and Japan.

The picture of a seamlessly integrated global capitalist economy is, thus, an over-simplification which falsifies the lumpiness and the national-centredness of economic relationships. So, too, the argument about skill trends is simplistic. Part of the argument has been linked in the literature to the theory of the 'New International Division of Labour' (NIDL), but whether or not the theory was ever universally valid, it is now being superceded (Castells, 1989; Schoenberger, 1989). The chief problem with the theory, as discussed above (Chapter 2), is that it places its emphasis on only one element in the process of profit maximising, namely wage costs. Other strategic factors continue to determine in favour of location in the advanced industrial world, and signal a continued demand for routine lower-level skills. We should not expect to find an inexorable and *universal* trend to high-technology, high-value-added production in the North. At the same time, the decentralisation of certain production facilities to the NIEs on the Pacific Rim is likely to continue. Apart from the tax breaks that remain attractive, and from the fact that as centres of growth these countries provide themselves a growing market, the NIEs on the Pacific Rim with their high emphasis on education are demonstrating the capacity to upgrade and operate the advanced technologies, thereby competing on the high ground with firms located in the North (Fong and Lim, 1989; Singh, 1994). Even with the relatively impoverished populations of Mexico it has sometimes been found possible to operate the most advanced plants. One factor here is that, even though the local stock of modern industrial skills may be limited, the costs of training people are also low like the wages.

# CONVERGENCE IN THE ADVANCED INDUSTRIAL COUNTRIES?

While global integration is far from a smooth and even process, is there at least a more even character to the integration that is taking place among the developed countries, such that from an economic standpoint these countries are beginning to look more and more alike? If so, are the skills used in these countries also coming to a greater uniformity?

The notion that there is a pervasive best-practice technology, coupled with an increasingly integrated world economy, is manifested in the hypothesis of traditional neoclassical growth theory that there will be a convergence of economic growth among those countries able to exploit it, chiefly the advanced industrialised countries. For these countries, it is said that competition has to be based primarily on the use of the technology to produce high-quality differentiated products. As Abramowitz has noted:

> Among the many explanations of the surge of productivity growth during the quarter century following World War II, the most prominent is the hypothesis that the countries of the industrialized 'West' were able to bring into production a large backlog of unexploited technology. The principal part of this backlog is deemed to have consisted of methods of production and of industrial and commercial organization already in use in the United States at the end of the war, but not yet employed in the other countries of the West. (Abramowitz, 1986: 385)

If the 'knowledge society' is becoming universal, and if the means of communication and diffusion are becoming so inexpensive, one might expect to see a reinforcement of this tendency towards convergence in the modern era (Baumol, 1986). This would be a realisation at last of the ideal world of the neoclassical growth model (Solow, 1956) in which all countries gravitate towards the same technologically-determined growth path and, concomitantly, the same degrees of physical and human capital intensity.[6]

Until recently, such arguments remained somewhat on a speculative plain, because of the sparcity of long-term growth data. Prompted now by the availability of new data sets covering as many as 15 countries back to 1870 and many more for the period after 1950, the notion of technological convergence has been re-invigorated by empirical testing. In particular, 'convergence' has in many cases been empirically examined in the form of a productivity 'catch-up' of Western nations with US best practice, whereby a country's productivity growth is strongly affected by its initial productivity or by the initial gap between its and the US's productivity levels.

Using a very long sample period, catch-up and convergence regressions of this type have been found to perform well (Abramowitz, 1986; Baumol, 1986). But such studies suffer from serious sample selection bias, in that only those economies that have grown substantially since the last century tend to be included in the sample (DeLong, 1988). By excluding those countries which did not grow very much, the impact of initial backwardness can be greatly overestimated. Studies over a shorter period tell a more complex story. Across a large range of countries post-1950, there is virtually no evidence of global convergence. Nevertheless, if the world is divided into three 'convergence clubs', according to current per capita income level, there is found to be a notable post-1950 convergence among 'rich' countries towards the focal point of the US. The convergence in the post-war decades was faster than earlier in the century, reflecting the increased role of trade and multinational investment compared to the inter-war period. Among middle-income countries there is less evidence of convergence, and there was no convergence at all among poor countries of the third world.

A key question concerns whether the convergence process among rich countries is continuing in the present era. After allowing for the diminishing or elimination of the gap between US and other countries' productivity levels, the theory of the knowledge society would suggest a quickening in the pace of convergence among all advanced industrialised countries. Various ways can be used to measure convergence according to how one measures the dispersion of growth rates,[7] but whatever the definition no such quickening has been detected. Baumol and Wolff (1988) and Abramowitz (1986) find that after the early 1970s the process of income convergence among OECD countries ceased. Dowrick and Nguyen (1989) adjust the data to remove cyclical movements, and find that convergence continued from 1973 to 1985 though at a much slower rate than previously. Their results show that after 1973 there was a slight increase in the dispersion of growth rates among the richer half of OECD countries, and a decrease in dispersion among the poorer half. Soete and Verspagen (1993) find that the slowdown or even reversal of the convergence process among OECD countries persisted till the late 1980s.

Three other major elements of macroeconomic performance also display some significant elements of cross-national divergence in the current era: unemployment, income distribution and wages. First, although there has been a widespread trend for unemployment rates to increase over the last 20 years, there remain five significant economies that have managed to traverse this extremely disruptive period without experiencing mass unemployment. These are: Japan, Sweden, Austria, Norway and Switzerland. There is also some variation among other countries. While it appears that current experience may be different in that, for the first time, Sweden is encountering problems of unemployment, the experience of two decades of divergent economic performance in terms of this key macroeconomic variable has significant implications for skills training.

Second, another area of divergence lies in the distribution of income (Gardiner, 1993; Green, Henley and Tsakalotos, 1994). Whereas some countries, most notably the US and the UK, have experienced substantial increases in income inequality since some time in the late 1960s or the 1970s, replacing a previous slow egalitarian trend, others have enjoyed either a roughly steady or even decreasing degree of inequality, including Austria, Canada, Denmark, Finland, Germany, Holland, Norway, Japan and Sweden. Since the US was unambiguously a less equal society than most even in the 1970s, the subsequent trend has widened the inequality gap. On the other hand, there appears to be less diversity in the direction of the trend in earnings distributions, with several though not all countries showing upward trends (Atkinson, 1993).

Finally, there is also considerable diversity in wages and labour costs between different countries, as Table 4.2 shows. Highest manufacturing wages and labour costs are in Germany and the Scandinavian countries, while the UK, Ireland and especially Portugal and Greece are low-wage countries. Such differences are a primary testimony to segmentation among national labour markets. As significant, however, as the level of wages, is their long-term growth rate. The simple neoclassical theory of growth predicts that, with everywhere the same rate of technical progress, wage growth should converge to the same rate in all countries.[8] The facts, however, are more complex. In the 1960s UK labour costs were, in contrast to Table 4.2, closer to European and Scandinavian levels, much greater than Japan's, but much less than in the US. Real wages in the US fell by over 10 per cent between 1977 and 1989[9] (Mishel and Bernstein, 1992), and by the end of the 1980s were comparable to the levels of other countries. Thus, if we include the US, the level of wages has tended to converge. But there remains significant diversity in the rate of growth of wages, with the US average real wages falling in absolute terms and the UK real wage falling behind in relative terms. Moreover, given the dispersion of wages in both the UK and the US, the average figures conceal the fact that very large numbers of lower-ranked workers have experienced decreasing real wage rates for some time.

*Table 4.2  Hourly Labour Costs in Manufacturing[a]*

|  | Hourly Earnings[b] | Total Hourly Labour Costs[c] |
|---|---|---|
| Norway | 160 | 168 |
| W. Germany | 132 | 167 |
| Switzerland | 164 | – |
| Sweden | 125 | 160 |
| Finland | 120 | 147 |
| Denmark | 166 | 136 |
| Netherlands | 127[d] | 136 |
| Canada | 132 | 133 |
| Belgium | 107 | 132 |
| United States | 129 | 131 |
| Japan | 154 | 128 |
| Italy | – | 125 |
| Austria | 94 | 122 |
| France | 99[d] | 114 |
| United Kingdom | 100 | 100 |
| Ireland | 94 | 93 |
| Greece | 43 | 50 |
| Portugal | 30 | 40 |

*Notes*
 a: Ranked by total labour cost, with the exception of Switzerland; UK=100.
 b: 1988.
 c: 1989; includes social charges.
 d: 1987
 Source: Ray, 1990.


A range of explanations may be given for diversity in economic performance.  On one hand there is the historian's concept of 'social capability' (Abramowitz, 1986) which alerts us to the likelihood that backward countries may not be able to catch up if they lack the relevant social capability – including education and other necessary political, financial and industrial infrastructures.  On the other hand there is a long tradition outside the mainstream that has stressed the role of cumulative causation, with Myrdal and Kaldor being most prominent in modern economic thought.  Kaldor built his theory on the assumption that there were increasing returns in the industrial sectors of modern economies, based on the technological and organisational advantages accruing to large scale and on 'learning effects'.  Faster rates of expansion would then lead to faster productivity growth, while slow rates of expansion would induce productivity stagnation – an unstable process of endogenous technical progress leading to divergence among countries that embark on different paths of expansion. Marrying this Kaldorian approach to an empirical model of social capability focusing on education and the capacity for innovation, Amable (1993) also finds a general pattern of divergence.

The Kaldorian tradition has recently been developed in specific ways by mainstream neoclassical theorists also with a mission to explain diversity (Lucas, 1988, 1990; Romer, 1990a, 1990b). These theorists also assume increasing returns to scale but do so in an individualistic optimising framework with ensuing equilibrium growth paths. A key feature representing an advance over Kaldor is to specify precisely the origin of the increasing returns in the production function. Lucas (1988), for example, assumes that a firm's output is affected not only by the human capital it employs but also by the general stock of human capital in industry. Thus, although constant returns are assumed for each firm (an assumption necessary to maintain consistency with perfect competition), the additional external benefits associated with the industrial stock of human capital deliver increasing returns. One result is that training and human capital acquisition will be suboptimal in the absence of state intervention. Another is that both actual and optimal growth rates would rise as a result of an improvement in the techniques of training. The consequence of these and other models in the same neoclassical vein is that growth rates and income levels in different countries can differ, even in a world with capital mobility and free trade. This represents an advance over traditional neoclassical growth theory which, till then, could explain very little about the stylised facts of growth.

Yet several criticisms of these neoclassical explanations have recently emerged (Ryan (ed.), 1991; Setterfield, 1993; Skott and Auerbach, 1993; Soete and Verspagen, 1993). One unsatisfactory aspect concerns the assumptions linking growth directly to R&D and the production of knowledge, whereas historical observation frequently finds that the ability to adapt technology, innovate and market new products is the key to economic success. Other disturbing features are the assumption of rational expectations and of (constant) exogenous preferences. Moreover, although the theories can explain dispersions of national growth rates, the focus on steady-state growth paths means that the theories have trouble explaining changes over time in national growth rates.

Dissatisfaction with the contrast between the reality of complex growth patterns across the world and the settled equilibrium ('balanced') growth paths that are the outcome of even the most technically sophisticated neoclassical growth models, has led other writers to opt for a disequilibrium approach to economic diversity. On the one hand, Soete and Verspagen (1993) approach the issue in a thoroughly empirical manner, and describe some of the patterns emerging among different growth clubs and patenting clubs.    And, in the same frame, but emphasising the importance of management structure and of the 'system of innovation', Tylecote (1992) develops the concept of diversity according to strict empirical criteria.    At the macroeconomic level these criteria comprise the rate of GDP growth and an estimate of its sustainability based on the balance of payments, debt and inflation.    These in turn are linked to more fundamental indicators, including industrial R&D expenditures, patenting rates and estimates of skill levels.    Tylecote argues that further European integration is likely to increase the diversity of experience between the core or semi-core regions (Germany, Switzerland, the Netherlands, Belgium, France, Austria, Italy and the Scandinavian countries) and the periphery or semi-periphery (Ireland, Spain, Portugal, Greece and the Eastern European countries).[10]

An alternative approach is to replace the individualistic assumptions of the neoclassical model with assumptions giving prominence to institutional and political forces.    Such an approach has enjoyed a long tradition among heterodox economists, dating back at least as far as Veblen and Marx.    One modern-day approach theorises the role of institutions within 'social structures of accumulation', focusing on the changing institutions and class forces necessary to support capital accumulation in different historical periods (Edwards, Gordon and Reich, 1982).    This approach has been applied mainly to the US, but the not-dissimilar approach of the French regulation school has been applied across a range of countries to account for diversity of economic performance (Leborgne and Lipietz, 1990).    Also with an emphasis on international comparative analysis, both political scientists and institutional economists have examined the role of corporatist institutions in modifying macroeconomic performance. Unionism, potentially a key force in a corporatist state, has itself been 'going different ways' in different countries over recent decades (Blanchflower and Freeman, 1990; OECD, 1994).    Corporatist countries – particularly the 'social corporatist' countries of Scandinavia that have practised an 'inclusive' form of social solidarity – have a far superior record in terms of unemployment and its trade-off with inflation over the 1970s and 1980s, compared to the more liberal economies (Pohjola, 1992). They have tended to exhibit greater degrees of macroeconomic flexibility, chiefly as a result of their centralised wage-bargaining structures, and their ability to broker political exchanges between employers, unions and the state.    And they have generally weathered the economic storms of the 1970s and 1980s without the U-turn on egalitarianism experienced so dramatically in the liberal economies of the United States and the United

Kingdom (Green, Henley and Tsakalotos, 1994). There is some more limited evidence too of how corporatist institutions have better facilitated the necessary restructuring for economic growth (Landesmann and Vartiainen, 1992).

There are, then, several dimensions of macroeconomic diversity among industrialised countries, which complement the uneven development of the world economy as a whole, and there is good reason to believe that national institutions are important determinants of these differences. If increased competition is cited as one of the well-springs of skill change, this is, after all, an insufficient basis *per se* for maintaining that skill trends across the world will converge to a uniform pattern. We should be sceptical, therefore, of grand simplistic claims about the general nature of skills needed to maintain competitiveness in the current era.

## IMPLICATIONS FOR SKILL DEMANDS

Indeed, in terms of skills, the general picture of continued politico-economic diversity is complementary to the conclusions so far at least of extensive debate among labour analysts. In an extensive of review of theory and evidence on technology and the transformation of work in the modern era, Wood concludes: 'The quest for general trends about the development of skill levels, or general conclusions about the impact of technologies, is likely to be in vain and misleading' (Wood (ed.), 1989: 4).

The argument for a general upskilling derives from assumptions about modern technology, especially the pervasiveness of micro-electronics in all industries, and the intensification of international competition. The result is a discernible pattern of replacement of old by new, higher-level skills. An example is the financial services industries, shaken up by macroeconomic disturbances, by deregulation and by the global revolution in telecommunications. Here, pressures for decentralisation, increased involvement by lower-level workers, increased interactions with customers and widespread automation of less-skilled tasks, have been leading to similar though not identical workplace transformations in a number of industrialised countries (Bertrand and Noyelle, 1988).

But it is simply incorrect to maintain that new technology *necessarily* increases skill requirements, as writers unacquainted with sociological findings seem often to assume. Many new technologies have historically been used to replace skilled workers – this being a central feature of Taylorist and Fordist production systems. It is far from obvious that such systems are obsolete, even though the theory that capitalist technologies are *necessarily* deskilling has been decisively refuted. Many writers are instead opting for some form of intermediate position, which involves both upskilling of certain sectors of the workforce and the downskilling of others. Such polarisation can be linked with processes of segmentation in the labour market.[11]   What we add to this set of conclusions is the proposition that the diversity in skills demand has its origins not just in technological diversity but in wider politico-economic differences across nations and regions.

Before we consider the argument and the evidence, we first address a confusion in the nomenclature. Not infrequently there is talk of the *skill needs* of modern technology and modern economies. This is a potentially misleading concept, which should be distinguished from *skill demands*. Whereas skill needs might be defined in terms of the skills that are required by humans to make the best self-enhancing use of the available technology, skill demands are those which employers demand of their workforces and in the market-place.   Skill demands may in turn be distinguished from the actual *skills in use*, since it is possible for those skills available in the market-place or in workforces, the *skills supply*, not to match what employers would like to employ. In that case there is a skill shortage or surplus. In the absence of skill shortages or surpluses, trends in skill use can be read as measures of trends in skill demands.   These distinctions, though elementary, are important to stress, in order to cut through some of the everyday rhetoric about education and training systems. For example, it is not unusual for surprise to be expressed at the disjuncture between the apparent 'need' for more scientists and engineers to handle modern technologies and the lack of evidence of increased supply to meet the 'need' – the truth being, in many cases, that in contrast to any proposed individual or societal need for such skills the practical demand for scientists and engineers (evidence for which could be higher pay and/or available jobs) may be lacking.

The evidence of economic diversity suggests that one cannot deduce skill demands or skills in use merely from a country's level of overall economic development in any simple manner. It may be, and often is, the case that catching-up countries in the modern era are placing far greater emphasis on education and training than some more advanced countries. One must expect to see diversity in skills in the advanced industrial countries reflecting, directly or indirectly, the diversity along various measures of economic performance and in their political and economic institutions.

To some extent the skills diversity will reflect different technological choices, and the conflict over these choices. Another factor is the different experiences of unemployment.   In those countries experiencing mass unemployment, the state has inevitably been drawn to ameliorate its social effects, in particular where youth unemployment is high. The state's actions to give some sort of job or low-level training to unemployed youths means that it is likely to be less successful in creating a climate for a more highly-skilled general workforce. A third factor is the very character of the state: as we shall show in Chapter 7, the 'developmental states' that have emerged for various historical reasons in newly industrialised countries have had decisive influences on the skill formation system. A fourth factor is the matrix of institutional links between and among firms and workers: for example, the presence or absence of active trade unions. A fifth factor influencing diversity in skills is the differences on the supply side. With an education and training system relatively autonomous from the state and from the economy, no amount of economic convergence would be likely to harmonise ET institutions and the levels of skill supply. Cultural patterns of social inclusion and exclusion, for example, are likely to be important.

## EMPIRICAL EVIDENCE ON SKILL DEMANDS

If a simple universal trend of skills demand and skills in use cannot be deduced from theoretical generalities either about production systems or about the economy in general, it becomes necessary to ask exactly what is known from empirical evidence. The short answer to this important question is: not very much. It would be ideal to be able to identify the various skill trends in different parts of the global economy: such information would be invaluable in developing the arguments of this book concerning the link between skills, skill acquisition systems and the economy. Unfortunately, there is relatively little data and what there is warrants very careful interpretation. It will nevertheless be useful to list the potential sources of evidence on skills and, without aspiring to comprehensive coverage, highlight aspects of the evidence relevant to the countries considered in ensuing chapters.

*1.* Qualifications and achieved educational levels may be taken as one set of measures of general skills supply. According to this approach, the average skill levels of the workforce have been rising in recent decades in many advanced industrial countries. In Japan, for example, the proportion of the population with just upper secondary education rose steadily from 14 to 46 per cent between 1950 and 1990, while the proportion with higher education rose even more dramatically from 3 to 22 per cent.[12] In the US, the proportion of over 25s who had graduated just from high school rose from 28 to 58 per cent between 1950 and 1992, while the proportion of college graduates rose from 5 to 21 per cent.[13] In the West German workforce of 1957 there were 42 per cent with no formal qualifications and only 3.5 per cent higher education graduates, but by 1991 there were only 20 per cent with no qualifications and over 12 per cent graduates.[14] The story in Britain is similar: data for 1980 and 1990 show the proportion of adults with at best A-levels rising from 20 to 25 per cent, while the proportion with higher education rose from 12 to 14 per cent.[15] Such figures are a direct reflection of the post-war expansion of education systems.

International comparison of skill levels using this method is a more hazardous exercise, because serious judgements have to be made about the comparability of qualifications gained in different countries. Nevertheless, with considerable care it is possible to come to some preliminary rankings, typically on a bilateral basis. For example, the British workforce compares unfavourably in this respect with Germany (O'Mahoney, 1992; Mason, van Ark and Wagner, 1994) and with Japan (Prais, 1987), but also with Canada (Ashton, Green and Lowe, 1993), with the Netherlands (Mason and van Ark, 1993; van Ark, 1990a), and with France (van Ark, 1990b; Mason, van Ark and Wagner, 1994). Multilateral comparisons show that, while France and the Netherlands have somewhat low proportions of the workforce educated to university level, the more serious deficiency in France, which is an even greater problem in Britain, is in intermediate vocational qualifications for craft workers and technicians, leaving more than half the workers in both countries having neither university nor vocational qualifications (Prais, 1993). Comparisons may also be made of the extent to which workforces have undergone training, irrespective of whether that training is certified. An EC survey of individuals in 1989 concluded that the proportion of 'skilled workers', those who had received vocational training of some sort, constituted about two thirds of the labour force in the whole community, but that the proportions varied considerably across countries.[16] It found that the Federal Republic of Germany ranked the highest at 87 per cent, while Denmark (76 per cent) and France (74 per cent) were not far behind. By contrast the skill level was low in the UK (48 per cent) and in the poorer nations, namely Spain (57 per cent), Portugal (50 per cent) and Ireland (50 per cent).

While qualifications or the achieved education and training levels held by the population are possible measures of skills supply, a measure of skills demand is the level of qualification required by employers for recruitment to jobs, about which there is a little information. For example, only about 55 per cent of US jobs are reported to have qualifications requirements, a proportion which did not change between 1983 and 1991 (Swaim, 1993). There was, however, a small increase in the proportion of jobs requiring educational qualifications or formal company training, indicative of an increasing importance attached to general and cognitive skills. We know also that there was a small increase in the average level of education achievement required for entry into American jobs over the 1970s but almost no increase in the 1980s, suggesting that skills demand in the US has been stagnating, and the projections for the whole of the 1990s show only modest rises (Teixeira and Greenberg, 1993). By contrast, in the UK, there may have been an increase since the mid-1980s in the proportions of jobs requiring higher-level qualifications (Gallie and White, 1993).[17]

There are, however, problems with identifying qualifications with skills. First, qualifications gained or required for getting a job are one thing, but a qualification where the associated skills are actually used is another. People may take jobs for which their qualifications are not an entry requirement. And where qualifications are necessary for getting jobs, there is the possibility of 'qualification inflation', whereby the minimum qualifications are steadily raised to ration access to jobs independent of the skills required to do the jobs. This becomes the more likely in an era of increasing supply of well-qualified applicants, and we must therefore interpret the above-mentioned findings of Gallie and White with caution. The phenomenon of qualifications inflation is perhaps more familiar to a North American than a European audience.

Second, the standards implied by qualifications may not be constant: in many countries it is not uncommon to hear claims about falling standards. Such complaints are notoriously hard to substantiate. In the US, for example, it has been fashionable to question the standards achieved by high school graduates. Yet research indicates that standards have at least remained steady over recent decades, if not increased, and that the US education system has held up remarkably well relative to the decline of other mass social institutions in that country, such as health and welfare (Bracey, 1992; Teixeira and Greenberg, 1993). It is no secret, also, that the standard implied by a degree in the United States is highly variable according to type of institution. US trends in the workforce proportions at degree level could therefore be misleading, if the mix of higher education institutions is also changing. In the UK, there is a wide sense of decline in higher education standards, but no adequate data is collected to evaluate such claims. Similar claims are made of basic literacy and numeracy skills in schools, but here careful analysis suggests the claims are unsubstantiated (Brooks, Foxman and Gorman, 1995).

2. An alternative to using national-based qualifications is to measure achieved skill standards directly using uniform testing methods. These methods have been used primarily to contrast educational standards of school children across nations, in areas of the curriculum that lend

themselves relatively easily to comparison – mathematics, science and reading literacy. Studies show the Japanese school system to be the most successful in terms of both mathematics and science achievements (International Association for the Evaluation of Educational Achievement, 1988; Robitaille and Garde (eds), 1989). With regard to maths, French and Belgian children also performed well, while Britain and the United States were around the average mark. With regard to science, English 10-year-olds and 14-year-olds on average lag behind children of the same age in most of 17 other countries. US 14-year-olds also performed poorly in Science, while the Dutch, the Hungarians and, again, the Japanese did best. Korean 10-year-olds were also among the best.[18] Such studies are useful indicators of the strengths and weaknesses of certain parts of national education systems, but no more than that. They only cover a proportion of the skills that are intended to be developed in an education system, and they relate only indirectly to the skills available in national workforces.

At the lower end of the scale, the proportions lacking basic literacy or numeracy skills are also important (Centre for Educational Research and Innovation, 1992). Possession of basic skills is presumably advantageous, if not necessary, for participation in modern capitalist economies.[19] Reading literacy among school children has been assessed in a range of countries, with Finnish children coming out on top, German children no better than average, and American children doing well at the age of 10, though more like average by the age of 15 (Elley and Schleicher, 1994). Illiteracy among adults is, however, the major cause of concern. It is frequently a source of some surprise to many to find significant proportions of illiterate adults in advanced industrial nations – for example, only 1 in 4 high school dropouts in the US could locate information in a newspaper, while only 1 in 5 could enter deposits and cheques and balance a chequebook. In Germany, adult illiteracy rates range from 0.75 to 3 per cent or even more according to some reports, this despite the fact that negligible numbers had not completed their schooling. In France, 2.4 per cent of the adult population cannot read, and 4.1 per cent cannot write. Meanwhile in Japan, illiteracy problems are considered so rare that no official data are collected (Felstead *et al.*, 1994).

Such international comparisons are not greatly helpful, however, since the national definitions of illiteracy vary a lot. Using a more limited but common definition of a literate person as someone who 'can with understanding both read and write a short simple statement on his or her everyday life', UNESCO assesses both comparisons and trends in illiteracy rates in a large range of countries (UNESCO, 1993a, 1993b). These show substantial declines in illiteracy rates in most countries, a gradual but far from complete convergence on the low levels of the richer countries. In

China, for example, illiteracy fell from 35 per cent to 22 per cent in just eight years from 1982, while in South Korea, illiteracy fell from 12.4 per cent in 1970 to 3.7 per cent in 1990. Even in Europe, later developing nations (Spain, Portugal, Italy and Greece) saw illiteracy rates cut by a half or more in the 1970s and 1980s. Only in sub-Saharan Africa did the total number of illiterate persons continue to increase.

3. Measures of skills in use can be obtained from an examination of the skills of the employed, and one method of approaching this is to survey employers in order to investigate the proportions of skilled workers they employ. An example is a 1989 survey of more than 25,000 firms across the EC, which found that skill use was especially low in the UK. It was highest in France, Italy and the Netherlands, while Germany was about average.[20] The precise conclusions need to be treated with caution because the notion of the 'skilled worker' is socially determined, and in particular may be interpreted differently in different countries. For example, Maurice *et al.* (1986) after a detailed study of matched plants in Germany and France, conclude that the German semi-skilled worker was the equivalent of the French skilled worker.

4. Skills in use have also been inferred from the industrial and occupational structure of workforces. Most industrialised countries have been experiencing a proportional decline in their manufacturing industries as their service sectors rise in prominence. At the same time, manual jobs have declined relative to non-manual jobs, or, what is approximately the same thing, production workers have declined relative to non-production workers (Berman, Bound and Griliches, 1994; Berman, Machin and Bound, 1994; Machin, 1995). In particular, there has been a long-term rise in the proportions in managerial and professional occupations. It is necessary, however, to be cautious in making inferences about skill trends solely from these changes, since many changes have been occurring within occupations. The same occupational designation can refer to greater- or lesser-skilled jobs after a period of time, especially where the designation is as broad as 'production worker'.

5. One way in which skill changes within occupations and industries may be investigated is through detailed case study. The most reliable would be via some form of participant observation, but the coverage of such a method is inevitably narrow. Alternatively, one may use in-depth interviews with employers and employees to elucidate the main changes that have occurred within a range of occupations over quite a long period, relying on respondents' power of recall. For example, Higgins (1993) using this method reveals a complex picture of both downskilling and upskilling, with the former predominant, among key occupations for youths in New Zealand: those of tailors and dressmakers, engineers,

automotive mechanics, plumbers, electricians, nurses, teachers, clerical workers and salespersons. She is able to explain these trends not just in terms of technology but also in terms of important institutional factors such as the relative strengths of union organization in different localities and occupations, and other characteristics of the local and national labour markets. This method is also able to bring out the multi-dimensional nature of the skills demanded by employers. Given the relative weights of the various occupations, Higgins was able decisively to refute the upskilling thesis as far as these New Zealand youths were concerned. Using a similar method, Penn (1994) also uncovers a story of conflicting trends, though here with more of an emphasis on upskilling, in the textile and engineering industries in Rochdale, England.

Such case studies are the more important, the broader their coverage. It is not hard to find examples which conform to any of the particular hypotheses concerning work transformation and associated skills movements. By the very nature of case studies, however, varying examples provide little reason for accepting or rejecting any arguments about general national trends.

6. A more comprehensive way to investigate changes in skills in use is to collect data on detailed skill requirements for all occupations, and plot over time both the changing pattern of occupations and the within-occupation skill changes. Such data sources have been available for some time in the US and Canada and have recently been used to tackle the issue of skills trends head on. Myles (1988) examines four measures of skills in use in Canada, known as General Educational Development (GED) score, the extent of Specific Vocational Preparation (SVP), the degree of 'cognitive complexity' and the degree of 'routine activity'.[21] He finds a notable upskilling in many industries in both the 1960s and 1970s, but also a considerable degree of polarisation and of segmentation. Similarly, in the US official statisticians have analysed and classified the skill requirements of a range of job titles, published as the *Dictionary of Occupational Titles* (DOT). Putting together the changes in the job requirements across a large range of jobs, Mishel and Teixeira (1991) and Teixeira and Greenberg (1993) find that skill requirements were increasing in the 1980s but at a very modest rate, and substantially slower than in the 1970s. Moreover, they project only a slow change over the 1990s. Cappelli (1993) criticises the use of DOT mainly on the grounds that successive reports may not be consistent over time. Instead he utilises job analysis data produced for commercial purposes by Hay Associates. The sample of firms is not representative of all firms in the economy, but Cappelli prefers this data set mainly on the grounds of its reputed consistency and reliability across establishments and across time.[22] He finds a notable upskilling between

1978 and 1986 in several though not all production jobs, especially in material handling and in inspection/quality control. The new skills can be related to the onset of 'lean production' systems, but the most common skills required in the new form of work organisation are found to be the behavioural, or social skills, necessary for working in teams (Cappelli and Rogovsky, 1994). In clerical jobs, by contrast, there is a mixed picture with some jobs such as office equipment and telephone operators experiencing deskilling.[23]

The DOT data do not cover the whole US workforce, and the Hay set probably less still. One is left with a mixed but incomplete picture on US trends. To our knowledge, no similar data are available outside North America.

7. An alternative way of measuring skills in use is on the basis of surveys of workers or employers. A particular advantage of this method is that it allows one to measure a range of types of skills. For example, questioning employers about the skills of their employees has shown a trend in the US towards the use of more 'complex' skills, linked mainly to changes in job content (Osterman, 1995). Associated with this trend is a move towards greater inequality, since it was the (less-skilled) manual workers whose skills were least likely to change. Looking instead at individuals, Rubery (1994) examines the differences between the self-perceived skills of British men and women in a range of dimensions. One can also question workers about their perceptions of skill changes. Using this method Gallie (1991) finds an average rise in individuals' skills in Britain over a 5-year period leading up to 1986, but at the same time some degree of skill polarisation: some 52 per cent had experienced a rise in skills in their jobs, while only 9 per cent had experienced a decline. A later survey found a greater skills increase, with 63 per cent experiencing a rise in skills from 1987 to 1992 (Gallie and White, 1993). There was also a statistical link between this subjective experience of skills increase and those who identified their jobs as requiring computing skills, and/or higher 'monitoring' and 'social' skills, and those who said that they were being required to work harder. Together, these two surveys constitute the strongest evidence yet that people *perceive* that their skills are increasing. As far as we know, equivalent data are unavailable in other countries.

It would be quite a leap, however, to regard this as anything like conclusive evidence for upskilling, because there may be a considerable disjuncture between perceptions and reality. We know, for example, that there are very large numbers of ordinary workers who nowadays work with computers. There is almost certainly a tendency to regard operating with a computer as an increase in skill, simply because it likely requires some retraining even of the most rudimentary sort. But computers replace both high- and low-level skills, so it is hard to be confident that what survey respondents perceive as skill increases represent the genuine article. We know, also, that employers and employees can have quite different perceptions of skills (Burchell *et al.*, 1994). Moreover, in any cross-section, some of the effect may be attributable to the maturing of the cohort included in the survey, rather than a genuine trend.

8. An indirect way of getting at skills is that favoured by many economists: assuming a link between skills and wages we could examine the more easily observed wage trends and infer what must be happening to skills. A number of recent studies have shown a fairly widespread increase in earnings dispersion, and associated with this a rise in the returns to educational achievement. The 'college premium', after falling in most countries in the 1970s, rose substantially during the 1980s in the US and the UK and less so in a number of other countries. In Japan, however, the premium stayed constant, while in Germany it declined further. With partial success, such changes in the education differential have been explained by changes in the supply of graduates and non-graduates, set against an (assumed) steady increase in the demand for skilled labour (Katz and Murphy, 1992). A 1980s slowdown in the expansion of graduates in the US is used to explain the rise in the premium, and similar explanations work for Australia, Canada and the UK, though not for France, Sweden and Italy (OECD, 1993). But such explanations, even where they 'work', are predicated upon an unproven assumption. An increasing college premium could as easily derive from a decline in the skills in the jobs of non-college graduates (Teixeira and Greenberg, 1993). It is potentially quite misleading, to infer *average* skill changes from changes in pay *relativities*. Rather, if the assumption that wages are correlated with skills is accepted, the increasing dispersion of wages is, if anything, indirect evidence for the polarisation of skills. If there is a decline in the value of the skills possessed by the low paid, the main question becomes whether the origin of the polarising trend lies in technological change, as Katz and Murphy (1992) imply or in increased trade with low-skill countries (Wood, 1994).

One might instead look to the average wage level in different countries as a very approximate internationally comparable gauge of average skills usage. Such an argument must be qualified in that wages and productivity can deviate according to the conditions of income distribution in each country. But if it is assumed that, in the long term, there is a tendency for labour costs to converge through international competition, then the level (and more weakly the growth rate) of wages should reflect in the long term the level (and growth rate) of productivity, which in turn can be linked to skills. The argument is consistent with the characterisation of Britain as on a low-skills route to accumulation. Wages in British manufacturing have been growing more slowly and are lower than in most industrialised nations. When social charges are included, hourly labour costs in 1988 were substantially lower in Britain than in 14 other OECD countries, (those with lower costs were Greece, Portugal and, marginally, Ireland) (see Table 4.2). At the same time Germany is a high-paying country, second only to Norway in total labour costs per employee. The US and Japan both lie roughly in the middle of the range. The difference between them is that the US, unlike other countries has exhibited decreasing hourly labour costs for a couple of decades. It appears to be on its way to low wages on average, even if it is not there yet. But it should be remembered that earnings dispersion is particularly sharp in the US and that there are many workers at the upper ends who have continued to gain during the last decades.

9. Finally, another indirect way to gauge skill trends is through data for education and training. Rises in education and training can, if they are assumed to lead to skill acquisition, be taken as indicative of an acceleration of skill levels. Sources of education data abound, and while great care has to be taken in interpreting cross-national variations, there is no doubt about the long-term expansion of education systems in the post-war period throughout the world. In the industrialised world the expansion is mainly at the tertiary level (see Table 4.3), since primary- and secondary-level education was already widespread some decades ago, while in the South it has been more at the primary and secondary levels. Table 4.3 also shows the particular emphasis given to tertiary educational studies in North America.

*Table 4.3 Number of 'Third Level' Students per 1000 Inhabitants*

|                | 1980 | 1991 |
|----------------|------|------|
| Canada         | 40   | 72   |
| West Germany   | 20   | 28 (1989) |
| Japan          | 21   | 23   |
| United Kingdom | 15   | 22   |
| United States  | 53   | 57   |

*Source*: UNESCO, *Statistical Yearbook 1993*, Paris: UNESCO.

*Table 4.4   Participation Rates of 16 to 18 year olds, 1987 (%)*

|             | Full Time | Part Time | All |
|-------------|-----------|-----------|-----|
| Australia   | 51        | 17        | 67  |
| Belgium     | 82        | 4         | 87  |
| Canada      | 75        | —         | 75  |
| Denmark     | 73        | 6         | 79  |
| France      | 69        | 8         | 77  |
| W. Germany  | 49        | 43        | 92  |
| Italy       | 47        | 43        | 92  |
| Japan       | 77        | 3         | 79  |
| Netherlands | 77        | 9         | 86  |
| Spain       | 50        | —         | 50  |
| Sweden      | 76        | 2         | 78  |
| UK (1989)   | 36        | 33        | 70  |
| US          | 80        | 1         | 81  |

*Source*: Employment Department, *Training Statistics 1992*, London: HMSO.

Educational comparisons are also of interest and relatively reliable when comparing the participation of specific age groups, especially young adults. Table 4.4 is a typical example, showing the relatively low participation of youths in the UK, especially on a full-time basis, and the high participation in Germany and Italy.

The expansion of training systems in recent decades is less well known, because of scarcity of data. Much training is carried on within companies, and is not separately accounted for in firms' accounts. This means that firms themselves often do not know how many resources they are devoting to training, and even if they do it is not at all easy to compile reliable estimates of aggregate training expenditures for any country as a whole. The validity of international comparisons is further vitiated in so far as different studies may include a different range of items as training expenditures. As for comparisons of training frequency, there is considerable room for variation in perceptions as to what counts as training (and whether that training results in skill formation), in the reference period and population coverage, and in survey methods.

Nevertheless, what solid evidence there is consistently points to an expansion of training activity across the industrialised world. In the UK, training participation has considerably broadened since 1979 (Felstead and Green, 1995; Greenhalgh and Mavrotas, 1993); in France, too, firms now spend a great deal more on training than in the 1970s (Verdier, 1994) and in Japan the same can be said of formal off-the-job training, where expenditure as a proportion of payroll rose by a third between 1975 and 1991 (Felstead *et al.*, 1994, Table 4.31). In the US, too, individuals reported an increase in training, particularly formal training, over the 1980s (Swaim, 1993).

It is much harder to make confident statistical judgements contrasting the intensity of training in different countries, for the above-stated reasons. Perhaps the only national ranking we can be reasonably sure of is between Japan and the US. If, for example, we look at the proportion of workers in the first year of their tenure in a job, we find that in Japan some 79 per cent received formal training, while only 8.4 per cent did so in the US (OECD, 1993). The picture is not so dire as this for the US, because there is also a substantial amount of informal training, which narrows the overall difference between the two countries (OECD, 1991a).[24] But there remains a substantial contrast between the two skill formation systems. This national-level difference is reflected in a careful industry-level study of training in auto plants, which showed that training intensity was greater in the NIEs, in Japan and in Europe (on average) than in the United States (Macduffie and Kochan, 1995). In the case of Japan, the high levels of training could be accounted for wholly by a firm's adoption of flexible production strategies. The same study reported that, within Europe, British and Spanish auto plants trained their employees the least.

The European Union now asks about job-related training and education participation in its annual Labour Force Survey. This has the advantage of consistency in terms of reference period, and to some extent in terms of survey methods, but the validity of comparisons remains in question because there is a real risk that the various countries' survey respondents interpreted differently what is meant by training. Nevertheless, because these data are not easily obtained elsewhere we present summary measures of training participation and intensity in Table 4.5.

These confirm that UK participation rates for youths are among the lowest, and the length of training for those receiving training is among the shortest, apparently preparing the young for a relatively low-skilled society. The incidence of training among UK adults is high, but, among those receiving any training, the proportion receiving more than 11 hours per week is relatively low. Other low-training countries appear to be Luxembourg, Greece, Spain, Portugal and Italy, that is, predominantly from the southern part of the Union. By contrast, Denmark, Germany and Holland are high-training countries.[25]

*Table 4.5  Training In The European Union*

|  | Participation Rate[a] | | Intensity[b] | |
|---|---|---|---|---|
|  | 16-24 | 25-59 | 16-24 | 25-59 |
| Belgium | 59.0 | 2.5 | 50.5 | 29.1 |
| Denmark | 65.1 | 17.2 | 90.3 | 52.6 |
| France | 62.2 | 3.2 | 80.0 | 55.9 |
| Germany[c] | 63.3 | 8.2 | 93.2 | 68.8 |
| Greece | 55.0 | 1.3 | 98.3 | 81.5 |
| Holland | 69.5 | 16.0 | 100.0 | 100.0 |
| Italy | 48.8 | 3.6 | 88.1 | 66.6 |
| Luxembourg | 45.0 | 3.1 | 78.8 | 40.0 |
| Portugal | 49.6 | 4.0 | 92.6 | 63.6 |
| Spain | 56.0 | 3.7 | 94.4 | 68.6 |
| UK | 47.4 | 12.9 | 61.5 | 41.1 |

*Notes*
a.  % of population receiving job-related education or training over previous 4 weeks
b.  % of trainees receiving more than 11 hours per week training
c.  Large number of no responses especially for adults.
*Source*: Data extracted from tables of the Community Labour Force Survey, supplied to authors by Eurostat.

## CONCLUSIONS

This chapter has set the analysis of education and training systems against the background of major developments in the global economy.  It has, in the light of these developments, considered the changing demands for skill that education and training systems are designed to meet.  And it has pointed the way to later chapters in which we examine the features of specific training systems in different parts of the world.

We have argued that, even in the advanced industrialised world, it is too simple to assume that all countries are converging to a common modern technology in which ever-increasing and broader skills are needed from modern national workforces.  We have brought together the evidence on a range of macroeconomic phenomena, including growth rates, unemployment, the wage level and income distribution, all of which tell a story of heterogeneity.  We have suggested that this is likely to be indirectly reflected in heterogeneity in the skills demands of employers, in the skills supplied by national institutions, and hence in the skills actually used in modern economies.  This led us, therefore, to review the evidence on skill trends.

There can be little doubt that the supply of skills, at least as gauged by the output of education systems, has been on the increase in most countries. In the industrialised world we see the widespread expansion of higher education and more recently of company training. In underdeveloped countries we see the expansion of schools. As regards the widely touted expansion of skills in use, the evidence is sparse and less strong: there has been some upskilling, but how widespread it is impossible to tell. There is also not enough evidence either to confirm or to refute detailed hypotheses about the particular role of institutions in different countries. It might seem surprising to outsiders that, on such a major question as this, which affects so many people's lives, comparatively few resources have been put so far into compiling the sort of data upon which social scientists can erect their theories and provide their policy advice. We hope to have provided the reader with a guide through the nascent literature on skills. But much work remains to be done in refining our measures of skill, in analysing the trends and variations in the various dimensions of skill, and in linking those skills with education and training and with work rewards.

Nevertheless, the evidence we have reviewed is consistent with some generally held perceptions about broad differences between the education and training systems of different nations. Thus, it is confirmed that Germany is a country whose workforce has a relatively high and rising level of qualifications, and high wages supported by high levels of productivity. These features are built upon a largely successful education and training system, with an expanding number of tertiary education students, and a training system that, at least for young adults commands high levels of commitment. These are some of the solid facts underpinning the view that German-based firms aim to compete, overall, on the basis of high skills, using advanced technologies, and in high-value-added sectors of the world market. Germany is, in other words, on a high-skills route to accumulation. Another major country classified in the same way is Japan. Here the evidence consists of a successful education system which enables high-level achievements by school children in maths and sciences, a broad participation in higher education, and a work system that requires relatively intensive participation in training. We shall consider the skill formation systems in each of these two countries in Chapter 7. There we shall pay some attention also to skill formation in the newly industrialised countries of the Pacific Rim, concentrating in particular on Singapore. While we have presented less evidence here about these countries, South Korea, for example, is marked by high-level participation in its higher education system, and as mentioned above it has some high levels of achievement in schools.

The contrast is typically made with the two largest Anglo-Saxon nations, the UK and the US. As the literature surveyed above has shown, the proportions of the UK workforce with qualifications is low, especially with respect to intermediate-level qualifications and the school standards in science achievements of those below the top are poor by international comparison. Educational participation rates, in spite of recent increases, remain relatively low for 16- to 18-year-olds, the proportions of skilled workers are low, and the wages are relatively low, reflecting productivity levels which still remain below those of other major competitor nations. In Britain, while there are many workers who achieve the highest-skill levels, the problem is that these achievements are not sufficiently broadly distributed across the population and workforce. One symptom of this is summed up in the following statistic: of a sample of 33-year-olds interviewed in the early 1990s, more than half (54 per cent) had experienced no training courses lasting more than three days during the previous decade.[26] On the demand side, in addition to the wage and productivity evidence, the relative failure of large numbers of British employers to use the Youth Training Scheme as a vehicle for serious upskilling of their workforces is often cited as evidence of a reluctance to demand high levels of skills. Commentators frequently point to the existence of large numbers of jobs in Britain which are said to require little skills and training, though the extent is hard to quantify in a meaningful way (Keep and Mayhew, 1995a, 1995b). What little evidence there is supports the view that investment by multinational companies in Britain is motivated by access to Europe from a relatively low labour-cost base and otherwise stable and conducive surroundings, rather than access to a highly skilled workforce, and that such multinational intervention tends to reinforce the low-skills orientation of local labour forces rather than impose any positive transformation of the skills base (Knell, 1993).

Set against this is the view that things are changing: that workers perceive that their skills are improving, and that participation in both education and training is rising. Nevertheless, although we think that there is no set 'equilibrium' in the UK ET system, it remains appropriate to characterise the UK as on a relatively low-skill route to accumulation. We examine the historical background to the UK skill formation in the next chapter.

Within the same chapter we examine, too, the US system, which has also been typically characterised as on what we call the low-skill route to accumulation. The evidence for this characterisation is, however, not quite so strong as in the case of the UK. We know, for example, that the science achievements of average US school children are relatively low, and there is evidence that the average skills being used in US industry are increasing only slowly if at all, and certainly slower in the 1980s than in the 1970s. Undoubtedly there are a large number of relatively low-wage jobs being created. And American firms sponsor low levels of (especially formal) workforce training compared to those in other countries. Nevertheless, wages are not yet low, by international comparison, nor is labour productivity; both remain high, buttressed by America's past affluence and its immense natural resources. Schools continue until age 18 for all but a minority of drop-outs, the system supports the highest levels of participation in higher education, and as a result large sections of the workforce are in possession of a Bachelor's degree of sorts. On top, there is a high-quality university system for a substantial minority, and in particular a world-leading system of management schools. These factors suggest that the characterisation of the US as on a low-skills route is less than accurate. It may be better to emphasise instead the polarisation and the divergence that is occurring within the country: the remarkable rises in income inequality, the enormous inequalities in access to education and the exclusion of most of the black population from affluence. Any single characterisation of the average US skill formation system seems likely therefore to be inadequate.

## NOTES

1. See, for example, Centre for Educational Research and Innovation, 1992; Employment Department, 1990; IRDAC, 1991; Johnston and Packer, 1987 and *Business Week*, 19 April 1988.
2. The experience of the NIEs has shown that one of the most powerful of these influences is the action of the state.
3. The data reported in this section are taken from World Bank (1991) and from *World Economic Outlook*, May 1992.
4. Existing research is sparse (Green *et al.*, 1994).
5. There is no evidence, however, that this is leading to a convergence, a supercession of national institutional frameworks for industrial organisation (Lane, 1991).
6. Note that, it is the *per capita* growth rates which are predicted to converge. The growth rates of aggregate income can differ if population growth rates differ.
7. Possibilities include the coefficient of variation, the standard deviation of the log, and Theil's entropy measure.
8. The wage level, however, would vary inversely with the exogenous population growth rate.
9. Total family annual earnings have held up, however, because of longer hours and increased participation by women in the labour force. Often two incomes are now necessary to support families (Mishel and Bernstein, 1992).
10. On this basis the UK is categorised in limbo as 'ex core'.
11. An interesting eclectic version is the 'compensatory theory of skill' advanced by Penn (1994).
12. Felstead *et al.*, 1994, Table 4.8.
13. *Ibid.*, Table 6.4.
14. *Ibid.*, Table 2.34.

15. *Employment Gazette*, March 1992, Table 2, p. 123.
16. *Ibid.*
17. This judgement derives from contrasting the results of separate surveys, whose comparability is assumed but not demonstrated by the authors.
18. Germany is not included in these studies.
19. There is, however, scarcely a drop of solid evidence which estimates directly the impact of literacy on production. Moreover, while employers may complain of illiteracy among their workforce, they generally spend little or nothing on trying to alleviate the problem.
20. *European Economy*, No. 47, March 1991.
21. The latter two measures are derived from factor analysis of the characteristics attached to jobs.
22. Note, however, that job analysis is far from a purely neutral 'objective' science. In addition to the inherent conflict over job definition between worker and boss, one complaint of job analysts is that, with modern personnel management techniques, employees are often encouraged to become both more involved in their jobs and to 'empower' themselves, leading them to talk up the skill content of their jobs as part of their self-esteem. This possibility raises a degree of doubt about the skill trends revealed.
23. See also Howell and Wolff (1991) and, for a study of trends in the US machine tool industry, Kelley (1989).
24. Supporters of the US system also point to the role of job turnover, especially for young adults, in matching people's idiosyncratic skills to the particular requirements of jobs (Heckman, Roselius and Smith, 1994).
25. The figures for adult training participation in Germany are low, but there were a very large number of non-responses to the training questions for this group.
26. See Arulampalam, Booth and Elias, 1995.

# 5  A Theory of Skill Formation Systems

We have shown so far that, just as there is persistent diversity among the economies of the industrial nations, so also there are substantial international differences in the levels of the skills being applied at the workplace. But we have also argued that no simple correspondence can be drawn between skill levels and levels of development. Our aim in this chapter is to begin to consider how societies arrive at a particular level of skill formation. We take as our starting point the critique of existing theories of the link between skill formation and economic development, which we pursued in Chapter 2. Our approach builds on the ingredients listed at the end of that chapter, and in particular places emphasis on the historical processes involved in resolving the conflict over skill formation.

The chapter contains two main sections. The first outlines what we hypothesise are the main institutional requirements for a capitalist economy with a high level of skill formation. Our analysis of these requirements is derived from our review and critique of the existing theories in Chapter 2, from our own research including empirical work on the process of skill formation in South East Asia, and from recent advances in the psychology of learning. One objective of this part of the chapter is to specify a broad institutional framework, against which normative judgements about the adequacy of any country's education and training system may be made. We shall use this framework in discussing some specific countries in Chapters 6 and 7, and in considering policy issues in Chapter 8. The second part of the chapter then sets out to produce a model of how the most important institutional conditions emerged at a specific juncture in history and how they are related through time. This dynamic model can then be applied to specific societies and so enable us to start explaining how and why different societies have achieved different levels of skill formation.

## THE INSTITUTIONAL CONDITIONS NECESSARY FOR ACHIEVING HIGH LEVELS OF SKILL FORMATION

We propose six related requirements concerning the institutions[1] needed for high-skill formation. Our hypothesis is that these six are necessary conditions for sustaining the high-skills route to accumulation in the modern era.

1. Fractions of the ruling class, specifically those in control of the state apparatus, must be committed to the goal of achieving a high level of skill formation and the innovative use of the productive system. The source of this commitment can vary, as we shall see later in this chapter, and need not be to achieve an objective of maximum economic growth.[2]   This commitment is necessary for two reasons. First it is hard to erect a system of skill formation without a solid educational base, and only the state can provide that.   Market-based systems of privately funded education reinforce inequalities and support only élitist education.

A commitment to a high level of education funding is not sufficient in itself, however, as the cases of Canada and Ireland testify.[3]   There, fractions of the ruling class committed the country to high levels of skill formation through heavy investment in education (Ashton, Green and Lowe, 1993), but this has not produced a high level of skill formation at the workplace.   This is because there has not been a corresponding development of the productive system.   Thus, it is not sufficient for the state to confine its activities to the provision of basic education services. For a high level of skill formation there must also be a commitment to develop the productive system.

2. As for the educational system itself, it must produce high levels of basic competence in language, science, mathematics and information technology among school and college leavers. By high levels of basic competence, we mean a large majority of school leavers achieving at least intermediate levels of qualifications in these areas. These are essential if future workers are to be in a position to develop their work-based skills further. Dore and Sako (1989) and Koike and Inoki ((eds)1990) have shown how such skills enable workers to make effective use of manuals and their own work experience to enhance their work-based skills. And we know from a great deal of empirical evidence that it is the better-educated workers who get selected for further training. The development of core skills is expensive and it is important that employers can assume that such skills are present when they are introducing new technologies and work practices, if employees are to make the most effective use of them. In the absence of such skills employers tend to use new technologies to deskill rather than upskill workers.[4]   In short the level of educational achievement/skill formation available in the labour force has an important effect in conditioning the ways in which employers utilise the technology available to them. If a society is to develop its productive forces to undertake high-

value-added innovative forms of production, either in the form of the Japanese system of flexible specialisation or the German system of diversified quality production then the majority of those in the labour force require these core intermediate level academic skills (Prais *et al.*, 1989).

3. Groups of leading employers must also be committed to the goals of high level skill formation. This necessity arises from the fact that skill-formation cannot be divorced from the workplace. The costs of training, whether formal or informal, are normally lower when located at work. In addition, however, there are important skills that are hard or impossible to codify, that are 'fuzzy' by nature, which it would be hard or impossible to impart in a classroom setting. No capitalist skill formation system, therefore, can do without employers, and a high-skill system needs high-skill-using employers to predominate, preferably in clusters of innovating organisations (Freeman, 1987), who also take the appropriate product market strategies.[5] An in-depth knowledge of modern technology can be acquired only through participation in the workplace. This limits the effectiveness of vocational education and class room teaching as an alternative means of producing a high-skills economy.

The recognition of the workplace as an important source of learning is now appearing in the work of psychologists. Until recently they have concentrated on developing general theories of learning which are then applied to the workplace. However, this approach to work-based learning is now being questioned. Billet (1992) argues that there are crucial differences in the social and cultural context between formal and natural (workplace settings), such that one cannot assume that learning acquired in the formal context of classroom can be easily transferred to the 'natural' setting of the workplace. Consequently he argues for the establishment of a separate theory of learning in workplace settings.

The fact that such a call can be made reflects the increasing concern of both researchers and policy-makers with the importance of the workplace as a source of learning (Fuller *et al.*, 1994; Koike, Pang and Woon, 1987). In some Anglo-Saxon countries this concern with work-based learning has been stimulated by the introduction of competence-based systems of certification. In some of the Asian countries it has been stimulated by attempts to introduce structured systems of on-the-job training based on the Japanese experience.[6]

The source of employers' commitment to skill formation may vary. On one hand, employers may be constrained to pursue the high-skills route through external pressure from a strong state. In this case, the emphasis must be on the word 'strong' because without the ability to coerce and cajole employers into compliance, independent-minded employers can mount political opposition by, for example, making training levies untenable or, in the case of multinational companies, by threatened or actual emigration. The state must be in a position to sustain the incentives for skill formation through suitable taxes, subsidies and regulations, and through the imposition of social obligations on employers. On the other hand, employers might acquire such a commitment from social convention in a consensual employee relations environment, with guidance from but without the heavy hand of the state. The essential ingredients are the ability and willingness to take a long view ahead, and this requires a degree of stability in firms' macroeconomic and financial environment.[7] But whatever the source is, the commitment is constitutive in part of a long-termist approach to business strategy.

4. While a limited social obligation is included in any such long-termist approach, our fourth institutional requirement is that there must be some form of regulation[8] and accountability in the process of skill formation at the workplace. This is necessary in order to over-ride the free market's inherent bias towards short-termism. To create a long-termist approach to training there must be mechanisms for overcoming the externalities associated with investment in training, mechanisms which induce employers to take account of the social benefits of training, which limit or preclude opportunistic behaviour, and which open up the process of training in ways that allow both employers and employees to assure themselves of the quality of the training provided. The relevant institutions will differ according to the structure and context of the labour market. In Germany, regulation derives from extensive external forms of explicit regulatory institutions, through Chambers of Commerce, legal regulation in the form of works councils and union regulations, all of which place pressure on the employer to adopt a long-term view of the employment relationship and the returns to be achieved from investing in training and development. In Japan, the lifetime employment system performs the same function placing pressure on the employer to invest in employees' development as they cannot easily be dispensed with during a downturn in the business cycle. In Singapore this is achieved by state intervention in the form of agreement with employers to reduce layoffs in return for tax reductions and incentives for employers to participate in training programmes for their employees (Ashton and Sung, 1994).

5. There must also be some means through which workers and prospective workers must themselves become committed to the goal of skill formation and continuous development at work. This must therefore be an integral part of the structure of labour markets and of the institutions of employee relations. The research mentioned earlier in Japan by Koike and Inoki ((eds) 1990) and in the US by Hirschhorn (1984) has shown that it requires a lengthy process of learning to master fully the skills necessary for the

effective utilisation of high-value-added forms of production. In addition, the development of the productive system which entails the continuous transformation of the technologies of production, requires employees to be prepared to acquire new skills as and when necessary. Thus employees must be sufficiently induced to stay with companies for a long period in order that the investment in their skills can be recovered.

Consent to the process of skill formation is most likely to be forthcoming when the inner rewards and incentives for learning are positive. Given the length and increasing complexity of the learning process no one can be forced to engage in it. Therefore, young people in school or college, at the brink of entering the labour market, must have an incentive to work hard, in order to improve their job prospects or their further education prospects. Adult workers' commitment derives potentially from a number of sources. One source is the provision of individual incentives as in the case of promotion from basic journeyman grade, in Germany (Lane, 1992). Another form of commitment is to integrate the employees into the values of the company, a phenomenon characteristic of Japanese enterprises and also many large enterprises in Western countries. Note, however, that even in Japan this method of securing ideological commitment is supplemented by a reward system that favours skill acquisition rather than just seniority (Brown, Reich and Stern, 1994). Another possibility is that individuals may be committed to national goals as in Singapore, regarding lifetime learning and upgrading as a national duty.

Workers must also be induced to participate in the workplace skill formation process as teachers, in particular to impart to younger workers those very skills that would be hard or impossible to teach in a classroom. Similarly, it is efficient if workers can be induced to share information they have gained about the production process with their fellow workers. Teaching, and information sharing, is fostered best in a secure and cooperative environment: secure, because workers are then not worried about job loss through productivity gains, and cooperative, because if openly conflictual there are incentives to withhold information. The Japanese Nenko system may be seen as in part a response to the need to encourage workers to teach others, and an important aspect of this system is the reward given to teaching (Brown, Reich and Stern 1994; Hashimoto, 1993). Similarly, in German enterprises the *meister* workers, qualified to be teachers of younger workers, receive extra pay.

6. Finally we propose a more detailed institutional requirement: that there must be a system in which work-based (on-the-job) learning can be complemented by off-the-job training in the knowledge base of the skills.

While, as we argued above, work-based knowledge and skills may become more important if employees are to operate in an innovative mode within the workplace, there is increasing recognition that if new skills for new techniques are to be developed, this is best done through a period of off-the-job reflection (Streeck, 1989; Koike and Inoki (eds), 1990). Periodic off-the-job training may also be needed to support the deepening of skills, in ways which enable workers to deal with unusual work tasks. Coming from a tradition outside the social sciences are the experiential psychologists, who emphasise the proactive nature of the learning process through the concept of the learning cycle. Kolb (1988), whose work has been influential in the field of training and development, stresses the importance of reflection in the learning process. Similarly, debates in the UK over the significance of competence approaches to learning are struggling with the need for practically acquired knowledge to be supplemented by theoretical underpinning knowledge (Hodkinson, 1991). In summary, there is a considerable body of evidence emerging about the importance of combining practical experience with theoretical or conceptual reflection if the process of learning the skills required for the more advanced forms of production is to be effective (Marquand, 1989).

Taken together these six conditions make high levels of skill formation possible. The institutions are linked in obvious ways: one can hardly sustain a high-performing education system without sustained support from ruling political elites, and the commitment of the latter also makes it more likely that employers become committed to high-skill formation. Moreover, once established these institutions can become self-reinforcing. Employers committed to high-skill formation can legitimate and reinforce the strategies of the state, and reward with rising wages and security the majority of workers, who accordingly remain committed to the high-skill strategy, and continue to 'justify' the employers' commitment. Whether this virtual circle has been achieved is an important characteristic to establish when assessing any education and training system.

# TOWARDS A THEORY OF THE INSTITUTIONS OF SKILL FORMATION

It also raises for us a complex theoretical and empirical question: what are the historical paths towards the establishment of the institutional conditions for high-skill formation? We consider next why the appropriate constellation of institutions may arise in some societies but not in others. To answer this question we must take one step back and examine broader processes of state formation, industrialisation and class formation, because it is these major historical factors which drive the process of skill formation.

The main thrust of existing social scientific enquiry has been in exploring the ways in which the development of the productive system is linked to the process of learning and skill formation within societies. Yet, as we saw in Chapters 2 and 4, this approach leads to the view that we should expect a general convergence of skill formation systems and skill levels as nations industrialise. The failure of this approach to provide a satisfactory explanation of why societies achieve different levels of skill formation lies, in our view, in the neglect of how the other driving force, the process of state formation, is also linked to the development of successive phases of the productive system. This requires a historical analysis of the institutions involved. Such an analysis is crucial if we are to explain diversity among the productive systems of nations (Wilkinson, 1983; Lane, 1992). Moreover, an understanding of country-specific deep-seated institutional legacies would seem to be a prerequisite for any appreciation of how if at all those institutions can be changed in the present.

Our focus will be on the commitment of the ruling elites to skill formation, and the historical legacy of the phase during which industrialisation took place.[9] Our contention is that the processes of both state formation and industrialisation determine, albeit in a complex and inter-related manner, the main functions and structure of the education and training system. We assume that state formation and industrialisation are relatively autonomous yet interdependent processes, and begin with a consideration of the former.

**State Formation**

Following Norbert Elias (1982) one can distinguish two aspects of the historical process of state formation. First is the establishment of the interrelated monopolies of force and taxation. The monopoly of taxation is essential in order that the flow of financial resources can be achieved to enable the central authority to maintain its monopoly of physical power, that is, the armed forces and the police. The second and related aspect is the progressive reduction in the number of competing territorial units. Through the course of history one can observe a process of competition between territorial units characterised by the gradual dominance of the stronger and larger territorial units over smaller and weaker ones, with the smaller being absorbed into the larger through the mechanism of military conquest (Mennell, 1989). The competition between territorial units and the resolution of conflicts through the use of military might is the driving force behind the process of state formation. In this approach, inter-societal competition and conflict is just as important in driving social development as intra-societal conflict (class conflict). Moreover, the political process of state formation is not reducible to economic processes.

It follows that, when it comes to explaining why it is that some states were successful in this competitive process and others failed, an analysis of inter-state relations is indispensable. Success in the sphere of inter-state competition is related to the military and economic power of individual states. It was in the process of forging the military machines that the absolutist rulers in Europe formed the first systems of national education. Only later did the rulers of Prussia seek to use their national systems to aid the process of industrialisation. Therefore, in order to understand how and why educational systems take on distinctive characteristics we turn to an examination of the international political context within which they emerged. As Andy Green (1990) has shown, one can best understand the origins and distinctive characteristics of national systems of education by starting from the premise that state involvement in education was propelled by the process of state formation.[10] Education systems were forged by the needs of rulers to maintain their sovereignty in relation to competitors from other societies and to control subordinates within their own jurisdiction.

The modern form of public education was prefigured in continental Europe during the absolutist monarchies of the eighteenth century. The relationship between the absolutist state and the development of educational systems is summarised as follows:

> The promotion of education clearly fitted in with the objectives of the absolutist state, particularly in its later years when the importance of expert administration and technical knowledge in the arts of war and industry became more important. Secondary schooling was increasingly important to provide the bureaucracy with trained and efficient staff, whilst technical and vocational schools could supply the military with capable recruits and the state manufactures and public works with expert engineers. Elementary schooling was likewise increasingly necessary to provide disciplined and loyal military and naval cadets and to promote patriotism amongst the people. The attempt to create universal, state controlled and bureaucratically administered national education systems can thus be seen as a typical product of state formation in the period of absolutism. (Green, 1990: 114)

The driving force behind the creation of the first continental systems of education was the military needs of the absolutist state. In the US, by contrast, the absence of strong military rivals meant that there was not the same pressure to establish the highly centralised administrative structures that existed in continental Europe. Following the defeat of the British, the only military threat came from the native Americans, whose collective lands were being expropriated and privatised, and who could be contained by a relatively small army. Consequently there was only a very limited centralisation of administrative power in the hands of the Federal government. Each state was responsible for the provision of its own education. However, a system of public education still emerged, driven instead by the urgent need to secure a political settlement following the Revolution (Green, 1990). From the period of the Revolution onwards education was seen to be uniquely important for the cultivation of national identity, for the maintenance of social cohesion and for the promotion of republican values among a heterogeneous population and many waves of immigrants. It was these needs, especially the urge to ensure that the new Republic had the support of the masses and could thereby secure its future independence, which led to the establishment of the public education system, in spite of the fact that control of education was decentralised in the hands of individual states.[11] But the requirements of the productive system, of the process of industrialisation, did not figure prominently in this agenda.

This brief discussion illustrates the variety of functions performed by the education system. It plays a crucial role in the socialisation of each new generation transmitting moral attitudes and technical skills under the control of the central authorities. This can be used for the delivery of disciplined recruits to the armed forces or to meet the needs of industry. It can also be a powerful instrument in building a sense of nationhood. Historically, the military and ideological functions have frequently taken precedence over the use of education for the transmission of technical skills deemed necessary for the development of industry. However, there is nothing deterministic about which of these functions were prominent at any one period of time.

The significance of any of these functions of education varies between societies and through time. The focus on the political functions of education does not preclude a consideration of the use of education to support the development of industry. In Prussia, as we have seen, a national system of education was introduced prior to the attempt to industrialise as part of the need to build up the military potential of the country and create the German nation. However, once established the educational system was later used as part of the drive by the state for 'forced' industrialisation (Green, 1990). In the US the use of education to consolidate the new nation coincided with the process of industrialisation and the education system became particularly important later in delivering the professional managers required for the introduction of mass production[12] and, later still, for providing the university-trained scientists that supported America's high-technology leadership in the post-war period (Nelson and Wright, 1992). In Britain the need to enhance the performance of the economy was one of the motives behind the 1944 Education Act which sought to establish technical schools. The use of education to perform both political and economic functions is just as evident in the new industrial countries of the Pacific Rim. Ruling groups in South Korea, Taiwan and Singapore have all faced political threats to the existence of their states and have used the education system for the purpose of nation building. Simultaneously, while endeavouring to build a strong economy in order to maintain their political independence, they also use education to fuel the process of economic growth.

So far we have concentrated on exploring the functions of education, but there remain important questions to be answered about the structure of national educational systems, and the institutional forms they take. The process of state formation is also important in helping explain differences in the organisational characteristics of the national educational systems. Scholars such as Muller (1993) have shown how the degree of centralisation of power in the state apparatus is important in explaining differences in the organisation of national education systems. Where the state's internal administrative apparatus is weak then education and other aspects of skill formation are organised on a private or communal basis. In such societies, social integration is maintained through a network of more or less autonomous institutions and associations. In these societies the state tends to leave the resolution of conflicts between classes to 'voluntary' institutional arrangements. Where the state's internal administrative apparatus is centralised then it will both supervise the education process more directly and control the provision of credentials in the labour market and the institutional arrangements for the management of class conflict. In these societies, the state is an active force incorporating its citizens through its institutions and imposing obligations on them to participate in national development (Muller, 1993: 11; Lee, 1994). Highly centralised internal administrative structures provide ruling groups with the ability to regulate the conflict the between capital and labour and to use the resources of the state to develop the productive system. Without a centralised state administration ruling groups are handicapped in any attempts they make to foster high levels of skill formation at work.

We noted above the importance of the regulation of employers behaviour for the development of a high level of skill formation. We can see the genesis of this regulation in the ability of the central state authority to regulate the behaviour of both management and workers. Where the state has developed a highly centralised system of internal administration it has achieved a high degree of autonomy in relation to the internal conflict between capital and labour. In regulating that conflict, as it has in Germany and Singapore, it has also played an important role in regulating the ways in which skills are acquired and certified. In Germany the state enforces the apprenticeship system and the qualifications which are a part of it, helping define the syllabus and define the skills covered by each trade. In this way it plays a major role in sustaining the institutional structures necessary for the reproduction of occupational labour markets (Marsden, 1986). Where the state is highly centralised, it can also play a more directive role in the distribution of skills. In Germany, the state plays an important role in structuring movement within the labour market. Thus Germany, while having a high level of skill formation, which was due in a large part to the apprenticeship system, also has one of the lowest rates of social mobility, that is, of movement between occupations. Once people enter the apprenticeship they tend to stay at that level. The need to obtain the appropriate credentials before entering a particular occupation means that movement within the labour market is limited. Research on the link between occupational (class) position and a person's educational credentials reveals that these links are stronger in countries such as France and Germany with their strongly centralised state structures and weaker in the UK and Ireland where the powers of the state are weaker (Muller, 1993; Blossfeld, 1994).

Where, by contrast, the central state relies on a decentralised system of administration, it plays a less significant role in the certification and distribution of skills. In societies such as Britain and the US, the state has largely confined its actions to the control of the education system and left employers and workers 'free' to organise training in the context of a more 'voluntaristic' system of industrial relations. The state has left the provision of vocational qualifications to private bodies and when it has attempted to intervene in the process, for example with the introduction in the UK of competence-based qualifications, it has sought to introduce these alongside rather than replace existing credentials.

In societies with a voluntaristic tradition, employers and workers are left to struggle over the organisation and distribution of skills. The state only intervenes in the case of the established professions by providing them with a licence to operate.[13] Where the state plays a minimal role in the process of providing credentials, there are fewer barriers to people moving between occupations and therefore greater social mobility.[14] In these circumstances, the state also has minimal influence over the form taken by learning at work.

## Industrialisation

Our emphasis so far on the essentially political nature of state intervention in education does not negate the significance of economic forces in shaping educational systems. While we have rejected the deterministic accounts of education and training which see ET systems, either as a response to the imperatives of the technology, or in terms of their functions in serving the needs of capital, nevertheless the system of production can have a powerful influence over the form and content of education and training. However, just as the political functions of education vary in accordance with the context within which the process of state formation takes place, so too the demands which the process of industrialisation makes on the education and training system vary in accordance with the development of the productive forces. We make a conventional distinction between three phases of development: the first characterised by craft production and co-ordination by the market; the second by mass production and microeconomic co-ordination by the large corporation and the third by high-value-added forms of producing goods and services and microeconomic co-ordination by both the state and the market.[15]

In the first phase, the early development of the productive forces did not require an educated labour force. Britain industrialised with one of the lowest levels of literacy in Europe (Lee, 1994) Workers requiring craft skills obtained these through the apprenticeship system or practical experience (Littler, 1982). In other instances, for example in textiles and construction, unskilled labour could be used which did not even have to be literate. As for management, the early entrepreneurs were able to utilise the market mechanism to co-ordinate production and did not require sophisticated managerial skills (Lazonick and O'Sullivan, 1994). Arguably, the lack of a need for education during this first phase of industrialisation has been embedded in a tradition of not harnessing education adequately to production in later phases.

During the next phase of industrial development which saw the introduction of mass production, employers' demands for knowledgeable craft workers were reduced. For the most part, the education system was only charged with the provision of the basic literacy skills needed to support increasingly bureaucratic forms of control used by employers. But there was a corresponding increase in the demand for professional managers to control the labour force and co-ordinate the process of production within the large corporation. The later emergence of 'new' industries such as electrical engineering and pharmaceuticals also placed reliance on the large corporation for the co-ordination of production. This reinforced the demand for new skills in managerial control: both sophisticated financial procedures and mechanisms for controlling worker behaviour, as industries such as automobiles and food production deskilled the labour process (Lazonick and O'Sullivan, 1994). In other industries, such as electrical engineering, the emphasis was more on the development of professional and technical skills.[16] The US economy came to prominence from early on in this phase, and again, arguably, this has contributed to its modern legacy of a relatively low level of intermediate skill formation coupled with a highly qualified managerial workforce.

In the most recent phase of the development of the productive system, the new technologies of aerospace, biotechnology and information technology, combined with the introduction of managerial techniques such as total quality management and lean production has meant that the demands on the education and training system are changing once again. In this latest phase we find many demands are for enhanced cognitive and conceptual skills and for 'softer' teamwork and human relations skills among workers (Marquand, 1989; Cappelli and Rogovsky, 1994). But the influence of these new technologies on skill formation is far from uniform.

The impact of the productive system on skills is heavily mediated both by the type of environment in which modern skill formation takes place (principally, the form of company organisation, but also the nature of the state) and by the existing historical legacy of the labour force and the education and training system inherited from earlier phases of industrialisation. Within the company, the organisation of personnel in relation to the technological base provides the material basis for the further development of skills. There are alternative ways of utilising new technology. The form of authority within the organisation, the extent to which job roles are clearly delineated, the system of payment and the provision for movement within the enterprise, all help to structure the distribution and utilisation of knowledge. Given trust between management and workers, weak role boundary definitions, mechanisms for information sharing and prospects for movement up the internal labour market, then workers are more likely to be trusted to use and control the new technology. Where these conditions are not met, then technology is likely to be used to control further the behaviour of workers. Here there will be little transfer of knowledge between groups (M.R. Kelly, 1989; Applebaum and Albin, 1989; Baran, 1988; Hirschhorn 1984; Koike and Inoki (eds), 1990; Nohara, 1987).

In addition, firms are much more likely to opt for high-skill forms of production when they can rely on a supply of adequate skills from the existing labour force and from the education system. The legacy of a poorly educated workforce is a limitation on the trainability of workers.[17] Realising this firms demand lower-level skills because they know that high-level skills are not available (Green and Ashton, 1992). Even in the latest phase, then, some firms find it profitable to pursue low-skill strategies.

Changes in the productive system and in skill requirements have been reflected in changing training methods and psychological theories of learning used to explain worker behaviour. In the first phase of industrialisation employers and their craftsmen relied on traditional techniques of practical, on-the-job training, as inherited from the medieval apprenticeship system. It was not until the introduction of mass production, in the second phase, that the demand for systematic training was developed as the new semi-skilled workers had to be trained to operate machinery and engage in the production process in the most efficient way, as defined by management. These needs were answered by the emergence and spread of behaviourist learning theory and behaviourist training techniques based on simple reinforcement (Hollway, 1991). In the latest phase, the demands for workers to be involved in the production process, controlling the technology and participating in 'management' decisions is making those theories and the techniques which they legitimated less useful. In response to the demands of the new phase of the productive system, developmental and experiential theories have emerged, providing the basis for new forms of worker and management training. In this third phase the emphasis is on the employees actively participating in the learning process and developing not only their cognitive abilities, but also their abilities to relate to others and control their own behaviour (Marswick, 1987).[18]

## Interaction Between State Formation, Industrialisation and Class Conflict

While the two processes of state formation and industrialisation exhibit a high degree of autonomy in relation to each other, they nevertheless interact in a number of important ways that can have an effect on skill formation. Firstly, the state can directly influence the development of the productive system. The establishment of the twin monopolies of force and taxation was a necessary precondition for the development of industry and without a stable legal system the development of capitalism would have been very difficult (Weber, 1947). In Prussia the state sponsored a process of 'forced' industrialisation (Green, 1990), establishing some industries and the necessary physical infrastructure for the development of industry generally, thereby rapidly moving German industry to the second phase in the development of the productive forces. This was followed by the Japanese state which was instrumental in steering industry through the initial phases and towards the third and most recent phase in the development of the productive system. Similarly in the Asian NIEs, the state has been a powerful influence in developing the productive system and moving the economy away from labour-intensive production to the production of high-value-added goods and services.

The interaction is, however, also reciprocal, in that the process of industrialisation influences state formation. Those societies which have managed to develop their productive system can exert more power in inter-state relations, Japan and the Asian NIEs being the most obvious recent examples (Chan, 1991). In the nineteenth and twentieth centuries the development of modern industry provided the ruling elites with the means of economic independence and enhanced their ability to develop armed forces capable of maintaining political independence. In short, the two processes of state formation and industrialisation are relatively autonomous: interdependent but not reducible to each other.

This brings us to the final point, namely the importance of the institutional arrangements which are used to regulate management/worker conflict and structure the process of skill acquisition. These are crucial in determining whether the skill formation process is geared to low- or high-value-added production. However, once these arrangements are in place, they require the power of the state to enforce them, or to create conditions under which the leading employers can enforce them, as in Japan. For this to occur, fractions of the ruling groups need to utilise the state's powers of force and taxation to regulate the conflict between manager and worker in the pursuit of a wider agenda. In Germany, this agenda was to ensure independence from their European neighbours and catch up on the military might of Britain and the US. In Japan, it was to ensure the independence of Japan *vis-à-vis* the West and Russia. This 'higher goal' legitimises the political elite's use of state powers to regulate the behaviour of both capital and labour. In materialist terms it provides the political elite with a degree of autonomy in relation to the struggle between capital and labour and thereby creates the conditions under which both can be subject to regulation. These are the conditions which have again been reproduced in the case of the Asian NIEs. However, it must be stressed that such accommodations depend upon the continuance of a particular constellation of forces and that further conflict between the parties can destroy them.

## CONCLUSION

One important conclusion of the foregoing is that education and training systems are subject to multiple determinations. There is no simple correspondence between the development of the productive system, as manifest in the process of industrialisation, and the development of the skill formation system.   In some countries the education system was developed before the process of industrialisation got established.  In others, such as Britain, the first phase in the development of the productive system was completed well before the state introduced a national system of education.   Industry developed without the 'assistance' of a state educational system.  In the Asian NIEs the ruling groups sought to use the provision of a literate, disciplined workforce as a means of initiating the process of industrialisation.  Only there do we witness the two processes of state formation and industrialisation moving more or less in tandem, achieving in forty years what it took some Western industrial societies 150 years to achieve.

In the first part of this chapter we have identified the main institutional requirements for the reproduction of a high level of work-based skills formation among the advanced industrial societies.   As such, these requirements should serve as broad benchmarks for the analysis of any industrialised country's education and training system, from the point of view of their adequacy in relation to creating a highly productive workforce.   In the second part we have identified the main processes responsible for their formation and the necessity for a historical analysis to understand the way in which these institutions are framed and are related in any one society.   We find that it is necessary to understand these processes in order to know why some nations' systems are currently more successful than others in establishing the related beneficial institutional requirements of success.

While these institutions, when established, can be self-reinforcing, we should note that for the institutions to be maintained through time requires the collaboration, either implicitly or explicitly, of different fractions of capital, of the political elite, and the compliance of labour.  Such alliances are impermanent because the contradictions and tensions between these groups can easily threaten the continuance of the overall process of skill formation.  The fact that relationships between the various groups involved are inherently conflictual also means that there is nothing deterministic about the process.  At a time of crisis or shocks to the system, conflict between the interests of the various parties can undermine the conditions necessary for the continuance of the process.  Societies which are currently pursuing a high-skills route could, in the event that conflict between the respective parties over-rides the continuance of collaboration in the skill formation process, find their industrial and service base changing direction and moving towards a lower level of skill formation.

Once we understand the nature of the processes involved then we are in a better position to understand the potential constraints facing reform of any of the systems. It is immediately obvious that piecemeal reforms that do not address the historical limitations, or which uncritically call for the importation of foreign institutions are unlikely to prove effective. Of more importance for improving the effectiveness of the overall productive system are the basic relationships we identify between the various institutions involved in the process of skill formation. In the following two chapters we move on to use this dynamic model to explain why some societies have achieved higher levels of skill formation than others and how different institutional forms have been created to meet the basic institutional requirements for different levels of skill formation. In the final chapter we return to the policy issues.

## NOTES

1. We are using 'institution' in its broad sense, as found for example in the framework of institutional economics, to refer not just to tangible legal entities such as unions or employers' organisations, but also to social conventions, attitudes and procedures.
2. Economic growth can be the target of governments even in a low-skills environment.
3. In Canada, the problem is chronic underemployment of educated workers (Krahn and Lowe, 1991); in Ireland the problem is the nature of inward investment which does not call for highly educated workers, the import of low-tech industry being matched by the emigration of graduate labour (Tansey, 1990).
4. There is a substantial literature on the impact of worker skill levels on the use made by employers of new technology, see for example Kelly (1989), Applebaum and Albin, (1989) Baran (1988), Cavestro (1989), and the work of the National Institute of Social and Economic Research in the UK, see for example Prais, *et al*. (1989). For a recent discussion of the US experience see Cappelli and Rogovsky (1994).
5. Not *all* employers need be high-skill users. In Singapore, a number of multinational companies refused to follow the government's call for a move into higher-value-added production. Nevertheless, though some of these just left for cheaper labour elsewhere, others stayed and joined with indigenous companies in the government's strategy.
6. In Singapore there has been an explicit attempt to learn from the work of the Japanese; see the report by Koike *et al*. (1987) for the National Productivity Board and the subsequent work by Dr Joseph Pious.
7. By macroeconomic stability we mean simply the avoidance of large business-cycle swings and associated uncertainty. By financial stability, we mean some protection from the ravages of stock market volatility, including opportunistic take-over activity.
8. For the broad sense in which we understand 'regulation', see Chapter 2, note 13.
9. The historical argument in this section thus corresponds directly to only some of the institutional requirements for high-skill formation but indirectly all those requirements are interrelated.
10. Green uses the work of Gramsci to inform his theoretical position. This variant of the Marxist tradition obliges him to seek the explanation of the characteristics of the different national educational systems in terms of the various ruling class alliances, which produce a particular form of class hegemony. This necessarily tends to direct the analysis to focus on intra-state relations. This is in spite of the emphasis in his empirical examination of the process of state formation on the importance of inter-state relations in explaining variations in the characteristics of national educational systems. The framework provided by the work

of Elias enables us to avoid this problem and focus more firmly on the part played by inter-state relations.

11. This refers to the northern states. The national system developed later in the southern states.

12. But note, however, that a significant aspect of management training in this era was the process of socialisation and ideological formation of the class of managers (Noble, 1977).

13. In the US and Canada this licensing by state and provincial governments has extended to some manual and service trades but the majority of workers remain outside the system (Ashton, 1986).

14. For a discussion of how this more structured system is experienced, as compared with the less highly structured UK system see Bynner and Roberts, ((eds)1991).

15. In the second and third phases the state is also, of course, central to macroeconomic co-ordination.

16. As we shall see in the next two chapters, these skill demands are mediated by the characteristics of the national education, training and business systems (Lane, 1992). The delivery of professional and technical skills is one area where national education systems have had a powerful influence on the development of the system of skill formation.

17. See the microeconomic evidence consistent with this in Chapter 3: the greater the education individuals have had, the more likely they are to receive further training.

18. In these new flat hierarchies employees are increasingly expected to monitor and control their own behaviour (Townley, 1991).

# 6 The Low-Skills Route

In this chapter we aim to use the historical model outlined in the last chapter to explain why it is that some societies arrive at a situation whereby the education and training system is only producing a relatively low level of skill formation. We use the history of two countries, the US and Britain, to put some empirical flesh on the theoretical bones. There is not sufficient space to provide a full account – our intention is merely to show how the ideas outlined above enable us to trace the interaction between the processes of state formation and industrialisation as they were structured through inter-state relations and the interplay of group and class interests and pre-existing institutional forms within the societies.

The form which institutions take on when they are first established can have a powerful influence on their subsequent development (Lipset, 1986). Hence we start the analysis of national systems of skill formation at the point in time at which, during the longer-term process of state formation, the societies in question embarked upon the process of industrialisation.

## BRITAIN

### State Formation

Two distinctive features of the process of state formation in Britain were the early establishment of the monopoly of physical force and taxation, which came about as a result of the unification of the English and Scottish crowns in 1606, and the weak form of the central administrative apparatus. For the British ruling class, the monarch and commercial aristocracy, success in the struggle between states and the maintenance of sovereignty in the eighteenth century was largely dependent on the strength and ability of British naval power. This ensured not only the security of the British Isles, but also access to foreign markets for British merchants (Hobsbawm, 1968).

A combination of reliance on the navy as the most effective weapon of inter-state relations and a strong commercial aristocracy produced a small central bureaucracy in Britain which had little interest in developing the

117

productive system as a means of ensuring national sovereignty. British naval supremacy which guaranteed access to markets for the country's exports in the late eighteenth and early nineteenth centuries was still based on the technology of wood and sail. Consequently there were few demands from the central state for the development of the productive system.[1] Developments in the productive system helped sustain British imperial dominance but the state was not driving the process of industrialisation.

Representatives of the new industrial class did not have access to positions of political power, while representatives of the commercial aristocracy were not always sympathetic to the interest of the new industrial bourgeoisie as witnessed by the struggle over the corn laws. Throughout the period, during which Britain moved towards industrial maturity, the aristocracy remained in firm control of the machinery of state, leaving the bourgeoisie to develop the productive system. The combination of innovations in social arrangements, the freeing of employers from the constraints of the Elizabethan apprenticeship system, organisational innovations such as the factory system and technical innovations such as mechanisation and the use of steam power – all these developed without substantial state intervention.

## Skill Formation

The lack of effective pressure on the political elite to provide for the transmission of technical skills for economic development had important implications for the emergent system of education. During this early period (late eighteenth and early nineteenth century) the main pre-occupation of the ruling elites with regard to internal affairs, was the problem of managing the lower orders. For the upper and middle echelons of society, education could be and was, left to each status group to run their own training, appropriate to the needs of their own particular group. In this context, one of the primary functions of education was to transmit not only the basic skills of literacy and numeracy but also the social characteristics which served to differentiate the various status groups (*Report of the Schools Inquiry Commission*, 1868). For the lower orders, the emergent working class, the ruling class felt safe in leaving educational provision to the discretion of the rival religious groupings who could be relied upon to instruct them in the appropriate moral virtues. For many, especially in the urban areas, this meant little or no education.[2] By European standards, Britain in the late eighteenth century was a badly educated society.

Although Britain industrialised without a national system of education this did not mean that training in technical skills was ignored. The skills necessary for production were transmitted outside the schools (Pollard, 1965) through a rapidly changing apprenticeship system (Snell, 1994). Other skills necessary for household reproduction and childrearing were transmitted informally through the family. As the skills necessary for industrial forms of production were introduced, employers and their representatives had to struggle to create new institutions (Pollard, 1965). Meanwhile occupational interest groups, the emergent trade unions and professional associations, sought to incorporate the transmission of existing skills and use them to bolster their position in the labour market and wider society. This created a permanent gulf in the education and training system between education and its concern with the transmission of skills 'appropriate' for each social strata, and training which was only responsible for work-related skills (Ashton, 1991). To summarise, although the education system was not controlled by the state, it continued to emphasise its function as an agent of social control rather than as a supplier of enhanced skills for the labour force.

The demands which the productive system made for skill formation could be largely contained within the transformed apprenticeship system. The early forms of factory and industrial organisation in Britain were a combination of craft skills together with the intensive use of unskilled labour, as in the iron and mining industries, textiles and engineering. In industries such as iron making, this placed the craft workers or equivalent in a powerful position *vis-à-vis* the unskilled labourers who worked under their control (Littler, 1982). In the textile industry male skilled workers were in a similar position *vis-à-vis* semi-skilled female and child labour (Turner, 1962). In engineering, the craft worker controlled large parts of the production process.

Throughout the greater part of the nineteenth century, payment of an entry fee to a particular trade and its secrets remained one of the main means of acquiring the knowledge required for production. For some trades literacy was important but for others it was not necessary. The skills required for the development of the productive system were transmitted through a system of on-the-job learning. Where employers did provide education this was very often for philanthropic reasons[3] and was confined to basic literacy and morality. There were no pressures on employers to provide anything more sophisticated for the majority of their workers.[4]

## Development of the Productive System

As for the production process, this was organised in some cases by the craftworkers who also organised the unskilled hands. In some instances, as for example in textiles, supervisors were used, but more often the organisation of production was through the use of sub-contractors (Littler, 1982). The different facets of production and distribution were co-ordinated through the market, with suppliers selling their products to transporters who sold them on to other manufacturers or retailers. Using these techniques, owners were in a position to organise the production process with a minimum of help from a small number of managers and a few clerical workers (Pollard, 1965).

This type of machine-based productive system, utilising worker skills and co-ordinated through the market mechanism, provided Britain with its competitive advantage in world markets. As the first machine-based system of production, the levels of productivity achieved surpassed those of other systems which relied primarily on labour power. However, it was a system with an absolute minimum of central control.

## Class Formation

Throughout the nineteenth and well into the twentieth century representatives of the aristocracy remained firmly in control of the machinery of state.[5] While the aristocracy could usually be relied upon to side with the bourgeoisie against the working class on political issues they were reluctant to let the state's military powers be used to suppress worker organisations. Throughout the first part of the century the main fear of the aristocracy was a repetition of the French revolution. This meant they had to be careful how they managed the lower orders. Employers could certainly use the courts to enforce discipline but the use of troops to suppress worker protest was restricted and military force only used as a last resort.[6] The new bourgeoisie were not to be trusted with control of the army for purposes of internal policing. However, apart from this one area, the political elite left the affairs of industrial production and employee relations to be regulated by employers and workers in accordance with their respective strengths in the market place, creating the distinctive system of voluntarism which characterised British industrial relations.

This provided the new industrial bourgeoisie with ample opportunities to transmit their property and cultural capital to their sons and some craft workers with sufficient opportunity to control access to their trades. For the generality of craft workers the situation was less secure, with pressure from employers on one side trying to reduce their income and on the other side from the unskilled wanting to gain access to their skills. This produced the phenomenon of the labour aristocracy and strong divisions within the working class. In terms of credentials, the apprenticeship remained the main credential, although during the course of the eighteenth and nineteenth centuries, some trades, such as the barber-surgeons (Campbell, 1747), were able to start differentiating themselves from the crafts to form the basis of the professional associations of the twentieth century. However, they continued to use the apprenticeship as their model for training, thereby enabling them to restrict entry and enhance their pay and status.

## Skill Formation in the Period of Industrial Maturity

When the political elite started to establish a national system of education for England and Wales, after the industrial mode of production had reached maturity, the interests of that elite in maintaining social exclusion and controlling the masses remained paramount. Scotland retained a degree of autonomy over its education system which still differs in important respects.[7] In England and Wales, education for the masses was provided through the religious schools with gaps in provision plugged by new state schools. Not all sections of the working class accepted these schools and during the first half of the nineteenth century many paid for their own education in the form of 'Dame' schools. Castigated by the middle class as inefficient, these schools provided a very basic education in literacy but under conditions controlled by working-class parents who paid for it. The child could attend during hours that were convenient for the parents and cease to attend when they had acquired the basic rudiments of literacy. This form of education was subsequently driven out as the state attempted to impose a national system of education (Gardner, 1984). Beyond the provision of basic literacy the delivery of this state education was based on the only model they knew, namely the curriculum developed in the 'public' schools as socialisation for the upper class and entry to the state and the liberal professions.

The development of the productive system in the second phase of industrial growth presented new demands for the skill formation process. Towards the latter part of the nineteenth century the needs of industry were again being transformed with the introduction of the new science-based industries of chemicals and electrical engineering. This change continued in the twentieth century with the belated introduction of mass production techniques in the automobile industry by American companies and the co-ordination of production through the corporation rather than the market mechanism (Hannah, 1983). Although this was a slow process, pressures were building up on the educational system to deliver the scientific and technical skills necessary for such industries. In part these were accommodated by the growth of the new universities in the industrial urban areas and through the introduction of colleges of advanced technology. Together these were to provide the skills for the integrated management structures which characterised the new industries and provided them with their competitive advantage. Attempts were also made early in the twentieth century to introduce more technical education for the working and middle classes but these were resisted by government (Eaglesham, 1967). Technical education for the masses, suitable for transmitting skills required for the productive system, was too expensive. It was cheaper to continue with the existing curriculum (Sanderson, 1994).

One other reason why the British political élite delayed the introduction of scientific and technical education into the main curriculum was the lack of demand from employers. The new mass production techniques transforming the productivity of American manufacturing industries were slow to enter Britain. Imperial and later commonwealth markets offered protection to British goods and the use of extensive systems of cartels meant that Britain was also slow to adopt the management techniques associated with the new American corporation. By the 1930s, it is estimated that no more than twelve major British manufacturing companies had management development schemes for university graduates (Hannah, 1983). Hence there was still little pressure for the introduction of management education. In the absence of such pressures the system of higher education was able, through modest expansion, to produce the graduates for the limited number of new 'managerial' positions that became available. However, access to the top positions in industry remained closed to those who had not received the requisite public school and Oxbridge education (Scase and Goffee, 1989).

During the Second World War the Labour Party fought for an extension of secondary schooling for the masses. This was granted but once again attempts to introduce technical education on a large scale were resisted on grounds of cost (Sanderson, 1994). Those members of the working class who were allowed access to higher-level jobs were channelled through grammar schools where they were re-socialised for entry to the middle levels of the emergent public and private sector bureaucracies. Provision was made for some mobility from the ranks of skilled workers into management through the use of night school and part-time education, the alternative route (Lee, 1968). The labour movement continued to reform education but this time the emphasis was to try and eradicate the association between social class and education through the abolition of grammar schools and the introduction of a system of comprehensive education. The political debate was about equity, equality of opportunity. Education for the masses was through a watered-down academic curriculum that bore little relationship to their needs as workers or citizens and which was not linked in any direct way to the technical needs of the productive system.[8]

The loss of imperial markets and the growing competition from American and German industry were not without effects on government. Training was an area where Britain was deemed to be falling behind its major competitors. The response in the 1960s was an attempt to impose some form of regulation on the behaviour of employers through the introduction of a levy on employers administered by newly formed Industrial Training Boards which provided a grant if training standards were met (Sheldrake and Vickerstaff, 1987). This was successfully resisted by employers and eventually abolished after two decades. Small employers complained that the system was costly, impractical and unfair. Many did not receive any grants. Others complained of the increasing bureaucracy associated with the Boards and some of the larger companies believed that the industry-based approach to training was unsound. However, there is evidence that both the quality and quantity of training was improved by the work of the Industrial Training Boards and substantial steps were taken in reforming the apprenticeship system with the introduction of a modular structure (Senker, 1992). The only other attempt at innovation in the field of skill formation, was the Manpower Services Commission, a tripartite, semi-autonomous structure charged with developing a national training policy. This met a similar fate, as the Conservative Party, now dominated by representatives of the bourgeoisie, sought to return control over training policy to employers (Ainley and Corney, 1990).

Within the labour market, the dominant form of training continued to be the apprenticeship system, although its focus as the centre of the training effort was declining. The growth of the service sector was creating new jobs which developed outside the apprenticeship sector. The emergence of large corporate bureaucracies with their own internal labour markets increased the importance of company-specific on-the-job training. In addition, the new colleges of further education started to provide extensive pre-employment training for white-collar work, especially for lower-level business administration such as clerical and secretarial work and for the burgeoning service sector in the hotel and catering trades (Gleeson and Wardle, 1980; Maguire, *et al.*, 1992).

The most recent phase in the interaction of the processes of state formation and industrialisation has been characterised by two major changes. The process of state formation has been affected by integration into the European Community, with the central state authority losing some of its powers to Brussels. One consequence of this has been the gradual introduction of European employment conditions within the UK. In the field of training, a process commenced whereby control over some aspects of government training policy moves to a federal level as the European Union starts to fund training programmes (Rainbird, 1994).

The area where even more dramatic changes took place was in the development of the productive system. The late 1970s and 1980s witnessed the opening up of British markets to the full impact of international competition, especially from American and Japanese multinational corporations. Initially, the remainder of the imperial markets were lost with the granting of independence to the colonies. This was followed by the loss of the Commonwealth markets as Britain joined the European Union where it faced enhanced competition from French, German and Italian industry. One consequence of this change, accelerated by the policies of the Thatcher government, was the rapid decline of the traditional heavy industries and the loss of British mass production companies in the automobile and white goods industries. Some of this productive capacity was replaced by the importation of foreign capital from Japan, America and Europe. With this came the introduction of new forms of management, including lean production and just-in-time production, and new forms of worker organisation such as teamwork and total quality management (Womack, Jones and Roos, 1990). Other areas of manufacturing where the British had previously competed successfully in world markets, in food manufacture, pharmaceuticals, and chemicals remained strong. In the retail sector British companies emerged with a competitive advantage over their European competitors, although in other areas of the service sector, such as hotels, the form of organisation remained uncompetitive with Europeans (Prais, Jarvis, and Wagner, 1989). In just about every sector workers experienced the wind of change through an intensification of their labour, and it seems likely that this, as much as the piecemeal reforms of production methods, was a significant factor explaining increases in productivity (Nolan, 1989).

From the point of view of the political elite and ruling fractions of capital, dominated for historical reasons by finance capital, the only way of enhancing the performance of the productive system was deregulation, leaving operation of the economy to market forces. Government intervention in industry was minimised and public sector industries privatised to enable them to compete on the open market.

Within the field of education and training the ruling elites remained lacking in their commitment to a system of high-skill formation. The capture of power by the representatives of the bourgeoisie under the leadership of Margaret Thatcher led to the centralisation of administrative powers as her government sought to curb the locally based power of the socialists. This led her to exert greater central control over the curriculum and over university education, but at the same time to introduce more diversified forms for the delivery of education in the guise of local self-management of schools. The brief attempt to increase the vocational component of education soon gave way to the traditional concern over standards and a new concern over parental choice. Attempts to introduce 'separate' provision of technical education through industry-financed technology colleges failed. The result was to reinforce existing inequalities (Brown, 1990).

Nevertheless, educational participation and achievement rates increased. In schools and colleges this was partly a consequence of the increase in youth unemployment (Raffe, 1992b; Furlong and Biggart, 1995) and partly a consequence of the reform of the public examination system. In higher education, expansion of the polytechnics and their subsequent incorporation into the university sector increased participation rates to about 30 per cent by the mid-1990s. These rises are testimony to an increasing commitment by working people to education. Yet, in terms of the educational achievement of the labour force as a whole, Britain remained well behind its major industrial competitors (see Chapter 4).

In the field of training the dismantling of the apparatus for the 'external' regulation of training was followed by an attempt to introduce a market based system of regulation (Ryan, 1993b). Against a background of the decline of the traditional heavy manufacturing industries this resulted in the virtual collapse of the remnants of the apprenticeship system. Meanwhile the state, through the colleges of further education and the polytechnics, was obliged to finance an increasing amount of pre-employment vocational training for the burgeoning service sector. However, companies were now left 'free' to organise training as they wished as employers were subsequently put in charge of the administration of government 'training' through their control of the Training and Enterprise Councils (TECs) and Local Enterprise Companies (LECs).

The undermining of the powers of trade unions, through the effects of industrial decline and the introduction of legal curbs on their powers, left employers and the state with greater freedom to determine the system of credentials. A system of individualised credentials in the form of National Vocational Qualifications was introduced, as part of the task of freeing up the labour market. This held out the promise of opening up all jobs to any person who could demonstrate their competence in a particular field, but started to founder when faced with the combined opposition of the professions and employers. The professions feared loss of control over their monopoly of skills and many employers were reluctant to finance training for skills which were not of immediate use to themselves. This together with pressures associated with the administration of the scheme led to a concentration on the certification of low-level skills (Felstead, 1994) and to serious public concern over the standards of certification (Smithers, 1993).

The result has been the increasing polarisation of the skills base of the nation. The system of higher education provided the technical specialist and the new generation of managers for those companies which remained in high-value-added markets. The collapse of large parts of the remaining manufacturing sector and the growth of deskilled jobs in the service sector led to a decline in the generation of intermediate level skills. The exclusion of unions from having any major say in the provision of training has diminished another potential source of change (Claydon and Green, 1994). The deregulation of the labour market has meant that many of those entering the new low-skilled jobs and unemployment are increasingly marginalised within the labour market (Ashton, Maguire and Spilsbury, 1990).

In terms of the hypotheses outlined in Chapter 5, Britain remains firmly located on the low-skills route. There are no signs of the political and leading factions of capital committing themselves and the nation to the high-skills route to accumulation. Regulatory mechanisms which might produce a high level of skill formation at the workplace have been dismantled and although central control over education has increased, educational inequalities have been reinforced and broad-based improvements in education have been sacrificed on the altar of market ideology and fiscal stringency. Educational participation and achievement has increased which may be indicative of rising commitment to high skills by the future workforce, but this still leaves Britain well behind other advanced European nations. And while participation in training has increased (Felstead and Green, 1994) much of that training is directed at the certification of lower level skills.

## THE UNITED STATES

The characterisation of the US as a low-skills route may still prove to be premature. As we saw in Chapter 4 there are some enviable aspects of the public education system, including a generous and flexible provision of post-compulsory education. There is still a dynamic part of the private sector competing at the leading edge of the more technologically advanced product markets. The economy as a whole, with its large domestic market and abundant natural resources is still rich. While it has been growing slower than other countries, it is too early to say whether it is likely to fall substantially behind other industrialised nations in the coming decades.

Nevertheless, there is a large section of the population at the base of the pyramid with declining real wage rates, poor levels of educational achievement and low-level skills and insufficient access to work-based training. Millions of Americans are managing to maintain their real incomes only by working hard and for long hours. It is the presence of this group which leads us to continue to characterise a large part of the US economy as following a low-skills route, and to seek an understanding of this position in its history.

## State Formation

The process of state formation in the US led, as in the UK, to the creation of a weak system of central administration, although for very different reasons. Once the struggle for independence had succeeded, the demise of the threat from Britain left the US government with only the Native American as their immediate competitor. There were no major pressures which would cause the political elite to use the resources of the state to follow a path of state sponsored industrialisation. Another reason for the emergence of a decentralised system of internal administration was the nature of the constitutional settlement. In the wake of absolutist rulers in Europe and the tyranny of monarchies, the Americans established a constitution which ensured that the powers of the President over internal affairs would be subject to checks and balances which made it difficult to impose a strong centralised system of administration. In addition the individual states jealously guarded their own independence *vis-à-vis* the central authority.

## Skill Formation

It was thus a considerable achievement that a universal public system of education was introduced, although the difficulties of introducing it in such a highly decentralised political system helps explain why it took a long time to bring in. The conditions of its introduction also explain why the functions it performed were different to those observed in the British system. Whereas the British aristocracy were afraid that the lower classes might rise against them and therefore required controlling, the American ruling class was afraid that the masses might not be committed to the ideals of the new republic and the new American identity. They wanted an education system to generate that commitment. Moreover, once established, the continued influx of immigrants meant that an educational system with this purpose needed to be sustained.

The consolidation of a US public education system started in the early

1830s in the North East.   Andy Green summarises the early development of the US system as follows:

> As in Europe, where education had proved to be the most powerful weapon for forming nations, in America public schooling proved to be a formidable tool for shaping national consciousness and it was largely in the pursuit of this that the initial impetus for public education lay.   From the period of the Revolution onwards, education was held to be uniquely important for the cultivation of a national identity, for the maintenance of social cohesion and for the promotion of republican values, especially so in a country of dispersed and heterogeneous communities and in the early years of a new and fragile republic.   As in Europe, the development of public education was a crucial aspect of nation building, and in its early phase performed a cultural and ideological role which was paramount over any other function. (Green, 1990: 171)

When the US started the process of industrialisation it did so with an emergent national system of public education geared to the inculcation of a national identity.   The requirements of industry were initially minor in comparison with this more urgent political task.   Nevertheless, there is evidence that, by the *ante-bellum* period, the emerging industrial bourgeoisie were becoming an important force driving educational expansion and reform.   Underlying their demands was the concern that children should acquire the appropriate habits and attitudes for participating in the economy as wage-labourers (Bowles and Gintis, 1976).

**The Development of the Productive System**

The federal state was instrumental in helping facilitate the process of industrialisation.   It played a part by subsidising some of the communications network, particularly the railways, and erecting national tariffs (Lazonick and O'Sullivan, 1994: 53).   This created a vast communications network across the continent linking the communities of small farmers and artisans, which were already commercialised, to create a market of millions.   Unlike some societies which were to industrialise at a later date, the American entrepreneurs did not have to break into world markets already dominated by others since their home market was sufficiently large to sustain the process of industrial growth.   One consequence of this was that the process of industrialisation in the US was more rapid than in Britain.

As in Britain, the initial craft-based production system made few demands on the education system.   The early American entrepreneurs also had to rely on the skilled worker to help co-ordinate production on the shop-floor.   However, unlike Britain, this reliance proved short-lived as did the phase of craft production. The high mobility of labour and the scarcity of skilled labour, caused by the opportunities for self-employment as farmers, created pressure on American manufacturers to develop skill-displacing technologies even before the emergence of the new science-based technologies of the second industrial revolution (Hounshell, 1984). Hence the references even at this early stage in the process of industrialisation to the 'American system of manufactures' (Lazonick and O'Sullivan, 1994: 58). The basis for transmitting skills was working on the shop-floor alongside experienced workers – an informal type of training that still characterises much of US industry in the late twentieth century. Such a system made few demands on labourers for whom three years' education in the three Rs and the development of appropriate values was thought enough: beyond that, cognitive and technical skills were not on the educational agenda (Bowles and Gintis, 1976).

Following the defeat of the South in the Civil War there was no opposition, as there was in Britain, to the bourgeoisie taking control of the reins of the state apparatus. Consequently the state apparatus, could be and was used to further the interests of manufacturers. There were, of course, small farmers who represented an important political force, but these were commercial farmers, whose fortunes were also tied up with the development of market forces.[9] As for the emergent working class, this was divided by racial and ethnic forces which made collective action difficult, especially when immigrant labour could be used to counter any attempts to control the process of production. Within this context of a rapidly expanding working class, whose growth was fuelled by immigration, the small groups of craft workers fought hard to retain control over access to their trades and differentiate themselves from the rest of the working class. However, their success was more limited and craft production only survived in enclaves such as construction. The introduction of the new techniques of mass production was part of a more widespread process whereby management was able to appropriate the skills of the craft worker and establish new industrial forms of production (Elbaum and Wilkinson, 1979). In this respect the process of deskilling was far more pervasive in the US than in the UK (Littler, 1982). The converse was that American manufacturers were the first to establish a new cluster of innovations, with the reorganisation of production away from craft to mass production, and the application of science to industry to generate the new industries of the second industrial revolution. The initial development of mass production techniques, and with them the growth of scientific management, created what was then the most productive system of industrial production hitherto developed. The US success was built on the associated scale economies, cheap raw materials and abundant, but low-skilled, labour (Wright, 1990; Marshall and Tucker, 1990).

The process of mass production, based on the extreme division of labour, created in turn the necessity for the introduction of modern forms of management co-ordination to replace the co-ordination skills of the craft worker and to diminish the role of the market (Chandler, 1977). The new mass production industries required the services of professional managers trained in the techniques of scientific management. Perhaps more significantly, these industries benefited from the humbler development of accountancy, secretarial and other 'lower' managerial skills. A further change of considerable significance for the process of skill formation was the separation of ownership from control. The owner-entrepreneurs gave way to the new professional managers as the Great Merger Movement got under way, creating the conditions for managers to move to the top of the hierarchy. The other major development with regard to the productive system was the establishment of the new industries of chemicals and electrical engineering. These were based on the application of the new scientific knowledge to the process of production. Together, the new science-based industries and the mass production industries created a significant demand for new technical and managerial skills.

With the bourgeoisie in control of the machinery of state there was no strong opposition to the introduction of new forms of knowledge into the educational system. The response from the educational sector was the creation of management schools and a significant growth of the higher education sector to supply the relevant courses. From the end of the nineteenth century the higher education system became geared to the production of the technical and managerial personnel necessary to staff the new bureaucracies. Existing educational institutions were adapted to meet these new needs. The Land Grant Colleges, originally designed to provide for the application of science to farming, became the centres for applying scientific developments to the needs of the new technologies being developed by the large corporations (Noble, 1977; Ferleger and Lazonick, 1993). After the turn of the century, the older classical colleges were increasingly obliged to take account of the needs of industry, especially when a substantial part of educational funding started to come from the fortunes of the entrepreneurs (Lazonick and O'Sullivan, 1994). Business schools flourished and higher education came to be closely linked to the needs and values of big business.

The new technologies and forms of organising production did not have the same impact on the education of the workers. One of the advantages of mass production and one of the reasons for its emergence was that it could utilise unskilled labour. Few demands were made on the intellectual skills of the employee, and there was no clamour from employers for more highly educated school and college leavers. It continued to be sufficient for the schools to turn out workers who could accept the demands of the new routines associated with mass production (Bowles and Gintis, 1976).

The domination of the state machinery by the bourgeoisie had other consequences. As in Britain there was no reason why the state should become involved in the process of certifying credentials. The distribution of knowledge and skills throughout the labour force was subject to the outcome of the struggle between employers and workers in which the employers had the upper hand. The result was a very open society by European standards in which emphasis was placed more on individual ability than on the prior acquisition of specific credentials. However, because of the extensive deskilling there were few demands for a system of qualifications for manual and service sector workers.

## Class Formation

Changes of such magnitude did not occur without a struggle. Once the new technologies did emerge, then employers used all the tactics available to undermine the power of craft workers and deskill the labour process, including repression. In this struggle they could rely on the state's monopoly of physical force to suppress worker protests. There was no aristocracy to restrain the behaviour of the entrepreneurs in their struggle to control workers and as a result the US had a far more violent history of industrial conflict than Britain. During the early decades of the century, employers won the struggle and established their full control over the production process, but this was at the cost of considerable bitterness. Future managers were separated out from future workers well before the latter left school, a social and political differentiation which was reinforced by the massive lay-off of blue-collar workers during the Great Depression.

The working class remained weak. Although craft unions had been largely destroyed, workers in the new industries successfully struggled to establish new industry-based unions with which the employers had to negotiate. When recovery came in the 1940s employers had to incorporate the new unions by offering welfare benefits, higher wages, and more secure employment as embodied in the seniority agreements. These ensured that workers acquired a small but steady increase in their wages as they progressed within the internal labour markets (Gordon, Edwards and Reich, 1982) – the political deal of Fordism. The remainder of the working class, ethnically divided, was confined to the secondary labour market.

During the 1960s and 1970s the contraction of manufacturing industry produced a bipolar pattern of employment growth with expansion occurring at the top (professional, technical and managerial workers) and bottom (clerical and service workers) of the occupational hierarchy. During the 1980s the trend was towards the growth of low-paid jobs and an increase in earnings and income inequality (Rosenberg, 1989; Green, Henley and Tsakalotos, 1994). In the absence of a developed system of public health and welfare provision and with the presence of institutionalised racial discrimination, these trends have tended to intensify existing inequalities.   One consequence has been the creation and persistence of racial ghettos.  As funding for schools is derived from local taxes this provides a mechanism for the reproduction and intensification of inequalities in access to skills.

**Skill Formation in the Period of Industrial Maturity**

In international relations the relative decline of the British economy left a void in international affairs which was filled by the Americans.  This had a powerful effect on the development of the US economy and society.  The rapid growth of the economy meant that, after the First World War, the US started to take on the role of the capitalist world's defender and policeman in international affairs, a role that was extended with the intensification of the Cold War after the Second World War.  This created the conditions for the US Federal government to develop the most powerful military machine in the world.   Given the structure of the Federal political system, this created considerable centralisation of power in the hands of the President, but only with reference to foreign affairs.  Internally, its impact was felt through the size of the Federal budget for military spending. Contemporary observers such as Mills (1956) and Galbraith (1967) illustrated how this stimulated the concentration of economic power which in turn provided an important central lever of control over the economy. However, these political pressures have now eased with the demise of communism in Russia and the growth of capitalist economies in the Pacific Rim.

With regard to the educational system, the pressure for it to maintain the socialisation of each new generation, especially the children of immigrants, into the values of the US was maintained.  There were occasional pressures on the system to increase general levels of achievement.  During the Cold War, the shock of the Russians launching the first person into space created a period of soul searching among many Americans which called into question the adequacy of their education system.  However, once they had regained the lead in the space race these pressures were removed. During the three decades following the Second World War the political and economic dominance of the US throughout the world meant that there were few other pressures to upgrade the system of primary and secondary education.[10]

Within the last two decades the efficiency of the American system of manufacturing has been seriously challenged as a result of new forms of organising production developed in Germany, Japan and the new industrial economies of the Pacific Rim.   During the period 1972 to 1982 the proportion of American-made goods subject to foreign competition increased from 20 to 80 per cent (Hampden-Turner and Trompenaars, 1994).   The success of imports threatened the existence of some of the largest and most powerful corporations.   The American multinational corporations were not slow to respond and sought to learn from the success of their foreign competitors, especially Japan.   Like Britain, the US lost many of its traditional heavy and labour-intensive industries, while the remaining mass production industries sought to restructure themselves, taking up the management lessons from the Japanese and other competitors (Applebaum and Batt, 1994).   As American companies sought to survive the intensified pressure of international competition there has been a spate of new management philosophies such as total quality management, process re-engineering and, occasionally, new flat forms of organisation. In some areas, such as computers and to a lesser extent aircraft, America appears to have retained a competitive advantage or, as in automobiles, regained one (Berggren, 1995).   Meanwhile it has developed a robust service sector, albeit one that has a heavy reliance on low-paid labour.

The relative decline of the economic power of the US and the challenges of the new forms of organising production being developed abroad have led to a re-examination of the US education and training system.   Successive reports have come to locate the source of economic decline in the inadequate skills of the workforce (Commission on the Skills of the American Workforce, 1990; Dertouzos *et al.*, 1989; Johnston and Packer, 1987; Marshall and Tucker, 1992; Reich, 1988), this concern culminating in the appointment as Secretary of State for Labor in 1993 of Robert Reich, a Harvard academic closely identified with this diagnosis of America's ills.   Although the US has developed a successful mass higher education system, the level of achievement of the average American child, especially in scientific subjects, is falling behind that of a number of other industrial nations.   The extreme polarisation of the labour force is mirrored by considerable inequalities in the quality of school provision, and relatively severe educational problems among its young college drop-out population.   With national drop-out rates of 17 per cent (US, 1990), and local rates in excess of 25 per cent of the age group, there is anxiety about whether this level of skill formation can sustain high value-added production or high performance workplaces (Applebaum and Batt, 1994).

And, as we saw in Chapter 4, there is no evidence that the average skill levels used at American workplaces are accelerating upwards. The system which succeeded in integrating a new nation and producing literate workers for mass production industries is not sufficient for the demands placed upon labour for the new forms of higher-value-added production.

The response of the political elite to these problems has been mixed, but to some extent split along party lines. Yet even if there were a consensus among the elites, history has dealt them severe constraints. The Federal government does not have the centralised apparatus or powers to intervene in education in the ways which the British government has. There are constitutional limits, even to the prospect of introducing national standards for educational and vocational curricula (Felstead *et al.*, 1994). Nor is it able (or willing) to constrain uncooperative employers to involve themselves with training: 'pay or play' training taxes (levy-subsidy schemes) are unlikely to gain widespread acceptance by the majority of employers not committed to an upskilling strategy. Moreover, given the fiscal squeeze, any money available for apprenticeship or other training schemes, other than those for the unemployed and various groups of disadvantaged workers, is sure to be small. State governments are also constrained in their ability to raise funds for education, through the need to compete on tax rates to attract businesses. Nor can any government, Federal or state, impose in the individualistic US environment even a modicum of regulation aimed at overcoming training externalities and associated short-termism of companies. Trade unions have too few members, and too little influence beyond the workplace, to be able to exert significant economy-wide control over the quantity and quality of training. Regulation is likely only to be achievable, therefore, in those large American companies that can adopt internal labour markets and provide reasonable prospects of career progression. Yet while there are many well-publicised flagships for the training lobbies, the prospect of using this route for upskilling large swathes of the American workforce remains limited and constrained by the relatively fluid US employment system (Brown, Reich and Stern, 1993, 1994).

One possible advantage of the current constellation of skill formation institutions is its flexibility: for the individual, who can with relative ease move in and out of education; and for individual state governments which are free to introduce innovatory regional schemes to boost training such as those in California and New Jersey (Batt and Osterman, 1993). A second advantage is the mass higher education system which not only is able to produce a highly trained managerial workforce, but also is able to provide further education through 2-year community colleges for large numbers of American workers. When linked to local industries, these could provide just that heady mix of off-the-job training to support the large amount of informal on-the-job training done by companies. But while the other institutional requirements are not met, it is hard to be optimistic about the US switching to a high-skills route.

## CONCLUSIONS

If we cast aside the sometimes hopeful rhetoric of policy discussion in the US and the UK, we find that the ordinary citizens of both countries are hampered by a considerable problem of skill formation in the modern global economy, a problem which bodes none too well for their future living standards. In neither country is there evidence of a commitment, on the part of ruling political elites or of the major fractions of capital, to a system of high-skills formation. In this chapter we have attempted to trace the origins of this problem to the processes of state formation and industrialisation of the two countries, and the resultant institutions that fail to match with those required in a system of high-skill formation.

In both the US and Britain, the ways in which the state formation process conditioned the formation of the educational system has meant that the provision of basic primary and secondary education has been dominated by the need to fulfil functions other than those associated with the transmission of skills required for modern forms of production. The longevity of institutional structures, once formed, has sustained these wider functions in the culture of education. It is only at the level of higher education (and only in the US) that the system was adapted and geared to the requirements of the major corporations as they established their factories of mass production.

The lack of commitment by employers to high-skill formation is by no means universal in the modern day. In the US in particular, many of the larger enterprises in the leading industries, have established an institutionalised system of workplace learning which enables them to continue to compete at the leading edge of world markets. Nevertheless, these remain something of an exception. Many employers continue to choose the low-skills route, since it is profitable to rely on cheap malleable labour. Their systematic opposition to proposals to fund skill formation from payroll or other taxes springs from this concern with their profits. The situation is not helped, especially in the US, by the institutional legacy of low regulatory intervention.

These structural factors point to the difficulties in making piecemeal transformations of the education and training system. Government in the US can only intervene at the margins of the training system. In Britain the centralised political apparatus makes the intervention of the state in the process of skill formation at least possible, even though its impact remains limited in an increasingly decentralised and unco-ordinated system of industrial relations. In the US the contradictions in the political system, the difficulties of enforcing a national policy and of raising the taxes necessary to fund it in a racially divided society mean that policies from the centre are unlikely to be effective, unless they are linked with a wider politics of regeneration that involves all communities with the project of skill formation and constrains employers to participate.

## NOTES

1. One exception was the demand for iron and the stimulus which the demands of warfare made for the development of the iron and engineering industries. Another important contribution made by the state to the process of industrialisation, was the development of early forms of bureaucratic administration (Dandeker, 1978). However, these were all the unintended consequences of the behaviour of the political elite. The state's powers were never used to drive the process of industrialisation as they were in Germany and Japan.

2. Adam Smith, however, despite his liberal philosophy, championed basic education for social control. Bewailing 'the gross ignorance and stupidity' of the 'inferior ranks of people', he maintained that the state 'derives no inconsiderable advantage from their instruction. The more they are instructed, the less liable they are to the delusions of enthusiasm and superstition, which, among ignorant nations, frequently occasion the most dreadful disorders' (Smith, 1976: 788).

3. This was the case for the Guest family who owned the world's largest iron works. The school started by the company was run on a philanthropic basis by Lady Guest (Elsas, 1960).

4. Management education was different, here owners often paid considerable attention to organising the technical and managerial education of their offspring (Pollard, 1965).

5. Although the political reforms of the nineteenth century enabled members of the industrial bourgeoisie to enter parliament, members of the commercial aristocracy still dominated the Cabinet well into the middle of the next century (Guttsman, 1968).

6. The Merthyr rising in 1831 was one such instance but troops were brought in only because of the fear of a general uprising.

7. For a concise account of these differences and their continued relevance see Raffe (1992a).

8. The use of a watered-down 'academic' curriculum for the children of working-class background contributed to their disillusionment with the education system (see Ashton, 1986; Ashton and Maguire, 1986 ).

9. A significant educational innovation in 1862 was the introduction of the Land Grant Colleges to integrate with agricultural development.

10. Another social impetus to educational reform in the 1960s was the Civil Rights Movement. But the success of the attempt to improve economic prospects for black people through education has been questioned (Bowles and Gintis, 1976).

# 7 The High-Skills Routes

## INTRODUCTION

In Chapter 5 we distinguished two main routes to capital accumulation via industrial forms of production, namely the high-skills and low-skills routes. In this chapter we retain this basic dualism, but within the high-skills route we make a further distinction between the routes followed by the second-wave industrial nations, taking as our examples Germany and Japan, and the route toward high level skills currently being pursued by the Newly Industrialised Economies (NIEs) of the Pacific Rim, namely Hong Kong, Singapore, Taiwan and South Korea. The former group have succeeded in establishing a highly skilled labour force, while the latter are well on their way.

Both sets of economies were faced with the task of emulating the nations of the first wave of industrial development. The attempt to catch up had a powerful influence on the relationship between the processes of state formation and industrialisation and skill formation. The political elite's use of the resources of the state to speed up the process of industrialisation led to a much closer set of linkages between the processes of state formation and industrialisation in these societies. One consequence of this was that the education and training systems that developed were more closely geared to the demands of the productive system and therefore had less autonomy than those which characterised the first wave nations. Because of the lateness of the NIE's bid to enter world markets, the autonomy of their education and training systems was lowest of all.

## THE SECOND-WAVE INDUSTRIAL NATIONS: GERMANY AND JAPAN

Germany and Japan had to industrialise in a world in which two great nations had already established powerful industrial economies. Therefore, at the political level, both had to catch up with the existing industrial nations of Britain and the US if they were to develop the industrial capacity to safeguard their independence in the competition between nations. A strong industrial economy was seen by leaders in both countries as essential if they were to compete effectively in the international arena, that is, in the imperial struggle for colonies and international domination. This produced a closer relationship between the two processes of state formation and industrialisation than was found among the first-wave industrial nations. This is an important factor in explaining the different routes to skill formation pursued by these countries.

This closer relationship was manifest in a number of different ways. If they were to establish an independent power base in international politics, both Germany and Japan required a strong industrial base to support mechanised armed forces capable of guaranteeing political independence (Laxer, 1989; Lash and Urry, 1987). The ruling groups in the two countries were aware of the link between the political independence of the state and the establishment of a strong industrial base, and therefore of the need for the state to play an active part in the development of the productive system (Laxer, 1989). In Japan in particular, the want of a tradition of relying on the market to decide at what level, and in which products, investments should be made, enabled businesses to break into the high-value-added world markets. If the Japanese could not rely on the unaided workings of the market to deliver economic growth there was no reason why they should expect the market to provide training. Indeed, the absence of strong occupational interest groups meant that there was no tradition of craft skills as being owned by individuals who could then sell them on the market. Therefore, there was no institutional basis for the existence of a market in transferable skills. Work-based skill formation was far more closely tied to the demands of the employing organisation and hence controlled either by the actions of the state or employers (Littler, 1982; Ishikawa, 1991).

When we examine the process of industrialisation, we find that, whereas the first industrial nations had industrialised on the basis of the old craft technology, harnessing it to steam power, for the second-wave industrial nations the 'new' process and mass production technologies of the second industrial revolution were available to them very soon after the start of their drive towards industrial maturity. Consequently, the process of industrialisation took a different form, which had important implications for the delivery of education, training and skill formation. Whereas the craft-based industries had been able to reproduce themselves on the basis of low levels of literacy, more of the industries of the second industrial revolution, engineering and chemicals for example, required a more highly educated and skilled labour force, especially at the higher levels.[1]

Therefore the pressure from the productive system in these countries was for a more highly educated and skilled labour force than those which characterised the nations of the first wave, at the same stage of their industrial development.

The combination of these various pressures meant that in both cases, the political elites were willing to make significant changes to the educational system as a means of contributing towards the goal of economic development. This stemmed in part from their commitment to industrialisation and their willingness to use the instruments of public policy to facilitate it. Moreover, they had the advantage of learning from the experience of the first generation of industrial producers and they could therefore observe the greater reliance of the more advanced industries on the availability of an educated and trained labour force (Amsden, 1989). In Germany, a national system of technical education was introduced, geared to the demands of industry (Lazonick and O'Sullivan, 1994). In Japan, modernising elites during the Meiji era were able to build on the high levels of education achieved during the Tokugawa period (Ryoshin, 1986).

The links between the processes of state formation and industrialisation were tightened during the crucial reconstruction phase after the Second World War. The economic and social dislocation caused by their defeat resulted in the removal of conservative elements from the ruling elites. In both countries there arose an alliance between major segments of the business community, state bureaucrats and the working class around a common agenda: to develop a partnership between the state and the private sector, planning for long-term growth, setting targets for technological breakthroughs, all within the context of a market system, producing what Laxer has termed enterprise intervention strategies.[2] Such a strategy drove all the parties in the alliance in the direction of higher-value-added production and the introduction of new ways of organising production in order to achieve a competitive advantage in world markets. Part of this agenda was to develop a highly skilled labour force on which to build the new industries. The innovation which both achieved, although in different ways, was to establish a combination of state provision of general education and employer provision of work-based learning.

The initial response of members of this alliance between state, employers and segments of the working classes was to make modifications to the institutional base of their existing systems of skill formation in order to accommodate the demands of producing higher value-added goods. The Germans further modified the medieval apprenticeship system to make it appropriate to the production of higher-level intermediate skills (Lazonick and O'Sullivan, 1994). In Japan, state educational provision was expanded. This provided a high level of mass achievement in the basic skills in mathematics, science, technology and language on which the firms would build a high level of work-based skills through the system of lifetime employment (Ishikawa, 1991).

## The Relationship Between State Formation, Industrialisation and Skill Formation

In this section we provide no more than an introductory sketch of how, in the two second-wave countries, these processes of change created distinctive institutional forms which focused on the enhancement of work-based learning, what we referred to earlier as systems of regulation.

## Germany[3]

### State formation
The military struggles in which the Prussian leadership had been engaged throughout the eighteenth century provided the impetus for the establishment of a strong centralised state apparatus, staffed by technically proficient bureaucrats.   This state apparatus was used in the field of economic and industrial policy to establish the Zollverein in 1834, which integrated local markets into one large German market.  This together with Bismarck's strategy for political unification provided the conditions for investment in a rail network and the construction of the transport and communication infrastructure.  The creation of a single internal market stimulated heavy machinery and associated industries such as railways, iron and mining industries (Chandler, 1990).  In addition to these political activities which fostered industrial development, the state was also a major customer for steel, chemicals and shipbuilding as it created its vast military machine.  In these ways the political powers of the state were used to stimulate and guide economic growth, a precursor of the enterprise-intervention strategy.

### Industrialisation
The process of industrialisation which the political unification of Germany stimulated and which subsequently provided the basis for the German military machine, went through an initial phase based on the skills of craft workers and the development of the textile and associated industries. Apprentices, trained in the German *Handwerk* sector, were the main source of supply for the small- and medium-sized enterprises which characterised this first phase.  As we have seen, this craft based technology was soon replaced by the more complex technology of the industries of the second

industrial revolution. Between 1870 and 1900 German banks played an important role in developing the capital-intensive industries and fostering industrial concentration. After that the companies raised their own money but representatives of banks still sat on the Boards, and acted as a break on any attempt to disperse wealth created by the company as opposed to using it to finance further development. The development of these industries provided the basis for the competitive advantage of German industry in world markets for chemicals, metals, electrical machinery and heavy general machinery. By the early twentieth century German industrialisation and exports were firmly based on the more technologically advanced industries.

**Skill formation**
This had clear implications for the process of skill formation. The development of more technologically advanced industries undermined the power of German craft workers, which had already been weakened by the political repression of the Prussian State (Lazonick and O'Sullivan, 1994). The new industries required scientific, technical and managerial skills, not those of the craft worker. When it came to manual work, the companies could more easily train their own semi-skilled workers than use the products of the apprenticeship system. The main demand on the education and training system was for the establishment of highly trained scientific and technical workers.

Although Prussia already had a national system of education, the higher-level skills it transmitted were primarily those of an academic nature. In the early nineteenth century universities had been similar to those in Britain, transmitting knowledge of classical culture. However, this system was called into question by the victory of Napoleon. In response to this political threat, Prussian leaders established technical institutes and a series of trade schools in the provinces (Lazonick and O'Sullivan, 1994). Initially these were developed outside the formal education sector and combined scientific knowledge with craftsmanship to create 'Technic'. However, by the beginning of the twentieth century they were awarding degrees. The German system of education was undergoing a substantial transformation. At the turn of the twentieth century the German engineering profession was split between the products of the two systems, that is between academic and practical engineers. The outcome of the ensuing struggle for power was the formation of a third group which won the day through integrating theory and practice. This group cemented links between German industry and technical education (Gispen, 1989). This marriage between technical knowledge and industrial activity became the basis of the German competitive advantage. The product strategy was not to compete with the Americans in the mass production of light machinery, but to produce one-off goods of high quality to the specification of governments.

Viewing the institutions of skill formation in historical perspective it is evident that political factors were very important in ensuring that the academic system of education was modified to meet the demands of industrial development. The modification of the academic system created the foundations for the German engineering profession which then played a crucial role in linking scientific knowledge and technical/managerial expertise to the development of the new industries. Those new industries required the skills of engineers, many to work as managers, to meet the demands of railroad, shipbuilding, iron-producing and mining companies (Chandler, 1990; Lazonick and O'Sullivan, 1994).

Although the German political elite had 'sponsored' the growth of industry there was no strong desire to regulate the relations between employers and workers. Attempts were made by Bismarck to introduce an elementary welfare system in order to counteract the socialists, but industrial relations at the workplace, including control of the system of skill formation, was left to the employers and workers to determine.

By the end of the nineteenth century many of the new industries of the second industrial revolution were dependent on a complex technology which was outside the control of craft workers, whereas this had not been the case with the industries of the first industrial revolution, such as textiles. The German *Handwerk* sector which had been the mainstay of the first phase of industrial production was undermined by these developments. The new industrial workers of the second industrial revolution were industry – not occupationally-based. This meant that by the end of the nineteenth century the German labour movement was more class conscious and less craft conscious than the British. Moreover, because the unions organised on industrial rather than craft lines, change did not threaten the workers' identity as it did in the UK.

In the early years of the twentieth century, German employers formed a powerful federation which was opposed to unions. This forced unions to adopt a more highly centralised structure which succeeded in making some agreements with employers, but the employers remained firmly in control of workplace skill formation. The apprenticeship system in the *Handwerk* sector supplied many apprentices for industry, but in the early decades of the twentieth century most of the large factories had their own apprenticeship schools and controlled the training of their own employees. In response to concerns that this would tie workers to the individual factory and undermine their collective solidarity, the unions pushed for the standardisation of the training system, regulated at national or industry levels.

Employers resisted workers' attempts to control the skill formation process, although works councils were introduced into plants with more than 50 workers in 1920. However, unions made some gains and were prepared to promote measures aimed at building up the competitive strength of German industry. In 1920 they supported scientific management, an early indication of the willingness of German workers to work with employers in the pursuit of common goals. However, the *Handwerkers*, fearful of the threat from the dynamic industrial sector and the socialism of the workers, supported Hitler. During the Nazi period the *Handwerk* sector was integrated into the German industrial economy in the interests of raising the productivity of the wartime economy. As a result training was standardised and regulated, creating the foundations of the modern apprenticeship system.

Following the Second World War there was a successful attempt to rebuild engineering and other industries in order to recapture world markets. Legal controls were introduced in association with the system of co-determination and the establishment of the dual system of apprentice training. These, together with a financial system which encouraged long-term investment, created the external pressures which pushed employers in the direction of high-valued-added production. The efforts of the state, employers and unions were directed at extending the process of skill formation down from the professions to the level of intermediate skills – a process which never occurred in the US and Britain.

The post-war re-alignment of political power in Germany enabled the political decision to be taken to develop the apprenticeship system as the basis for the system of worker training. In this new accommodation between the state, capital and labour, the state continued to play a central role and employers accepted as legitimate the role of trade unions in worker training. The state took an active part in the management of relations between capital and labour, imposing a dual system of worker representation between industrial trade unions at national and regional level and worker representation at plant level on the works councils. The administration of training was kept much as it had developed during the war, but the unions were integrated more into the governing and regulating bodies – the vocational training committees of the Chambers, together with relevant government ministries and employers' associations. At enterprise level the Works Councils had the right to negotiate the structure of the in-firm training programme. Here we have the foundations for the German combination of off-the-job and on-the-job training.

The off-the-job training financed by the state is intended to convey the theoretical knowledge necessary for the trade and also a basic education in the requirements of citizenship. The on-the-job training is characterised by its systematic nature, as defined by the syllabus and the presence of the *Meister*, trained in the arts of teaching, to guide the apprentice through on-the-job training.

One of the unintended consequences of this system was that it placed pressure on employers to adopt product market strategies which would enable them to make the most of these highly trained workers and to use the technology to develop systems of diversified quality production (Sorge and Streeck, 1988). This was particularly the case with the large employers in the engineering industry. In this way the institutionalisation of the German system of skill formation after the Second World War directly influenced the development of the productive system.

Employers were no longer able to gear training programmes to the requirements of the individual firm. They were now forced to consider the needs of the industry as a whole. As Lazonick and O'Sullivan (1994) observe, this was particularly appropriate in industries with a historically stable technology, but may not have been so in industries where the pace of innovation was rapid. This training system has also enabled many of the medium-sized enterprises, which do most of the training, to compete in niche markets in those industries with a stable technology, for example precision machine tools and laser optics. They can compete successfully because of their excellence in design and the production flexibility that result from their workers' and managers' skills.

Another mechanism which placed constraints on employers was the powers of the works councils to reduce the employers' ability to hire and fire, thereby forcing them to consider training as a longer-term investment. Workers were no longer factors of production which could be easily dispensed with and therefore employers were obliged to consider strategies which could be used to secure the continuity of production. All these mechanisms served to place pressure on employers to move into high-value-added production (Streeck, 1989).

There are problems associated with the German system of training. The co-operation of the *Länder*, the Federal government and the chambers of commerce in the process of training does mean that change is slow (Casey, 1991; Blossfeld, 1994). Nevertheless, the system has been simplified with a reduction in the number of recognised trades and successful attempts have been made to upgrade the syllabus of many of the trades. However, females remain under-represented (Heinz, 1991) and many young people fail to achieve entry to the jobs for which they have trained. Moreover, there is relatively little provision for those who wish to change trades in later life (Auer, 1992), and there remain shortcomings in the provision of continuing education and training of adults (Mahnkopf, 1992). There are rigidities, too, in the system of higher education, with comparatively excessive times taken to achieve higher qualifications and limited access to privileged professorial posts.

## Japan

### State formation
As we saw earlier the Japanese state played an important part in stimulating the process of industrialisation for the same reasons as in Germany. The threat of foreign invasion meant that if the country did not industrialise rapidly and obtain modern armed forces, it would be vulnerable to foreign domination. In order to secure its political sovereignty, the Meiji government used the resources available to the state to find ways of fostering industrial development in the latter half of the nineteenth century.

### Industrialisation
Although textiles was one of the leading industries in the first phase of development, if the state was to be secure then heavy manufacturing had to be developed to provide the material means to establish a modern industrially-based defence force. Therefore, such key industries as steel and shipbuilding were initially run by the government, and foreign workers were invited in to ensure the transfer of skills (Ishikawa, 1991). The government's interest extended beyond just the financial provision for such industries; the policy was to ensure that the knowledge to run such industries was embedded in the Japanese labour force. This provides some indication of the extent to which the political elite were willing to go, in order to guide the development of the productive system in the early stages of industrialisation. However, having once set up such industries, the state had no intention of remaining in control: the industries were later transferred to the private sector.

One of the most important agencies through which the Meiji government operated were the Zaibatsu families who were given concessions for minerals and who set about establishing the basic industries of the second wave. The Zaibatsu families started building their enterprise groups at the turn of the century and continued to develop them until the end of the Second World War. During this time, members of these families delegated considerable powers to their managers who built up substantial organisational structures (Lazonick and O'Sullivan, 1994). This created a demand for educated professionals and managers.

As in Germany, defeat in the Second World War led to a re-alignment of the political, business and labour elites. This had a profound effect on the development of the productive system and the subsequent process of skill formation. The Allies insisted on the break-up of the old Zaibatsu families' holdings, but the enterprise groups stayed intact. In the 1950s the Japanese business community undertook cross-shareholding – a move to ensure that ownership rights for companies stayed with other enterprises rather than with individuals or institutions. This ensured long-term reinvestment in industry, which continued to be dominated by the large corporate entities – Mitsubishi, Mitsui and Sumitomo, joined by others such as Toyota and Sony which have emerged from the automobile and electronics industries. The dual economy of large and small enterprises was reproduced, with labour-intensive activities being placed with satellite companies on a sub-contract basis, leaving core companies free to innovate and pursue new investment strategies. These companies can organise cooperative investment strategies across enterprises. Here we see the conscious attempt by companies to move in the direction of higher-value-added production.

After the war, the state remained a powerful influence on the direction of investment. In particular, the MITI played a significant role in encouraging investment in selected industries, many of which were in new forms of high-value-added production. The resources of the state were used to establish and develop these industries until they were capable of tackling world markets. Part of the success of the Japanese approach to the development of industry depended on the availability of long-term finance. This provided a set of conditions in which employers could concentrate on the achievement of long-term objectives for which the development of their human resources was vital. Thus, rather than having a set of institutional structures which forced employers to concentrate on longer term development of the enterprise and its employees, as in Germany, the Japanese state helped create a set of circumstances in which such behaviour among the main employers was the norm. The success of these strategies, together with that of employers in incorporating the interests of labour at the level of the company, created the conditions necessary for a high level of skill formation at the workplace.

The state helped in the development of industry in a number of ways. It protected the home market while businesses built up the ability to compete internationally. Certain industries such as automobiles and electronics were targeted for development. Competition between existing companies was initially encouraged and those who came out on top were encouraged to invest in the latest technology and build up the industry ready for competition in world markets. This process encouraged firms to incur the high level of fixed costs necessary to compete internationally. In addition the state promoted cooperative R&D among Japanese companies. Imports in those products selected for development in Japan were discouraged through protectionist measures, and favourable long-term finance made available for the establishment of the latest manufacturing capability. The older more labour-intensive industries were run down through the introduction of cheaper foreign imports and attention focused on those products where it was felt that the Japanese could obtain a competitive advantage. Periodically the MITI would review this policy and a consensus would be developed on the next set of industries to be targeted (Johnson, 1982).

In addition to this 'industrial policy' the state also facilitated the process of industrialisation by maintaining a stable economic environment and high levels of employment. This not only facilitated the investment of private capital but also enlarged the market for consumer goods (World Bank, 1993).

As a result of this new stimulus given by the state to the development of the productive system, and the consensus achieved among senior bureaucrats and business leaders about the direction in which the Japanese economy should move, Japanese industry outperformed America's in mass production of consumer durables, especially automobiles and electronic equipment. It also mounted a major challenge in steel and the capital-goods industries of machine tools, electrical machinery and semi-conductors. In the process they have also pioneered significant improvements in the enhancement of quality and in the refinement of the productive system through the introduction of techniques such as lean production (Womack, Jones and Roos, 1990) and just-in-time production.

These advances in the development of the productive system have been created by, and have in turn created changes in, the process of skill formation. In particular they have involved making full use of the cognitive skills and personal commitment of all male members of a company's permanent labour force. The state has aided by extending educational provision for all to age 18 and expanding provision of higher education. However, the main basis for the establishment of the Japanese system of work-based skill formation has been the incorporation of all male permanent employees in the large companies into the core labour force with the security of lifetime employment.

### Skill formation

The political leaders were conscious of the need for an educated population. Following the Meiji Restoration the state built up the educational system and within two decades had a universal system of public education. Compulsory elementary education for four years was introduced in 1886 and extended to six years in 1907 (Ishikawa, 1991).

Although the educational system was based on an academic curriculum the government modified the system of higher education to produce engineers for the private sector in order to meet the demand for scientific and professional personnel from the new second-wave industries. They also sought to provide technical education for foremen and technicians. In fact these changes extended to an attempt to introduce craft training in the schools in 1880, but this system was not accepted by employers. A later attempt in 1920 to use public institutions as a basis for craft apprenticeship training was also successfully opposed. Employers preferred to rely on work-based apprenticeships for their supplies of skilled workers, and in the later stages of industrialisation they built on this with a system of continual in-house retraining of craftsmen. The educational system remained as a route to higher status occupations.

Here again the government, as in Germany, was willing to make substantial changes in the education system to meet the needs of industry. Moreover when these failed, as they did in the case of craft apprenticeship training, the government sought to legislate to control the training of apprentices by employers which it did in 1916 and later in the 1930s when the needs of the wartime economy pushed the government into further action (Ishikawa, 1991). Following the Second World War the education system was expanded to enable increased participation at the secondary and tertiary levels. As a result Japanese people emerge from school with some of the highest levels of academic skills. Their particular achievements lie in maths and sciences, and in spreading their achievements across the ability spectrum, so that there are few who fail altogether in their schooling.[4] Within the educational system, vocational education was integrated into mainstream education for aged fifteen plus. There is now no difference between the courses offered in the schools and in the public vocational institutions (Ishikawa, 1991).

One result of the government-induced changes in the education system was that the schools-to-college route took on a function as a general intelligence sorting mechanism (McCormick, 1988). Unlike the British schools which sought to inculcate social skills, the Japanese schools sought to develop cognitive skills. As Dore (1974: 5), expresses it:

> What the schools did impart was knowledge; what they sought to guarantee in their products was not 'breeding' but cognitive skills. And this implied strict regulation of entry into elite institutions according to demonstrated 'merit'. They were created, after all, by a modernising government, not to perpetuate the dominant culture of an established class, but to 'mobilise all the talents' for the development of the nation.

During the feudal period the Japanese had relied on an apprenticeship system which was similar in many respects to that which emerged in feudal Europe, based on the master–servant relationship, with the master providing accommodation but no pay and the apprentice acquiring the skills over a long period of time. This was used in handicraft production and in commerce. During the early period of industrialisation this same apprenticeship system was used to provide the training of industrial workers. It was this system which the state tried to encourage management and labour to accept. However, it was not considered by employers as appropriate for the new industries and the workers did not have strong enough organisations to impose it on industrial employers. Employers did not have to wrestle with the craft workers to obtain control of their skills, as in Britain or the US. Thus, in spite of government attempts to introduce elements of craft training in schools, employers insisted on replacing the traditional apprenticeship by a system of factory apprenticeship as industrialisation got under way (Ishikawa, 1991).

The government intervened in the process of skill formation more directly in the early stages of industrialisation. In order to acquire knowledge from the West the government attracted foreign workers to whom they attached Japanese nationals. Model factories were set up where Japanese workers would acquire the new skills and then leave either to set up their own businesses or to be employed in one of the new private businesses (Ishikawa, 1991). However, according to Ishikawa the learning process was not very effective and the new workers were not good enough to train other workers. In addition, there was a high level of labour turnover associated with these new workers who moved from firm to firm seeking better pay. The response of entrepreneurs was to find new ways of training and retaining their new employees, especially craftsmen. Firms started to recruit inexperienced school leavers and provided planned training over two to three years, after which they were bonded to the firm for a period of time. However, this did not work as the companies still suffered from high levels of turnover and poor training. Yet the large combines persevered in their efforts to retain key workers who would be adaptable to changing production technologies.

The solution which the larger employers developed through time was to integrate such employees into the organisation through the implicit promise of lifetime employment. This was a system which had been used in the early twentieth century to attract college graduates away from government service and into management. This was the first attempt by Japanese managers to create an internal labour market. After the First World War this practice became institutionalised among large firms (Ishikawa, 1991). The Nenko system of lifetime employment, as it became known, extended downwards to supervisors and key skilled workers before the Second World War in order to retain former sub-contractors who had recruited and trained the labour force for the larger enterprises.

The representatives of labour were incorporated into this new system, not so much by involving them at a national level as through the development of company-based unions and including the voice of labour at the level of the enterprise. Following the Second World War, unions sought to establish strong nation-wide organisations. The employers' resistance produced bitter conflict between the sides. The employers were victorious but in order to avoid such conflicts in the future they helped initiate company-based unions which would tie the interests of the workers to the company rather than to the industry, especially in manufacturing.

The other element of the employers' solution to the problem of industrial relations was to extend the system of lifetime employment to all male blue-collar workers in large enterprises. The result of the interaction of these developments in the product market and the productive system, with management's attempt to handle the problems of industrial relations, and the state's attempt to enhance the skill level of the labour force, was the establishment of the unique Japanese system of employment-based skill formation. Workers were offered lifetime security of employment but, crucially, were rewarded not just for their present level of performance but for their contribution to the company over time. This meant that if workers continued developing their skills within the organisation they could be rewarded in financial and status terms through promotion (Dore, 1973; Koike and Inoki (eds), 1990; Brown, Reich and Stern, 1994).

Traditionally Japanese workers had been given discretion over the control and monitoring of the flow of work in the workshop. This discretion, together with lifetime security of employment and a system of financial rewards which reinforced workers' commitment to the organisation, and which rewarded continuous learning, contributed towards the successful introduction of flexible manufacturing systems. The work of Koike and Inoki and others has revealed how this system has also contributed to the development of workers' knowledge and skills both in terms of breadth and depth. Workers were able to broaden their knowledge of the functioning of the organisation through movement between departments and also deepen their knowledge of the technical basis of production. The security of lifetime employment also meant that it was possible to raise the incentives for training fellow workers and for sharing knowledge with peers and subordinates. And the very fact of long-term employment meant that the company's investments in skill formation were not lost through labour turnover. The companies not only built this experience into the training of workers over time but crucially their organisational structure enabled them to reward such workers with promotion. In these ways the company became a place of lifetime learning

(Ford, 1987; Dore, 1993).

Within the manufacturing sector this constellation of arrangements provided the institutional basis for the extension of the system of intensive skill formation to workers with intermediate level skills.[5] However, it did so in a manner which left employers in firm control of the skill formation process. In the service sector the transformation was not as thorough and there a somewhat different, more traditional constellation of institutional arrangements was maintained (Bertrand and Noyelle, 1988).

The Ministry of Labour was also established after the Second World War and, through statutory means, sought to control standards of training in industry. Employers were slow to respond but the Ministry did have some success especially with its attempt to introduce a system of training within industry, based on the US experience. However, once industry accepted the system, the government withdrew. In addition, the emphasis shifted from government programmes for training the unemployed to programmes aimed at providing more intensive training for specific trades. In 1958 it attempted to systematise vocational training: existing vocational guidance centres were renamed vocational training centres aimed at providing both the basic and higher-level skills required for the new industries. A national system of trade certificates was introduced in an attempt to raise the status of blue-collar workers.

During the 1960s the move to higher-value-added forms of production gathered pace and the demand for skills changed accordingly, moving away from the conventional manipulative skills to conceptual and theoretical skills. The public system of training was slow to respond, with the result that larger employers made their own provision and public institutions moved in to serve smaller employers. The state aided this process of upgrading through legislation on training and by continuing the system of public provision. However, the primary responsibility for training was placed with employers and public provision limited to the retraining of adults and upgrading the labour force. This systematic revision of training provision to keep pace with the demands of industrial and commercial change led to a further revision of the law. The Vocational Training Law of 1969 was replaced by the Human Resources Development Promotion Law of 1985. This was in response to the widespread adoption of microelectronics technology and the growth of the service sector. The emphasis was now on assisting employers to provide learning opportunities for their employees, expecting leading firms to become 'learning companies'. Employers were encouraged to plan for the development of learning opportunities for their employees and to ensure that this systematic provision suited employees at each stage of their career. Smaller employers were provided with subsidies to encourage them to participate in the process of training and development. In addition the government and, to a lesser extent, employers' organisations, continued to control the certification and testing of detailed skills, thus preventing the capture of these processes by private professional training organisations (Dore, 1993). What is interesting from a theoretical point of view, is that this is a systematic attempt to upgrade state provision in line with changes in the productive system.

Despite these efficiency-enhancing characteristics of the Japanese education and training system, not all is rosy. Two major issues appear to trouble the system: the large barriers that limit women's access to skill formation, and the controversial pedagogical methods in schools that rely on learning by rote. Women are largely excluded from the lifetime employment system, and suffer unusually large workplace discrimination compared to western industrial economies. By their role in the family women do play an exceptional tacit role in the education process (providing tuition and moral pressure to succeed in education); nevertheless it would appear to be socially inefficient, from the viewpoint of the productive system, to fail to make use of the potential of half the population. The problems of excessive learning by rote have been recognised for some time, it threatens to stifle creativity later on at the workplace, and with the associated pressures to succeed in school, the stress it creates for teenagers is recognised as a social problem. But the political processes necessary to introduce change have been stifled by lack of consensus (Schoppa, 1990).

The Japanese system is based on intensive initial training of new recruits which is expected to provide the basis for further learning through refined on-the-job learning and job rotation supplemented by occasional off-the-job training. When new technology is introduced, Ishikawa reports that it is usually used to build on and enhance the skills of the workforce rather than simplify them. Employers have responded to the intensification of international competition and the increase in value of the yen by increasing their investment in training and development. Increasingly larger employers are adopting long-term plans for the provision of systematic training and career development for their key personnel, although the size of that key labour force is starting to shrink (Ishikawa, 1991; Berggren, 1995).

**Conclusions on the Second-Wave Nations**

In Germany and Japan, the various conditions for high-skill formation have continued to evolve to the present day. These two countries have been ruled for substantial parts of the last two centuries by elites who saw it as important for their own purposes to develop the skills of their workforces. In the most recent phase of industrial development they saw to it that their industries were developed in ways that would demand skilled workers, and that their education systems were able to supply the necessary flows of personnel. Meanwhile employers were induced, through their relations with both the state and with workers, to adopt appropriate strategies for high-skill formation, and workers were provided with strong incentives to participate in the process. While the processes of regulation are quite different in the two countries, they have both allowed the externality and opportunism problems associated with training to be superceded.

This evolution should be seen, not as a consequence of any long-term political strategy, but as a resultant of conflictual historical processes. While, for example, the state in Japan played an important part in stimulating and later in guiding the direction of product market development and in ensuring that the requisite education-based skills were in place, there are strict limits to what can be attributed to the foresight of politicians. Indeed, some key facets of the process of skill formation which we now see as distinctively Japanese were not the results of a conscious skill formation strategy. This can be seen, for example, in the development of the system of lifetime learning and its extension to manual workers in manufacturing industry. As we have said, this was at least in part a result of management's attempt to handle conflict with the unions. In both Germany and Japan the emergence of the system of work-based learning which was central to this latest phase of growth, was largely the result of the unintended consequence of government, employer and workers' actions. In neither case is there any evidence of a long-term strategy on the part of government to establish such a system.

Nor are the German and Japanese education and training systems ideal, even from the limited point of view of industrial efficiency. We have noted already the problems facing women, especially in Japan. In addition, it remains the case that education and training policy in each country is only loosely linked to industrial policies. In neither country is there an overarching body which co-ordinates the two sets of policies. In Japan, those departments responsible for education (the Ministry of Education) and training (the Ministry of Labour) do not have mechanisms for co-ordination, with the relationship between them being characterised by competition rather than cooperation. However, as long as the major competitors were European states, the fact that there was an element of co-ordination, with the state adjusting its education and training policies in the light of demands from the manufacturing sector, was sufficient to provide the Japanese with a form of competitive advantage. In the new industrial order of the twenty-first century this may no longer be sufficient.

Finally, it is important to point out that the Japanese system of work-based learning has been concentrated in the manufacturing sector. Development of such skills has not necessarily taken place in the service sector, and even in manufacturing we find the 'ideal' system mainly among the core firms rather than among their smaller supply satellites. By contrast, the apprenticeship system in Germany has ensured that skills across both manufacturing and service industries have been developed, although as we noted, the German system lacks a strong component of lifetime learning. In view of this we may expect that, if education and training becomes more closely related to economic growth and provides an increasingly important element of a country's competitive advantage, then other countries may well emerge with a different system of institutional arrangements which will produce a more comprehensive system of skill formation and thereby out-perform Japan. In the next section we consider the prospect that this may already be happening among the Asian new industrial economies.

## THE ASIAN NIES' VARIANT OF THE HIGH-SKILLS ROUTE

### A New Model of Skill Formation

We now move on to consider a third way that leads to high levels of skill formation, that is currently being forged by the newly industrialised economies of the Asia Pacific Rim. It is not uncommon to see these countries as developing in the wake of Japan's growth, using the metaphor of the flying geese. In education, Japan, Taiwan and South Korea are said to have evolved a common model distinct from that prevailing in the West, and this is thought to be a key aspect of Asian economic success (Cummings, 1995). However, we shall argue here that, when we examine the processes of skill formation which are wider than just the education system, the NIEs may be evolving a distinctive model in themselves. Like the second-wave nations, these countries – Singapore, Taiwan, South Korea and Hong Kong – share many features in common, especially in terms of the relationship between the processes of state formation, industrialisation and skill formation. We provide a brief general outline of these key relationships before we consider the case of Singapore in more detail.

**State formation**
The Asian NIEs route emerged from the same struggle to establish a system of skill formation linked to the requirements of the same industrial system of production that we witnessed in the older industrial countries. Traditional agrarian elites had to be replaced by modernising elites. In the case of Hong Kong and Singapore the foundations for this were laid by British colonial rule, while in South Korea and Taiwan the Japanese performed the same function (Whitley (ed.), 1992b). This was followed by the establishment of efficient, modern systems of bureaucratic administration staffed by technically competent officials. This aspect of the process of state formation ensured a public system of administration run independently of the vested interests of employers and other groups within the society (World Bank, 1993). Such an efficient system of state administration ensured that the political and industrial policies of the rulers could be implemented relatively free of widespread corruption and also of the immediate interests of capital and labour.

**Problems facing the political elite**
Like the second wave nations, the Asian countries faced a world prior to their industrialisation in which markets were already dominated by advanced industrial nations. After the Second World War they had to create an industrial base and break into international markets already controlled by European, Japanese and American companies, an even more daunting task than that facing the second-wave nations. For the leaders of the new industrial economies, this meant that the state had an important role to play not just in providing the appropriate infrastructure, but also in influencing the type of productive base to be established. As was the case with Japan, there was no time to leave the process of economic growth to the unaided working of the market: resources of society had to be mobilised to achieve that goal.

In the case of Korea, Singapore and Taiwan, the need to enhance the efficiency of the state apparatus, build up effective armed forces and proceed with the process of industrialisation had added urgency because of external threats to their independence. In Singapore those threats came from the possibility of incorporation into Malaysia, in Taiwan and South Korea from the mainland communist Chinese (Castells, 1992). These threats provided the impetus for political leaders to make their priority the establishment of a powerful central state apparatus and the creation of those conditions necessary to ensure rapid economic growth.

**Industrialisation**
Unlike the second-wave nations, the third-wave countries had a different

prior model of the process of industrialisation available to them, one which did not rely exclusively on the operations of the 'free market'. Japanese industrialisation had provided them with a form of state intervention which appeared to speed up the process of industrialisation. It provided an example of how late developer countries could, through concentrating their efforts on selected products, successfully break into world markets. It also provided an example of how the state could facilitate the move from low-value-added to high-value-added production (Amsden, 1989). Yet while the NIEs used the Japanese model, their experiences differed in important respects from those which characterised the Japanese. Like the Japanese but unlike the Germans, they did not have a strong craft-base tradition on which to build a training system and control the activities of employers. However, neither had they (apart from South Korea) an extensive network of large indigenous employers, as found in Japan, who could be relied upon to provide a system of lifetime skill formation at work. What the leaders of the NIEs did was to use the Japanese model to guide their overall strategy.

The precise character of their economic development strategies varied considerably, Singapore relying in the early stages on attracting foreign multinationals, Taiwan on the development of an indigenous entrepreneurial class and South Korea on the development of indigenous heavy industry. While their strategies varied, all have been conscious of the need to modify those strategies constantly to adjust to the demands of world markets (Castells, 1992). After initial attempts to protect home markets, all switched their strategy to one of manufactured export-led growth. Initially the drive was to establish modern, often low-value-added forms of production. Even in Hong Kong, renowned for its reliance on market forces, the state intervened through a massive system of public housing subsidies which kept the price of labour low in the initial stages of economic growth (Whitley (ed.), 1992b; Castells, 1992). However, once the basics of the industrial system had been established, the political and/or business elites moved the economy in the direction of high-value-added production (Castells, 1992). Thus the process of industrialisation has been strongly influenced by the activities of the political elite and has therefore taken a different form from that characterised by the first- and second-wave industrial nations. As a result the link between the process of state formation and the development of the productive system became even closer than it had been for the second-wave nations: a feature which has important implications for the process of skill formation.

**The relationship between the processes of state formation and industrialisation**

One of the ways in which scholars have attempted to conceptualise this link between the process of state formation and industrialisation among the NIEs is through the concept of the developmental state (Johnson, 1982). This refers to the use made of the state apparatus by the political elite in furthering their aims of economic growth. The state has become virtually dedicated to the task of securing economic growth. Given the external international pressures on the leadership, they sought to achieve levels of economic development in one generation which it took the older industrial nations three generations to achieve.

To reach these objectives, the political elite used all the resources available to the state, following the logic of the Japanese model but taking state intervention further than the Japanese. The result has been the systematic and comprehensive involvement of the state in many aspects of economic growth, including the strategic guidance of national and multinational corporations. In order to achieve this task the state has been proactive in adapting the economy to changes in world market conditions. As new higher-value-added industries developed, the state adapted the productive base in such a way as to enable it to compete in the new world markets.

The developmental state assumes as its principle of legitimacy, its ability to promote and sustain such development. In such a state there is no rigid division between the state and civil society or between the state and the economy. Market forces are just one of a battery of tools which the state can use to achieve its objective of economic growth. It is therefore the function of the state to monitor and anticipate changes in world markets and in the productive system and to manage the internal transformation of the society and economy to accommodate to them. This also involves managing the process of skill formation in a way not encountered in the second-wave nations. Whereas the nations of the second wave have tried to link changes in the education system to changes in the productive base, in the NIEs this has been taken a stage further. Here the state has attempted to manage and co-ordinate changes in the two areas with the aim of reducing 'wasteful' investments in education and thereby enhancing the speed of economic growth.

An integral part of this project for the developmental state is the need to anticipate the type of skill formation required for any upgrading of the productive base and to ensure that an adequate skill base is available. Here the Asian NIEs have been innovative. To achieve this objective meant developing an effective education and training infrastructure which, in addition to providing a mechanism of social (moral) control, accomplished three other tasks.  The first was to provide the basic skills in mathematics, language, science and technology required by industry.  The second was to ensure that the technological skills required for the most advanced forms of production were transferred from older industrial countries and their multi-national organisations and reproduced internally. As Amsden has pointed out, successful late industrialisation is premised on learning the production and procedures that are characteristic of the advanced economies (Amsden, 1989: 215).  The third and perhaps most important task was to anticipate changes in the skills required for the next phase of adaptation to world markets and to provide the mechanisms whereby these skills could be generated in anticipation of the demand for them from employers.  The political leaders of such a state could not afford to leave the process of work-based learning to the actions of employers as had the leaders of older industrial economies who followed the high-skills route.  The result has been a massive investment in human resource development (World Bank, 1993).  In this respect it is possible that the NIEs have changed the relationship between investment in education and training and economic growth that characterised the older Western countries.

Another distinguishing characteristic of this route is that the fruits of such rapid economic development are relatively equally distributed throughout the population, far more so than in the case of the older industrial nations (World Bank, 1993).  The achievement of constant improvements in living standards requires the population to make present sacrifices and to follow the lead of the government.  As a result the goal of economic growth figures far more prominently in the political agenda of these societies than it did in either the first- or second-wave nations.

The success of the Asian NIEs contrasts with the experience of the Latin American countries of the 1950s and 1960s which failed to make the transition to higher-value-added production in the 1970s and 1980s.  This was due to a number of factors, such as the debt crisis and the actions of the International Monetary Fund but a significant difference between the Latin American countries and the Asian NIEs was the level of investment in education among the latter (Barro, 1991).

The success of the Asian NIEs meant that the different phases of industrial development occurred far more rapidly than in the first- and second-wave nations.  The craft phase which had been central to the industrialisation of the first wave nations was bypassed altogether and replaced by a short period of reliance on labour-intensive forms of production.  Thereafter the NIEs rapidly moved to the status of advanced industrial nations.[6]  This extremely rapid development of the productive system created equally extreme demands on the system of skill formation.

**The management of capital and labour**

There are other areas in which the experience of the NIEs differed from that of the second-wave nations. First, they industrialised rapidly, in the course of little more than one generation, from societies which were largely agrarian in character (Whitley (ed.), 1992b). In western societies commercialisation already had a profound effect in transforming the economic base of the old agrarian society prior to the onset of their industrialisation. In the traditional agrarian societies from which the Asian NIEs emerged, commercialisation had not had the same impact. There, rapid industrialisation meant that many of the secondary associations which are to be found in the West, such as trade unions, professional organisations and local political authorities, were either absent or very weakly developed (Whitley (ed.), 1992b). It was easier for those in control of the state to use its resources to manage both capital and labour. Put another way, the state had achieved a higher degree of autonomy in relation to the interests of both capital and labour. There were a number of important consequences which followed from this for the process of skill formation, not the least of which has been the ability of NIEs to manage the process of skill formation and link it directly to the process of economic development in a way which it has not been possible to do in societies which industrialised earlier.

The autonomy of the state was facilitated by the fact that there were few strong vested interests opposed to the actions of the political elites as they sought to achieve high levels of economic growth. From the perspective of skill formation, there were few secondary interest groups, no firmly entrenched trade unions or professional associations, who had the power to utilise the process of skill formation for their own interests or to resist the actions of government. Trade unions were suppressed or incorporated into the political system (Goh-Tan, 1995).[7] Education and training, apart from providing a form of moral control, was therefore dedicated to the task of enhancing the level of skill formation perceived as necessary for rapid economic growth.[8] Secondly, the process of skill formation could be centred around the needs of economic growth, rather than having to compromise between the needs of occupational interest groups as in Europe. Similarly employers, while they represented an important interest group, were precisely that, and their needs were catered to only in so far as it facilitated the process of economic growth.

The Asian NIEs are also distinctive in that they operate within the framework of a Confucian culture which has succeeded in creating a distinctive form of Chinese capitalism (Lever-Tracy and Tracy, 1992; Whitley (ed.), 1992b). There is considerable debate about whether the impact attributed to Confucianism is a product of that particular set of beliefs or whether it can be attributed to other distinctive features of the Asian experience (Whitley (ed.), 1992b). Yet there are distinctive features of Confucianism which stress the importance of the collective good as a precondition for the achievement of the individual's potential, the acceptance of authority and the moral duty of political leaders to maintain those values. Political leaders have been able to use the acceptance of these values by the masses to mobilise support for the political goal of economic growth.

## The Singaporean Experience

### The autonomy of the state
In the case of Singapore the ability of the state to achieve a degree of relative autonomy in relation to the internal vested interests is connected to the political threat facing the country in its early years. After securing independence from British colonial rule the Singaporean political elite were concerned with ensuring the political survival of Singaporean society and creating a national identity in the face of possible threats from neighbouring Muslim countries. This provided the impetus for the establishment of a strong state apparatus staffed by technically competent officials (Castells, 1992), based on the administration bequeathed by the British.

The fact that the political elite were able to detach themselves from the immediate interests of capital and labour enabled the government to use the resources of state to pursue its 'vision'. This vision then became of central importance in directing the country's trade and industry policy. Industries had to be attracted in the first instance. Thereafter, old industries had to be relocated and new investment brought in that would enable the vision to be realised. If new industries are to be attracted then the human resources essential for the successful performance of those industries have to be in place, and this provides the basis of the dynamism which characterises education and training policy. What is especially distinctive in Singapore is the way in which the government has co-ordinated the changes in education and training policy to facilitate the successful execution of its policies on trade and industry (Ashton and Sung, 1994).

### Industrialisation
One can distinguish three broad phases in the development of the Singaporean economy. In each of these the state has played an important role in bringing about changes in the economy. The first phase was

characterised by the introduction of labour-intensive industries. These made minimal demands on the education and training system, and indeed investment in education in Singapore was behind that of some of the other NIEs. The aim of the politicians was to achieve full employment. The second phase was characterised by the introduction of higher-value-added production. During this phase the government attempted to reduce the significance of low-labour-cost industries in the economy and restricted inward investment to capital necessary to establish high-value-added production. To ensure that the human resources were in place it widened the provision of secondary vocational and technical education and developed a training infrastructure. The third phase has been characterised by the growth of knowledge-based service industries. Government policy has been to place less emphasis on manufacturing and more on making Singapore the financial centre of the region. Manufacturing capital was encouraged to move into the lower-labour-cost areas of the hinterland. In this phase the emphasis has shifted to expanding the provision of higher education and enhancing the provision of work-based skills through structured on-the-job learning (Ashton and Sung, 1994).

One of the means by which the future of Singapore was to be assured was through the establishment of a strong industrial economy which would help guarantee political independence. On achieving independence, the rate of unemployment was in the region of 17 per cent. In order to achieve economic growth the first task facing the government was to create full employment. Thus, in the first phase of Singapore's development (1950s to 1970s), the government sought to attract inward investment from multinational corporations in order to establish a strong manufacturing base, founded on the availability of low-wage labour (Low, 1993).

In the late 1970s, the growth of equally attractive low-cost labour in other parts of the region meant that Singapore was losing its competitive advantage. The government, fearful of this and of losing its political independence, used the resources of the state to help change the direction in which the economy was moving. To do this it launched the 'Second Industrial Revolution' in 1979. The aim was to reduce reliance on low-wage, labour-intensive industries and replace them with capital-intensive, higher-value-added industries (Wong, 1993) that is to change the economic base of the society and transfer the production of labour-intensive products to the hinterland.

Towards the end of the 1980s, the political leaders produced a new vision of the future of Singapore, which prefaced a third phase of economic growth in the 1990s. To stay ahead of their competitors in the region, the government set out to match the economic performance of the best industrial economies. This current 'vision' is set out in the document

'The Next Lap' (Government of Singapore, 1991). The implications of this vision for the economic development of the country were detailed in 'The Strategic Economic Plan' (Ministry of Trade and Industry, 1991). The aim was to achieve the same standard of living for the Singaporean people as that achieved by the Swiss.

To achieve the status and standard of living of the Swiss by the year 2020 or 2030, the economy was to continue to attract companies planning to invest in the production of high-value-added goods and services. However, in order to sustain economic growth it was felt necessary for Singaporean companies to move out of Singapore into the Asia Pacific region and form a 'second ring'. This would enable them not only to take advantage of cheaper labour outside Singapore but it would also place Singapore in the centre of the region's drive for economic growth. Singapore would move from 'Singapore Incorporated' to Singapore International Incorporated (Low, 1993). This is the direction in which the economy is currently moving.

The precise role of the government in creating this rapid economic transformation is the subject of debate. World Bank economists tend to view the role of government as that of facilitator adopting a market friendly approach (World Bank, 1993). Other economists, such as Castells and the proponents of the developmental state thesis, see the part played by the state as central to this transformation. On the basis of existing evidence our view is more in accord with the latter position.

**The system of skill formation**
Parallel with these changes in the productive system, the government introduced changes in the education and training system. During the first phase of economic growth, there was minimal state involvement in the process of skill formation. The type of industry attracted required unskilled and semi-skilled labour which could be trained on-the-job to perform routine operations. All the state was required to do was to provide a literate population capable of following basic instructions. Consequently, basic literacy was provided through primary education with only limited provision of secondary and higher education. The emphasis was on providing a disciplined labour force in the context of a politically stable environment.

In order to attract the higher-value-added industries required for the second phase, the education system was upgraded and a new training infrastructure put in place under the auspices of the Vocational and Industrial Training Board (VITB). However, the speed of Singapore's development had meant that many of those who left the education system in the colonial era and in the early stages of Singapore's independence still had literacy and numeracy deficiencies. As late as the 1980s, 61 per cent of Singapore's non-student population had an educational level of primary six or less (Ministry of Trade and Industry, 1991). Because they could not wait for changes in the system of initial education to increase slowly the stock of skills, they adopted a second front and sought to act directly on the employed adult labour force and improve the basic skills of those already in work. To tackle these problems a series of programmes were launched aimed at enhancing the skills of mature workers. The programmes, delivered in modular form through institutes and employers, provided a progression route for such workers either to continue their education to secondary school level or to provide a basis for the enhancement of their work-based skills. By 1990, illiteracy rates had been reduced to 10 per cent of the total population and 1.4 per cent for the 20–24 age group (Felstead *et al.*, 1994).

The foundation programme, Basic Education for Skills Training (BEST), introduced in 1983, had by 1992 reached 78 per cent of the potential target pool of 225,000 workers, in a total labour force of 1.4 million workers (ITE, 1993: 25). However, not all these people completed the full programme. On the foundations laid by BEST a whole series of programmes were used to improve the basic skills of the labour force. In 1986, the Modular Skills Training programme was introduced aimed at enhancing the skills of semi-skilled workers. In 1987, Worker Improvement through Secondary Education was introduced to General Certificate of Education level and by 1992, 42 per cent of the target pool of 122,000 had been reached (ITE, 1993: 25). The Core Skills for Effectiveness and Change was also introduced in 1987 aimed at service sector workers and covers two-thirds of the low-income labour force.[9]

In addition to enhancing the skills of those already in the labour force, the government also sought to use the knowledge of the multinational corporations to set up a series of joint industrial training centres. As part of the deal to attract multinational corporations the government persuaded them to set up joint ventures which would ensure that the skills required by the new companies were available locally and that additional training was done to embed those skills in a broader population and make them available to other businesses (Wong, 1993).

In the third and most recent phase the education system has been upgraded with the aim of bringing it in line with the most advanced systems in the older industrial countries. Emphasis was placed on upgrading technical and intermediate-level skills. In addition, training policy has been re-focused to concentrate on enhancing intermediate work-based skills and, crucially, on improving the use of the workplace as a source of learning.

To achieve these new educational goals the government studied educational practices in Germany and Japan, which it considered to be the most advanced, and found that the teaching of the working language and mathematics amounted to 50 per cent of curriculum time in the primary school (Yip and Sim, 1994). However, in Singapore the problems posed by bilingualism (English and the mother tongue) meant that if children in primary schools were to have a sufficient exposure to both languages then there would be less time left for other subjects. The solution, currently being tried through the 1990 reforms, is to introduce a preparatory programme for all five-year-olds in order to compensate for the heavier demands made by the bilingual requirement.

In order to ensure that school leavers had mastered the basic skills necessary to enable them to develop further at work, it was decided that all young people should have 10 years minimum general education and enhanced forms of technical education. The VITB, renamed the Institute of Technical Education (ITE) in 1992, now only takes on young people for technical training after they have completed this basic education, thereby enhancing the status of technical education. The ITE now offers much higher skill content courses, which enable those following the vocational route to proceed to further education in the polytechnics and universities. For those already in the labour force, the lowest level of National Trade Certificate (renamed National Technical Certificate in 1992 and roughly equivalent to the UK NVQ level 1), disappeared in 1995. The lowest level will then be equivalent to the standard of the competent craftsman. The aim of these reforms is to ensure that everyone entering the labour market will have the requisite base on which today's skills and those of tomorrow can be built. In line with this objective, the types of skills transmitted in the educational system are starting to shift from the 'harder' technical skills to the 'softer' office and business skills (Low, 1994). As participation rates in education are already high, with over 90 per cent of 15–19-year-olds in education and 26 per cent of 20–24-year-olds in tertiary education (Low, 1994) these reforms are aimed at creating a system of education comparable with the best in the West.

In the third phase, the programmes the government had established to enhance the skills of those who missed out on their primary and secondary education (BEST and MOST) are starting to run down as the target pool declines in size. The emphasis has now moved towards enhancing the process of work-based learning. It became evident in the late 1980s that while improvement in the quantity of training undertaken by employers was important, the new growth industries of the 1990s demand not just competence in technical skills but also in the ability of workers to achieve greater flexibility and develop the skills to tackle new unforeseen problems. In these new circumstance learning at work took on greater importance. Studies of the German dual system and the Japanese and Australian systems of on-the-job training helped suggest ways in which this might be achieved.

One of the lessons learnt from the German dual system was the need to integrate on-the-job and off-the-job elements in training if it was to provide the quality of learning experience and the depth of skills required for companies to compete effectively in world markets. The significance of this policy shift is underlined by the findings from a number of studies which suggest that some of the skills necessary for companies to compete in the markets for high-value-added goods and services can only be acquired through a combination of on-the-job and off-the-job learning (Streeck, 1989; Koike and Inoki (eds), 1990).

Improvements were made to the apprenticeship system by the introduction of the New Apprenticeship Scheme in 1990. Modelled closely on the dual system,[10] it was targeted at employers with the ability to train their own workers. Like the German dual system it required pedagogically qualified trainers (*Meisters*) and both on-the-job and off-the-job training. The same idea of integrating on- and off-the-job training has been used to inform the new 'Hybrid' apprenticeship system. This was launched in 1992, aimed at the small- and medium-sized enterprises (SMEs) which have traditionally avoided apprenticeship training.[11] The objective of enhancing both the on-the-job and off-the-job training of mature workers (aged 20–40 years with below 'O' level qualifications), was tackled by the ITE's Adult Co-operative Training Scheme introduced in 1992. This is based on the new apprenticeship model, and so workers have to be sponsored by their employers, but they then receive on-the-job and off-the-job training in the company's time (ITE, 1993).

While the apprenticeship model was the preferred form of providing education and training, not all employers would adopt it and therefore other forms of intervention had to be found if the labour force as a whole was to have its skills enhanced. The Skills Development Fund[12] (SDF) had experience of funding company-based training through the skills programmes introduced during the second phase of economic development, with the number of training places supported by the fund increasing more than 12 times from 32,600 in 1981 to 407,900 in 1991 (NPB, 1993: 44). This has been further enhanced in two ways. First, employers were provided with a series of programmes which offered help and assistance for them in learning how to organise and implement their own training. Second, after studying other countries, ways were found of helping firms enhance the quality of their on-the-job training.

The task of helping employers to learn how to organise and implement training was done through the Training Grants Scheme, under the auspices of the National Productivity Board (NPB) and funded by the SDF. This comprises a series of schemes focused on helping employers improve particular aspects of training. The Training Grant Scheme, provides grants to employers of between 30–90 per cent of the cost of (re)training workers through in-plant programmes to upgrade their skills. The largest of the schemes, the Worker Training Plan, encourages companies to undertake systematic training through an annual plan. This was responsible for 61 per cent of the total training places supported by the SDF in 1991 and accounted for 88 per cent of the total SDF spend (SDF, 1992: 12). The trainee recipients of all these schemes tend to be workers with average or below average educational levels; 72 per cent of training places were filled by workers with 'O' levels or less (SDF, 1992: 38).

Other schemes have been established to help companies ease their cashflow problems when investing in staff training, to embark on systematic training based on the results of company-wide training needs analysis and to make the services of good quality training providers available to small companies who do not have the resources to develop their own training programmes. In addition, other schemes are in place to enhance the training infrastructure, for example by helping managers improve their ability to train and by providing training in the delivery of quality in the service sector.

Another way to improve the quality of training, identified by the NPB, was the more widespread use of structured, on-the-job training as this was seen as the most cost-effective form of training. Research by the NPB in 1986 revealed that 90 per cent of companies in Singapore engaged in some form of on-the-job training (OJT) but this was not necessarily structured. As a result it was found that 'more often than not, OJT meant that workers were left to chance to acquire skills during the course of their work' (NPB 1992: 9). A task force was therefore set up with the Economic Development Board and the Institute of Technical Education to identify the core skills needed to be developed through OJT schemes. Following this the NPB introduced a programme aimed at identifying industry-based blueprints or model OJT schemes. These are being developed with leading companies in a variety of industries and are then used as a base model for other companies to emulate. The long-term plan is to get 100,000 through OJT by the end of the decade. In addition steps are being taken to train OJT instructors. This will complement the off-the-job training undertaken by the ITE and will be available for firms in service as well as manufacturing industries.[13]

Good quality OJT, while providing workers with the skills required for today's companies, will not necessarily equip workers with the skills required to cope with the demands of the new markets and industrial restructuring associated with them. In line with the vision of where Singapore hopes to be by the year 2020, the focus of the government's concern with on-the-job training has shifted from the provision of flexible multi-skilled workers to the task of skills deepening. The result is a skills-deepening programme.

Swiss workers are seen as extremely well trained in technical skills and 'equipped with the foundation for drastic retraining should industrial restructuring take place' (NPB, 1993). Following a study mission to Switzerland in 1992, the NPB is working with other government departments to identify the leading edge companies with potential for skills deepening. These are seen as the industries experiencing rapid growth and having the potential to compete in regional and international markets. The NPB is working with such companies to develop and design training programmes to deepen core job skills, using OJT techniques. The aim is to train workers in these companies, not just with the technical skills but also the deeper intellectual skills necessary to cope with the drastic retraining they will have to undergo to enable them to handle industrial change and restructuring. Core areas of the economy, such as precision engineering, have been targeted for the implementation of a programme of skills deepening.

The other area where the government sought to upgrade skills was from the multinational corporations and foreign governments. In the mid-1980s the Economic Development Board decided that the knowledge-intensive and technology-intensive industries necessary to achieve the government's vision would require resources in excess of those that single partners involved in the joint industrial training centres could provide. It needed to access expertise on a global rather than a single-country basis. To achieve this it sought agreement from three governments with whom it already had agreements to incorporate other multinational corporations into the institutes. These reformed institutes would then provide the necessary 'hardware, software and teachware' required for the establishment and development of knowledge- and technology-intensive industries. In this way the EDB sought to set up training in anticipation of the needs of the new and emerging industries (Wong, 1993).

Much of the above review of government training strategy has been based on discussions with officials and public statements of policy. Whilst we are confident about the accuracy of our presentation of this strategy, it is difficult, at this stage, to evaluate its effectiveness. To our knowledge, such an evaluation remains to be done. The reason we have given the government shemes such prominence here is that they provide evidence of a different strategy towards the process of skill formation to that hitherto pursued by governments of the older industrial states. Moreover it is a strategy which appears, on the basis of fragmentary evidence, to have created a commitment to training on the part of employers and workers, at least in the larger organisations (Huam and Jewson, 1995; Yun, 1995).

The difference between this strategy and those followed by some of the older industrial societies such as the UK and Germany, is evident in the two-pronged nature of the Singaporean strategy. In the older industrial countries the main thrust of attempts to improve the level of basic skills has come from reforms of the education system or the vocational education and training provided for young people entering the labour market. In those societies, provision for adults has been largely confined either to facilities for liberal self-development or for the unemployed to assist them back into the labour market. In this new model, the focus is also on enhancing the general level of skills of the total labour force. Continuous education, of the type recently advocated in the West, has been a feature of their policies from an early stage and is directed at upgrading the skill levels of those already in work as well as those just entering.

### The state, class relations and skill formation
The relative autonomy of the state in Singapore has enabled the political elite to adopt a much more pro-active role in regulating the relationship between capital and labour than has been characteristic of any of the countries of the first and second wave.[14] In the first phase the vision was confined to establishing the independence of the country and securing full employment. At this stage the efforts of the political elite were directed at attracting the MNCs with a promise of cheap, disciplined labour and political stability.

With regard to labour, the resources of the state were used to suppress those factions of labour organised under the Communist Party which sought to extract immediate gains from capital in the form of higher wages. In order to establish cooperative relations between capital and labour the People's Action Party formed a close alliance with the National Trades Union Congress (NTUC). In the early stages of this relationship efforts were made to find ways of reducing the conflict between employers and unions and find ways of enhancing cooperation in pursuit of national goals (Goh-Tan, 1995). The NTUC is now used to represent worker interests in government and to explain the government's development policies to workers. In the early stages of economic growth the NTUC acted to contain labour costs in order to promote low-value-added production (Deyo, 1989).

In the second stage, the government had to entice new companies which could introduce higher-value-added production to Singapore. This meant operating contrary to the interests of employers intent on maintaining low-value-added production. Such employers were encouraged either to leave Singapore and move into surrounding areas of low-cost labour or to move into forms of higher value-added production. To this end the government, working in conjunction with the NTUC, encouraged the growth of worker income by 20 per cent for a three-year period and imposed a levy on low paid labour, both measures being designed to discourage companies from continuing to embark on low-value-added production (Wong, 1993). This levy created the Skills Development Fund (SDF), which was used to finance a series of programmes aimed at improving worker skills and employers' ability to train. When some elements of capital, particularly some of the multinational corporations, resisted such guidance, the government switched tactics and sought to make Singapore the financial centre of the region. The government's role in this latest phase has been to make a massive investment in the information technology infrastructure and to monitor incoming investment to ensure that it contributes toward the achievement of the current vision.

**The implementation of a national human resource policy**
One consequence of the attempt by the government to regulate both capital and labour is that it claims the authority to identify the country's training needs. Unlike the situation in the UK, the US and other advanced industrial societies, the starting point for the analysis of those training needs is not the needs of employers or of individuals. On the contrary, the needs of individuals are seen as secondary to the collective needs as defined in the government's vision. Employers are used to deliver work-based training through the various government programmes, but they are not given an exclusive right to identify the nature of the country's training needs. Employers' immediate needs are just one component of a much longer-term plan to up-grade the quality of the labour force. What drives the Singaporean system is the future needs of the economy as defined by the government.

To achieve this integration of skill formation and trade and industry policies requires a high level of co-ordination at government level. The current vision as set out in 'The Next Lap' requires that the appropriate human resources are in place not just to accommodate to the existing demands of employers but crucially the demands of inward investment and tomorrow's leading edge companies. In order to achieve this integration a series of important links have been made between the various departments involved in assessing national human resource needs and the departments charged with the task of ensuring that these national needs are met.

The goals as defined in the vision provide the targets which inform the work of the Ministry of Trade and Industry and the Investment Board. The Ministry of Trade and Industry is a powerful ministry responsible for ensuring that the economy is geared to the demands of the international market and is therefore in a position to achieve the government's vision. To identify the future human resource needs it relies on agencies such as the Investment Board, which sells the benefits of investing in Singapore and while negotiating with foreign capital is in a position to identify the future demands on the country's human resources which that investment is likely to make. The Ministry of Trade and Industry then collates such information on the future demand for human resources and these are mapped against the projections from academics about the likely state of labour (human resource) supply. The results provide the basis for the identification of the country's skill needs.[15]

The Economic Development Board translates this information about the country's skill requirements into targets for the Council for Professional and Technical Education. First established in 1979, this is a national body, chaired by the Minister responsible for Trade and Industry, which sets targets for education and training at all levels. This Council institutionalises the link between trade and industry policy and the education and training system (Selvaratnam, 1989) and thereby ensures that human capital demands of the new industries inform the targets.

The Council breaks down the overall target into specific targets for the universities and polytechnics, schools and the Institute of Technical Education and ascertains whether these targets can be met or whether new institutions or policy initiatives will be necessary to meet them. For this exercise they require feedback from the education and training authorities. If the government cannot meet the targets from indigenous institutions then they look to import the requisite skills. In this way each sector, higher education, schools and the Institute of Technical Education, has its own targets for student numbers and for levels of achievement. The current targets for the educational system are by the year 2000 to have 25 per cent of young adults either in junior colleges or universities, 40 per cent in polytechnics, 25 per cent in Institute for Technical Education programmes, with a drop-out rate of 10 per cent. However, the drop-outs are not regarded as lost to the system for they are targeted, once they have had some work experience, through government programmes aimed at enhancing their work-based skills.

Other government departments and agencies are also involved in ensuring that the human resources required to achieve the government's vision are in place. Thus, while the National Productivity Board has a different focus, being concerned with employer-based training, it too has its targets. One of the NPB's current 'vision goals' is for organisations to double their training investment from 2 to 4 per cent of the payroll by 1995, the amount which it is believed the better corporations in the world spend on training (NPB, 1993).

The quotas for numbers and targets for performance are implemented by the higher education institutions, schools, the ITE and the NPB in their own plans. The performances of the respective institutions are then systematically evaluated against the targets. Within the ITE, training plans are formulated on a five-year basis but these are rolled over every two years. When any revision occurs the Trade and Industry Ministry has a significant input. This ensures that the future demands of the economy are constantly fed back and inform any revision of targets. In this way it is intended that the education and training system as a whole will respond to the future human resource development needs of the economy.

In addition to these mechanisms which ensure collaboration between government departments there is another set of links between the major institutions of government, unions and employers. These are known as a tripartite system but it is a different form of tripartism to that practised in the West. It involves the familiar system of employers, unions and government undertaking joint consultation with regard to major policy issues but in addition it involves the exchange of personnel. Thus the head of the NTUC may subsequently become the head of the National Productivity Board. The idea behind the system is that this will provide an institutionalised mechanism to help ensure that those involved with representing sectional interests will be made aware of the over-riding importance of national goals (Goh-Tan, 1995).

It will be obvious that this process of human resource planning differs from traditional manpower planning based on manpower requirements forecasting using input–output analysis and growth forecasting techniques. The Singapore process is closer to but still differs from 'market-oriented manpower planning', as now advocated by the World Bank (Middleton, Ziderman and van Adams, 1993, Ch. 5). In that approach to education and planning, the case for public investments in schooling and training is to be based on comprehensive labour market information, but 'can be reduced to situations where markets fail to perform their allocation task' (*ibid.*: 148). However, the point about the Singapore case is that, rather than regarding market failure as an exception, markets are encompassed by and superceded within the policy process. The institutional integration allows the planning of skills supply to be integrated with the policies which influence future skills demand.

There are of course problems attached to the Singaporean approach to skill formation. In the first place there are the high risks involved in the attempt to identify the next generation of leading edge industries which will ensure a continuation of the high rate of economic growth. If mistakes are made here the stability of the whole system could be brought into question as the rate of economic growth falls, as has happened in Japan (Berggren, 1995). Moreover, as Singapore enters the ranks of the most advanced nations it becomes ever harder to predict the industries in which high rates of future growth can be expected. In this respect it is difficult to evaluate the effectiveness of the latest investment in work-based skills as the results from such an investment will not be known until some time in the future.

There are other problems associated with the strategies adopted by the Singaporian government. While the Skills Development Fund was meant to ensure a higher level of training among the smaller companies, it is still the larger companies which tend to take advantage of the training subsidies it provides. In importing capital through multinational corporations and creating an educational system geared to producing high-level administrators for the state bureaucracy, Singapore has failed to develop a large group of indigenous entrepreneurs. By contrast, in Hong Kong the exclusion of the indigenous population from the upper ranks of the civil service meant that the efforts of the local population were more focused on the development of local companies.

## CONCLUDING REMARKS

We have singled out the experience of Singapore here for some more detailed analysis because relatively little is known outside that country about the reasons for its remarkable success in terms of economic growth and skill formation, and because with its distinctive features it appears to exemplify a new model, a third way after the internal labour market and the corporatist models, through which high-skill formation can be achieved.[16] We have focused on a number of features. The first is the integration of education and training policies with trade and industry policies. While elements of this were a feature of the German and Japanese examples, in neither case were there mechanisms similar to those in Singapore, for integrating the two sets of policies. Secondly, in Singapore the government was in a position to learn from the second-wave nations and identify the development of work-based learning as of crucial importance for this third phase. This enabled the government to formulate a long-term strategy to implement a policy of enhancing work-based learning which the second-wave nations were not able to do, and which may prove crucial to the further development of those companies seeking to operate at the cutting edge of world markets. The third feature has been the policy of the Singaporean government to develop its two-pronged attack on the problem of enhancing the skills base of the nation, using changes in the educational system combined with programmes aimed at enhancing the skills of those in work. The result has been the systematic adjustment of the education and training system to the changes taking place in the productive system. This ensures that neither are resources 'wasted' in over-educating the population for any given stage of economic development, nor is the provision of education and training allowed to hinder the process of economic growth through inadequate investment in the creation and reproduction of skills, thereby creating skills bottlenecks as found in the UK. On the contrary the education and training system is used to anticipate future skill needs and ensure that they are in place in order that the new industries can develop.

We suggest that as a result of these innovations there is likely to be a tighter relationship between changes in the education and training systems and the development of the productive system than that characteristic of societies which industrialised earlier. In this respect we can expect that the relationship between investment in human capital and economic growth will prove to be stronger in the NIEs than in the older industrial societies, precisely because the relationship has been managed from the centre.[17]

Just how far this remains true of the other NIEs remains to be explored. While we have focused on Singapore, there is some evidence that in its essentials the model we have presented here is also replicated in the other NIEs, although this must remain a question for future research. In Hong Kong the Vocational Training Council has performed a similar function to the VITB/ITE in Singapore (Ashton, Maguire and Sung, 1991). In South Korea and Taiwan, the state has attempted to match the new requirements of the productive system at each stage of its development through appropriate education and training policies (Amsden, 1992). However, it is not clear whether this has been as tightly managed as it has been in Singapore.

What remains true, nevertheless, of all the models discussed in this chapter – those in Germany, Japan and the Asian NIEs – is that in every case we find ruling elites demonstrably committed to high-skill formation, the conscious creation of a high-quality education system, the means to cajole or constrain employers to invest in work-based skills, the means to regulate this process, a more or less adequate system of ensuring workers remain committed to their learning, and, finally, a realisation of the importance of skills deepening through periods of off-the-job training. These institutional facts, it would appear, are needed for taking the high-skills route to accumulation in modern capitalism, even if there are significant differences in their historical origins.

## NOTES

1. Not all the industries of the second phase required more highly skilled labour. Mass production as a system of production was set up in part to exploit unskilled labour. The important point is that more of the second-wave industries required an educated and trained labour force.
2. For a discussion of these strategies see Laxer, 1989: 149 on the German and Japanese cases, and Whitley (ed.), 1992b: 121–7 on Japan.
3. Part of this section draws substantially on the work of Lazonick and O'Sullivan (1994).
4. See Chapter 4 and Felstead *et al.*, 1994.
5. The process whereby the interests of the employee are locked into that of the company is of course more complex. We use the term lifetime employment to refer to this, which includes the system of remuneration which links the individual's income to the success of the enterprise as well as his/her commitment to the enterprise; the same is the case for the system of symbolic rewards and promotion.
6. In 1993, Hong Kong and Singapore entered the ranks of the ten richest countries in the world as measured by national output per head adjusted in terms of purchasing power parities by the World Bank economists. In terms of gross national product per capita Singapore overtook the UK while the figure for Hong Kong was only marginally below that of the UK (World Bank, 1995: 163).
7. In the case of Singapore the role of trade unions changed during the process of industrialisation, moving from a confrontational stance to one of collaboration in the achievement of national goals. In the most recent phase the Singaporean Unions have played an important part in placing pressure on employers to enhance the level of training they provide (Goh-Tan, 1995).
8. One possible alternative explanation of the high level of skill formation is that this is a product of the Chinese family business typically found in these economies. In Hong Kong and Taiwan the typical Chinese business is relatively small in size with a distinctive, fragmented form of business organisation, which distinguishes it from both the Anglo-Saxon and Japanese form of business organisation (Lever-Tracy and Tracy, 1992; Whitley (ed.), 1992b).
9. For a case study of how this programme was used to train workers who had few qualifications and little formal education see Huam and Jewson (1995).
10. Specifically, on the system found in Baden-Wurttemberg.
11. This scheme was hybrid in the sense that the lack of broader-based skills training available in the SMEs was overcome by the introduction of a period of block release to provide initial training in these skills before entry to the narrower on-the-job training within the company. In this programme the government wholly fund the off-the-job training.
12. The SDF is built up from the levy imposed on employers who pay workers less than $750 per month and is used to enhance work-related learning.
13. Information supplied during interviews with NPB officials, 1994.
14. Here we focus on the conflict between capital and labour. The other sources of conflict which the government had to address were those between the ethnic groups. There the aim has been to recognise cultural diversity and seek agreement around common Singaporean values.
15. Information on the operation of policy has been obtained from interviews with NPB and ITE officials.
16. While we hypothesise that this third way is likely, given their similar environments and the common developmental state model, to apply with variations in the other Asian NIEs, this remains the subject of ongoing empirical research.
17. However, it is still important to remember that the continuance of any coalescence of interests is not inevitable and can be disrupted by conflicts both within the society in

question or in the broader set of international relationships.

# 8 Conclusion: a Framework for Policy Analysis

## INTRODUCTION

The aim of this final chapter is to consider the implications of our approach for the formulation and delivery of policy. Although our subject has a geographical domain spanning all nations, in one volume we cannot hope to examine the implications for all the many country-specific policy initiatives across the global economy. We can, however, ask what can be learnt about the general framework of education and training policy-making at the turn of the new millennium.

Let us begin by setting the terms of this evaluation. We survey a medium-term horizon, say that of a generation or so. This means that, while short-term changes in policy or economic performance are largely irrelevant for these purposes, we do not envisage any fundamental change in the nature of the socioeconomic system. A second assumption which we would like to make explicit is that, as far as the industrialised countries are concerned, we shall be considering policy frameworks for following a high-skills route to accumulation. It is necessary to make this explicit because, as we have argued, there are alternative routes to accumulation that do not involve high skills, high wages and high-value-added production, which may be viable for some advanced capitalist countries in the medium term, and which from the point of view of the businesses aiming to maximise their profits may be just as, or even more, desirable. The choice between these routes, complex in reality, is the stuff of politics. A major theoretical point that we have urged at various stages in the book is that skill formation issues are inherently subject to conflict.

That the phrase 'high-skill, high-wage economy' has become something of a cliché reflects the fact, however, that there has now arisen in many countries a potential or actual coalition among a range of parties for an expansion and improvement in the quality of education and training in capitalist societies. The possible coalition includes: citizens as parents, who increasingly expect a decent education for their children; citizens as workers who want to participate more in the use of modern technology, to advance their job prospects and to fulfil themselves more in their daily

176

work; fractions of employers who realise that participation and skill can convey profitability and competitiveness; and the employees of the education and training systems whose job satisfaction and security is raised in a society which values their contribution.

Not all parties subscribe to this coalition. On one hand there are those who, when they are honest, do not hold to the view that it is necessary to raise significantly the education levels of the majority of the population; for them it might be considered best to let minorities of able or privileged persons achieve high levels of education while the large majority fit into a more 'flexible' labour market. On the other hand, from a polar political perspective among some left-wing thinkers, there are those who hold that, in the current conflict between capital and labour, the call for workers to participate in a programme of upskilling is a distraction from the real need to confront capital in an organised manner. In this viewpoint upskilling workers, even if successful, would not provide a bulwark against the threat of increased competition from capital operating in the third world. It is only a matter of a brief time before workers in third world countries are equipped with equivalent skills, and it is said to be in all workers' interests to concentrate on resisting the forces of capitalist competition. In any case, it would be a delusion to imagine that a high-skill route to accumulation would be stable and free from contradictions.

While we would agree that no route, not even the high-skill route, is free from contradictions (we have discussed them elsewhere in this book), we nevertheless hold that a medium-term successful period of capital accumulation, relatively free from crises, is feasible. It behoves us therefore to consider the policy context that could frame such a period. We believe that the constituencies in favour of education and training are now both broad and deep within many countries. Our remarks are concerned with how to establish the viability of this option in any given country.

## POLICY OBJECTIVES

Because education and training issues are conflictual, any policies for high-skill formation need to have the support of a strong enough coalition. In particular, it may be insufficient if a policy is decided on by government if that policy does not have the backing of other sections of society. Political support needs to extend beyond a parliamentary majority. It will not, for example, be possible to sustain policies for high levels of good quality training if a large proportion of employers is unwilling to cooperate with the policy. Or it may not, to take another example, be possible to impose a particular pedagogical policy on a relatively autonomous teaching profession.

Supposing, however, that support exists for policies of high-skill formation, our analysis in Chapter 5 has pointed the way to the additional institutional requirements which those policies must reinforce: an education system that is capable of inculcating in the large majority of school children at least intermediate-level academic skills in core subjects; a system of social or legal regulatory practices which compel or cajole individual employers to provide good quality workplace training; a means of maintaining incentives for individuals across the social and the ability spectra to participate actively in their own and others' skill formation; and an institutional means to allow continuing work-based skill formation to be complemented by periodic spells of off-the-job training. These are the common objectives which, in a nutshell, should form the basis of an evaluation of the skill formation system in any particular country. In addition to the checklist of requirements, however, we have also stressed how it is important to see the development of education and training institutions in a historical context. With this perspective one can better assess the possibilities for institutional change.

Though national diversity precludes a discussion here of the detailed policies of individual countries, it is safe to say that certain policies may be particularly difficult to implement in some countries. Governments might find, for example, that it is possible to bring about reforms in parts of the education system (especially those that require less funding), but that it is much more difficult to influence the level and quality of skill formation in the workplace. Our analysis of the differences between the first-, second- and third-wave nations suggests that the first-wave nations face some of the most difficult problems in adjusting their institutional base in such a manner as to facilitate the move toward the generation of a highly-skilled labour force. But there are in addition many second-wave nations, especially in Europe, whose skill formation systems face considerable changes if they are to match up with the comparatively successful systems in Germany or Japan.

## POLICY DEBATES

### The Policy Debate in the Older Industrial Nations

In addition to institutional barriers to change, which differ from country to country, new policies may also be held back by the limitations of mainstream policy debate, which shows certain common features across the industrialised world. The terms of this debate tend to be too narrow to permit realistic radical policies to emerge.[1]

Education and training policy debates involve diverse issues, including academic standards, creativity, and 'traditional' versus 'progressive' classroom pedagogies, but, most of all, they concern the level of government 'intervention'. The debate about intervention is hinged on a conventional left-right political axis with fixed parameters. These parameters limit the debate to a clash between two opposing sets of assumptions. From the point of view of the left, the origin of the problem of training is seen as the behaviour of employers who will not invest in long-term training unless subject to external constraint. The solution is for the state to design a means of intervention in order to enhance the level of training undertaken in order that the broader needs of the society as a whole can be taken into account. From the point of view of the right, the assumption is that only employers are in a position to define national training needs, as only they are in a position to know what training their staff require. The solution is for the market to provide the answer to the problem of training by leaving employers and individuals free to negotiate what is best for them.

Within the framework of the first set of assumptions, a number of 'solutions' have been tried by governments seeking to constrain the behaviour of employers. The most common has been the imposition of a levy or tax on employers which can be used to reward employers who are training and to penalise those who are 'free riders', living off the investment in training made by the 'good' employers. In the UK this took the form of the Training Board Levy, introduced in the 1960s through a series of decentralised, industry-based, training boards, which were subsequently abolished. In France the *taxe d'apprentissage* was initiated in 1925 and has been substantially modified since then. Increasingly the tax has been used to support forms of entry-level training other than the apprenticeship. In the field of continuing education and training (*formation professionnelle continue* – FPC) the legislation of 1971 and 1984 put in place a system whereby all enterprises employing ten people or more have had to allocate a specified minimum proportion of their payroll to expenditure on FPC. In Australia a training levy, based partly on the French experience, was introduced in 1990, in the form of the Training Guarantee Scheme aimed at increasing the level of employer expenditure on training. Unlike the French scheme it encountered strong opposition from employers' organisations and was suspended in 1994 (Senker, 1995).

Associated with the attempts to enhance employer-led training have been the developments associated with the apprenticeship system, the most dominant and successful of which has been the German apprenticeship scheme discussed above. Similar well-developed apprenticeship schemes have been established in Austria and Switzerland. A less well-developed scheme (The Modern Apprenticeship Scheme) has recently been introduced into the UK.

Within the framework of the second set of assumptions, an alternative set of policies has been tried. These included the attempt by the US government to encourage employers to take the initiative in improving training provision through the introduction of Private Industry Councils (PICs) later to be taken up and copied by the UK government and introduced in the form of Training Enterprise Councils (TECs) in England and Wales and Local Enterprise Companies (LECs) in Scotland. The purpose of these reforms and associated institutions was to enable those government resources devoted to training, to be controlled in their delivery by employers who would be more sensitive to the demands of the market.

More recently the UK government has attempted to carry these reforms further and stimulate the emergence of a training market by empowering individuals with Training Credits, which enable them to purchase training provision from employers.

Within the same framework, another alternative approach has been for the state to leave the training of younger and older adults almost entirely to the employers but to invest heavily in education in order that those entering the workforce will have high levels of achievement. Once these have been provided it is assumed that employers will then build on them in enhancing the skills base of their labour force. This has been tried in Canada and Ireland where substantial investments have been made in their education systems.

But to limit the debate to questions of too little or too much state intervention is to restrict the scope of what is at stake. Education and training policies in the industrialised countries do not differ merely as alternative means to the same socially agreed objective of achieving a high-skill workforce. They may differ also in relating to different objectives. Crudely speaking, if the objective is to follow a low-skill route to accumulation, the requirements of the education and training system are likely to be for appropriate forms of education and training: reasonable levels of universal basic skills (literacy and numeracy, conformity and communication skills) plus a small proportion of the workforce well-trained to technician and higher professional levels. Even if it is seen to be the objective of policy to aim for a truly high-skilled workforce, the too-little versus too-much state intervention axis may miss the essence of the problem. That analysis lacks the politics to validate the policies. If, for example, a government decides on a policy of raising training by 'intervention' to impose a training levy, the policy might fail not because in abstract principle it is incorrect, but because it wanted for sufficient political support. A major limitation to the achievement of such support in the liberal (non-corporatist) nations derives from the difficulties of achieving a consensus among the key agents involved in the skill formation process. A recent case in point is the above-mentioned failure of the Australian levy system. Moreover, as our analysis has shown, the establishment of a high-skill formation system requires that policies are also in place to influence the demand for skills. The policy debate should therefore encompass this objective.

The political institutions of the older industrial nations function to intensify the conflictual nature of the policy debate. The two-party system encourages conflictual politics through the provision of alternative interpretations of events. In legitimating this arrangement, they thereby help institutionalise the conflict between the groups concerned. Under these circumstances, it is difficult for the political elites to step outside their concern with the interests of those groups they represent, in order to adopt a more consensual approach. In some instances where such a consensus has been achieved, as in the UK with the establishment of the Manpower Services Commission, the attempt to introduce a longer-term perspective proved short lived in the face of employer opposition (Ainley and Corney, 1990). In the more corporatist nations among second-wave industrialisers, it is precisely that necessary consensus which, through a process of brokered political exchange, the corporatist institutions have been able to achieve, even if the consensus is neither complete nor permanent.

### The Policy Debate in the NIEs

Given the radically different model of skill formation now being developed in the NIEs, it is not surprising to find also a different type of policy debate there.

To recap briefly: the NIEs have succeeded in forging a new role for the government, as 'guardian' of the long-term interest of the community; they have pioneered the use of trade and industry policy to direct investment and used their education and training policies to ensure that the requisite skills are in place, consistent with that trade and industry policy; and they have forged new mechanisms for creating an awareness of common goals and co-ordinating the component parts of government administration. We have only touched on such mechanisms in this short study, but it is clear that the distinctive use of tripartite consultation, the movement of personnel between the organisations which represent different class and sectional interests are successful means by which the Singaporeans have been able to generate a high degree of consensus around national political goals. Finally, they have pioneered a policy of continuously adjusting the provision of training in line with that demanded by the productive system at a particular stage in its development. They have addressed the problem of enhancing the amount of training as well as ensuring that such training is related to the demands of the productive system. They have shown how there is no point in investing in higher education and sophisticated training if the productive system is demanding unskilled labour. Currently the skills demanded for high-value-added production require intensive on-the-job training, but it is no good for the government to encourage this if employers are reluctant to move into markets for the production of high-value-added goods and services.

Under these conditions the policy debate in the NIEs concerns the identification of ways in which the parties involved in education and training provision can contribute towards achieving higher levels of economic growth. It is a debate about how the government, employers and (sometimes) unions, can best collaborate to enhance the fit between the output from the education system and the requirements of the productive system. There is no assumption that employers' interests determine the national interest or that government action represents some form of 'intervention' in what is rightfully the province of the employers. The debate is over what is the appropriate role of each of these parties in contributing to the national goal. Thus, in the case of Singapore, the opposition parties accept the need for a national vision to determine policies; the political debate is in terms of which party has the most appropriate vision and policies for achieving that vision. In terms of education and training, one aspect of the debate concerns whether the curriculum, with its reliance on rote learning, is appropriate to deliver the more creative minds required for the knowledge-intensive industries (Chee Soon Juan, 1994). In terms of our analysis, the parameters of the debate are whether the content of the education being delivered is appropriate for the next stage in the development of the productive system.

At this stage in our knowledge we are not absolutely certain how far the experience of Singapore is replicated in all the other NIEs, or indeed, elsewhere. In both Taiwan and South Korea, human resource development has been identified as an important factor in accounting for their high economic growth rates (World Bank, 1993; Amsden, 1992) but the extent to which skill formation policies have been integrated with general economic policy formation in these countries awaits further research. In Hong Kong, which is typically seen as the most 'market' oriented economy, the Vocational Training Council has provided an important mechanism whereby employers' interests in training and development are reconciled with the political elite's overall requirements for the economy. However, one of the major differences between Hong Kong and Singapore lies in the absence of a strong union voice in the debate. In Malaysia, government strategy and the policy debate have many elements in common with the Singaporean experience. The lack of big indigenous industrial concerns has pushed Malaysia to adopt the Singapore route of making use of multinational corporations to drive economic growth and upgrade technology. At the same time, Malaysia appears to have learned from the Singapore experience in resisting being dictated to by the multinational corporations (Jomo, 1994), and it is developing a human resource policy linked to technological change entitled Vision 20/20, which is similar to Singapore's 'The Next Lap'.[2] The containment of the debate to a discussion of the respective roles of the parties in achieving national objectives does not mean that class interests have somehow been eradicated. Conflicts of interest are recognised, and hence there is a need for mechanisms to ensure a reconciliation of such interests with the broader national goals. The success of such measures is in part reflected in the more equitable distribution of income in these societies and the high levels of capital accumulation.

Yet successful as these societies are in achieving high levels of economic growth, they are not without their problems. One of the most important of these is the position of the ruling elite. A consequence of the relative autonomy of the political system in such societies is the danger that the vested interests of the political elite could displace the wider national goals in the political agenda, as happened with the nationalist government in China and the Macarios government in the Philippines (World Bank, 1993). If that were to happen, the social cohesion, which is an important feature of the political regimes in the NIEs, could rapidly deteriorate into major political repression. The tension between economic growth and democracy is indeed always a potential contradiction, a source of instability. As individuals become more affluent they may demand greater freedoms to rebel and to criticise establishments. Such tensions could be exacerbated by economic crises brought on in the NIEs by their integration into the global economy. From a Western perspective the lack of autonomy of different sections of society goes against the grain of democracy. The ability of professional associations, trade unions, certification bodies and schools to pursue their own agendas is constrained by the requirements of the national goals. In many areas of civil life, collective goals take precedence over individual goals. The limitations thereby placed on individual 'freedoms' amount to a shift in values which many in the West find difficult to accept. Moreover the force of western culture can hardly be shielded from an increasingly sophisticated citizenry, many more of whom spend time in Western countries. For the present, any comprehensive evaluation of these societies must recognise that there is a social balance sheet of achievements, with both minuses and pluses. Against those elements of repression and what are regarded in the West as undemocratic practices, range the historically remarkable developmental achievements which have liberated many people from economic oppression. In the current epoch it would be foolish for those in the West who oppose the political systems characteristic of the NIEs to dismiss out of hand the emergence of this new model of skill formation which is fostering such high rates of growth and eradicating the problems of poverty and unemployment previously experienced in such societies.

However, it is largely because of these immanent tensions between the economic, the political and the international spheres, that we limit our timeframe of analysis to the medium term.

## CROSS-NATIONAL IMPLICATIONS AND POLICY BORROWING

### Policy Borrowing Within the Older Industrial Countries

Our analysis of the route to high skills among the 'second wave' nations also has implications for 'policy borrowing'. A narrow notion of policy-borrowing refers to setting up similar initiatives in one country that are thought to work successfully elsewhere. A wider notion, which we prefer, simply refers to the notion of learning from the experience of other countries. First, our analysis reveals the fallacy of attempting to borrow a set of reforms from one country, and expecting them automatically to solve the skills problem of another. The interrelationships between the different institutional spheres means that items cannot be dragged from one society and imposed on another and then expected to perform effectively, whether they are PICs, the German apprenticeship system or the French levy system. What can be more effective is the use of specific policies which are then modified to suit different national institutional structures and which form part of a coherent strategy. In this respect the UK Conservative government's attempt to establish TECs and LECs has been more successful in so far as they are part of a more general strategy to develop a training market. Such a market is likely to deliver training for skills in use, reproducing the existing skills base. It is unlikely to help steer the economy toward the production of high value-added goods and services.

If the policy objective is to move the economy in the direction of high-value-added production then the hypotheses which informed this study would suggest a number of important policies, which could be borrowed from the more-successful systems and adapted to the context of less-successful countries. The following are some examples. The first is to ensure that the educational system is producing high levels of achievement in the field of basic intermediary level skills, such as language, maths, science and technology, on which work-based learning can build. If this basic education is deficient then the task facing employers in their attempt to produce highly skilled employees is much more daunting and expensive (Koike and Inoki (eds), 1990). A second policy imperative would be that the training system is focused on integrating practical on-the-job learning with the learning of theory.[3] Here the German apprenticeship and the Swiss system of skills deepening have important lessons for other countries. Third, policies should fully involve employers in the delivery of the skills necessary for high-value-added production but should not leave them in a position to monopolise the definition of the nation's skills needs. Fourth, systems should be in place to encourage and reward employees' commitment to lifetime learning. Just what form such policy initiatives take will differ from one country to another, depending on whether existing institutions could be modified or whether new institutions will have to be introduced. And, to repeat, such initiatives cannot merely come from government, without the political support from other sections of the community.

## The Implications of the Education and Training System in the NIEs for the Debate in the West

One of the main points we have been arguing is the need to understand the new systems of skill formation in the NIEs in their historical context. In these NIEs the close linkages which have been achieved between the education and training system and the productive system, underpin the high levels of skill formation. In view of their different histories it would be impractical to suggest that the older industrial societies could learn from the NIEs just by copying their institutions. But we believe that it is always possible to learn something about possibilities for one country by examining how things work elsewhere. Indeed, governments in both Singapore and Hong Kong have systematically and successfully borrowed specific policies that were operating elsewhere, and adapted them to fit in with their own institutional structures. Now the lessons may go partly in the opposite direction: the experience of the NIEs raises important questions and issues for the older industrial countries.

The first issue concerns the ability of the NIEs to achieve this close linkage between the education and training system and the productive system. If we are correct in our finding that this is a contributory factor to their high levels of economic growth, then this in itself has important implications for the policy debate in the West. It suggests that if the Western nations are to enhance their rate of growth, then measures must be taken to create a closer set of linkages between their trade and industry policies and the main components of their education and training systems. This raises acute policy issues for some of the Western countries, especially those such as the UK, US and France, where policy questions concerning education and training have traditionally been treated in isolation from any consideration of trade and industry policy, if such a policy exists. This reflects the autonomy of the education and training system. Whether the debate has been about improving standards in education or constraining employers to train more, policies have been devised in isolation. Education policies are rarely related to training policies, with the exception of Germany, and both sets of policies are governed by agendas which do not link the objectives of the policy with any broader strategy to develop certain types of industries. We feel that this is where the experience of the NIEs has a great deal to teach the older industrial nations. For if they are to compete effectively in the next generation of high-value-added product markets, then their ability to do so will be related to the success of their education and training systems in providing the appropriate skill base. This is a question, not of slavishly copying the experience of the NIEs, but merely of learning that the high levels of skill formation necessary for such industries to compete effectively in world markets will require the co-ordination of education and training policies in a manner not hitherto practised in the West. Moreover, both education and training policies will need to be driven by the goals of an agreed trade and industry policy.

The ways in which such a trade and industry policy would be established and the mechanism through which it could be linked to the education and training policies and systems would be determined by the particular characteristics of the national system in question. However, such a policy is also likely to receive opposition from existing class interests, particularly those of employers. This is because it undermines the claim that their interests in the field of education and especially training represent the national interest. However, by forcing the policy debate to consider the linkage of the education and training systems to each other and to broader national goals, the experience of the NIEs would give a new dimension to the policy debate and raise the possibility that the education and training systems of some of the older industrial nations could contribute more directly to higher levels of growth.

The second implication is that reforms aimed at changing the education and training system must be related to the demands of the productive system at the appropriate phase of its development. Given the present market-driven approach which characterises the US and the UK, any attempt to link education and training to the demands of the productive system as it is, would merely reproduce the low level of skill formation for a significant proportion of the population. Therefore, to contribute effectively towards the establishment of a high-wage economy, reforms of the education and training system must be geared towards creating the skill required for the next stage in the development of the productive system. Here the experience of the NIEs can be of more direct relevance as they have shown how the workplace can be used as a foundation for enhancing the nations skills base, although how this has been done varies from one country to another.

The other lesson they offer in this respect is the use of government-sponsored programmes to enhance the learning abilities of adults. In the older industrial countries there is a tendency to rely on improvements in the educational system, in the flow of people into the labour market, to improve the level of basic skills. This leads many observers to argue that improving the base-line skills of the labour force, the stock of skills, is a long slow process. Not so in the NIEs where they have directed learning programmes at adult workers, even those in their forties and fifties. By using what we referred to above as a two-pronged approach, governments have been successful in enhancing the basic skill levels of adult workers and thereby brought about a radical change in the stock of skills.[4]

But there are inevitable and obvious limitations as to how far the NIE model of skill formation could be adapted in the West. The relative autonomy of education and training institutions makes it hard to pursue a detailed manpower policy, even if such a policy is considered desirable.[5] The content of education is typically controlled at some remove from central government, while the also circumscribed control of funding is a blunt instrument. In addition, governments may be opposed by the vested interests of the education and training community, whose control of the output of the system (for example through the process of certification of standards) enables them to extract greater material rewards and status and generally more resources for education and training, in ways that may not be justified in terms of national economic performance. The weakness of the state in mature Western democracies also precludes the sort of centralised encouragement, direction and prescription for employer behaviour which is made possible by the developmental state. These problems are exacerbated in the older industrialised nations, especially the US, where there is a very weak regulatory structure, and endemic ideological opposition to statism.[6]

## Implications for Developing Societies

In so far as the NIEs represent a new route to high levels of skill formation and high value-added production, a route forged in the context of contemporary international markets and relations, they represent a model which could also become relevant for the needs of developing countries. The institutions of the Western countries were formed in a much earlier period of international relations, before capitalism had become a truly global system. Such institutions may not be appropriate for producing the skills required for effective competition in the global markets of the twenty-first century. The ability of the NIEs to link education and training to continuous change in the development of the productive system provides a model which offers institutional flexibility and the possibility of catching up fast on the older industrial nations.

Such a promise might make this new model more appropriate for countries like South Africa with a large unskilled labour force, with low levels of literacy, and a political imperative to create a more equitable distribution of income. Having modelled their education and training and industrial relations systems on those in Western industrialised countries, there are problems of co-ordination between the systems, with few institutional linkages in place: predictably, industrial strategy is left to the market. What our analysis suggests is the need for a new trade and industry policy which should be linked to an effective national human resource development strategy. This would mean organising the education and training and industrial relations systems to meet the human resource requirements determined by the trade and industry policy. If the first political requirement is to create full employment, this may mean attracting capital for labour-intensive forms of production. The next task would be to put in place the institutions required to produce a disciplined literate labour force. Once this is accomplished other objectives can be pursued.

However, there may be limits to the applicability of this new model of skill formation, in that some of the developing countries are not yet in a position to generate the basic institutional prerequisites, such as an efficient and stable system of state administration, required for the establishment of a developmental state (World Bank, 1993). The analysis of training should reflect the basic material differences between impoverished developing countries and the industrialised world. Not only are developing countries overwhelmingly agrarian, but also there is a considerable institutional poverty. Training is often much less differentiated in both content and delivery from education than it is in developed countries, and where it is differentiated the numbers being trained tend to be small. Training systems are liable to be evaluated also with a different mix of objectives in mind, and in particular to give more weight to equity considerations. And although the effect of training may be great for the individuals concerned who receive the training, the overall impact on the economy is bound to be limited. A particularly important objective of training policy analysis is likely to be to redress the institutional poverty: to set up and improve the efficiency of private and public organisations concerned with the analysis of training needs and the development and execution of training initiatives.

Nevertheless, education and training schemes constitute a major channel for international aid flows to developing countries, as a result of which considerable attention has been devoted to determining the most effective skill formation policies in such countries. The advice and practice of such organisations as the World Bank tends to be informed largely by the liberal, human capital approach to education and training policy (Middleton, 1988; Middleton, Ziderman and van Adams, 1993). The approach tends to focus on identifying the most productive forms of education and training, measured in terms of the impact on the ability to find employment and the rate of return. In the 1960s this was seen as investment in primary education. In the 1970s investment was recommended in secondary vocational education and in the 1980s in the use of non-formal training centres, along the lines of the Latin American model (Ducci, 1988). These training centres, such as those developed in Brazil, have strong links with industry, provide a steady flow of skilled labour and are able to adjust more rapidly than schools to changing labour market conditions (Middleton, 1988). Such flexible systems are seen as the most appropriate model for developing countries to follow. At the same time governments are advised to practice 'market-oriented' manpower planning – facilitating the work of private and public trainers by encouragement and by the dissemination of labour market information (Middleton, Ziderman and van Adams, 1993). Taking a long-term perspective, the certification of quality and ensuring flexibility are among the pragmatic watch words of this approach.

While not wishing to deny the importance of creating flexible institutions, it is important to point out that the predisposition towards market-based solutions may lead to contradictions and may miss an essential part of the task facing developing country's skill formation problem. The problem it creates is that associated with the liberal model of training, namely of treating the education and training system in isolation from the overall development of the productive system. Thus, while it may seem like an admirable recommendation to ensure that the output from the training institutions adjusts to changes in the labour market, such systems are only likely to reproduce skills in use. They are unlikely to create the skills necessary for entering the next phase of economic growth.[7] Moreover, the advice does not extend to linking policy to attempts to influence the demand for skills. These factors may explain why, although the Brazilian model is arguably an efficient education and training system for a developing country (Middleton, 1988; Ducci, 1988), being flexible, decentralised and providing employers with what they demand in the way of trained labour, the Brazilian economy has not been able to move into high-value-added production in the same way as the Asian NIEs.[8]

## CONCLUDING REMARKS

For many of those countries in the advanced industrial world that are currently not following a high-skill route to accumulation, it is a feasible task to move towards this route. Despite the barriers we have alluded to, we have stressed the political issues involved. Developing a workable consensus among the ruling political groups and among the majority of leading employers would seem to be the *sine qua non* for a successful high-skills strategy. That done, a variety of policies are in principle available to support the regulation of skill formation at the workplace, and the state can assume the major responsibility for financing the raising of educational levels. The difficulties are not technical, but political, and in particular the opposition of group or class interests which do not wish to see, even less to fund through taxation, a rise in education levels. Yet, if we are also right that the linkages between education, training and the economy have intensified in the modern era – to the extent that without developing that linkage economic performance for the mass of citizens will be poor – there should develop at least the materialist basis for building a political coalition in favour of education and training.[9]

We wish to conclude our excursion into the realms of policy philosophy, and our complete analysis, by re-asserting the modesty of its scope. Considered broadly enough, the case for education and training is the case for self-development. Many eloquent writers have articulated this case. Yet, in a book such as this which focuses on the relationship between education and training and economic growth, it is inevitable that our discussion of education and training is pre-occupied with the ways in which they can enhance the productive capacity of the economy. Of course, education and training have functions other than the transmission of the skills necessary for work. They are also a powerful means for ensuring personal development and the full realisation of human capabilities. But it remains true that such freedoms and potentials cannot flourish on a bed of poverty. The history of the industrialised world has shown that the 'luxury' of a full and adequate skill formation has hitherto only been available to a minority of the population. There is, now, a rare moment of optimism that, in at least one feasible path of economic development over the next few decades, we could see a substantial expansion of the freedoms that accrue to a well-educated and highly trained population.

## NOTES

1. The situation is not helped by the absence of a clear multidisciplinary policy philosophy.
2. We are indebted to Johnny Sung especially at this point for his report and discussion of Malaysia's case. Johnny Sung has also highlighted the case of Cyprus, which faced similar political threats to the four Tigers and has produced a national HRD strategy similar to that of Singapore in that it makes explicit administrative links between education and training provision and national economic policy goals (Samuels, 1995).
3. This is one of the main problems with the UK competence approach which tends to undervalue the learning of theory at the level of intermediate- and higher-level skills.
4. This refers to Singapore where the government programmes mentioned earlier have made a substantial impact. For an analysis of one such programme and its impact on enhancing the learning abilities of disadvantaged workers see Huam and Jewson (1995).
5. 'Manpower forecasting', as used to be regularly attempted, based on output forecasting coupled with input-output techniques, is now out of favour as a general policy tool in many countries. The underpinning theoretical assumptions were not usually valid, and frequently insufficiently well informed by labour market data. Nevertheless governments do, for example, attempt to control student numbers in total and in various subjects, which is a looser form of manpower planning.
6. A country like France, with its étatist traditions, might be in a better position in this respect.
7. The need for some public investments in training is conceded, in the World Bank approach, as an exception in cases where, in the opinion of well-informed planners, the labour markets are failing to 'predict accurately the emerging skills requirements of new industries and production technologies'; where such skills are judged to be of strategic importance to economic development, the public sector is allowed to step in (Middleton, Ziderman and van Adams, 1993: 149). Our difference from this approach may appear to be one of emphasis, in terms of the frequency with which this 'exception' arises, but if the exception becomes too common, too much like the rule, then it ceases to be valid to characterise an approach as 'market-oriented'.
8. Even more, these factors can explain the stultification of the training system in Qatar where, despite an avowed concern to generate an adequate skill formation for a new technological age in the indigenous workforce, little attempt has been made either to influence employers' demand for skills among Qataris or to construct institutional links between employers and the training system (Devlin and Jewson, 1995).
9. Auerbach (1992) frames this proposition as the essence of a modern socialist agenda.

# Bibliography

Abramowitz, M. (1986), 'Catching Up, Forging Ahead, and Falling Behind', *Journal of Economic History* **XLVI** (2): 385–406.

Acemoglu, D. (1993), 'Labour Market Imperfections, Innovation Incentives and the Dynamics of Innovation Activity', paper presented to conference, The Skills Gap and Economic Activity, Centre For Economic Policy Research, London.

Addison, J.T. and Siebert, W.S. (1979), *The Market For Labor: An Analytical Treatment*, Santa Monica, Goodyear.

Ainley, P. and Corney, M. (1990), *Training for the Future: The Rise and Fall of the Manpower Services Commission*, London, Cassell.

Alba-Ramirez, A. (1994), 'Formal Training, Temporary Contracts, Productivity and Wages in Spain', *Oxford Bulletin of Economics and Statistics* **56** (2): 151–70.

Amable, B. (1993), 'Catch-up and Convergence: a Model of Cumulative Growth', *International Review of Applied Economics* **7** (2): 1–25.

Amsden, A.H. (1989), *Asia's Next Giant: South Korea and Late Industrialisation*, Oxford, Oxford University Press.

Amsden, A.H. (1992), 'Taiwan in International Perspective', in N.T. Wang (ed.), *Taiwan's Enterprises in Global Perspective*, New York, M.E. Sharpe.

Applebaum, E. and Albin, P. (1989), 'Computer Rationalisation and the Transformation of Work: Lessons from the Insurance Industry', in S. Wood (ed.), *The Transformation of Work*, London, Unwin Hyman.

Applebaum, E. and Batt, R. (1994), *The New American Workplace: Transforming Work Systems in the United States*, Ithaca, New York, ILR Press.

Armstrong, P., Glyn, A. and Harrison, J. (1991), *Capitalism since 1945*, Oxford, Basil Blackwell.

Arrow, K.J. (1973), 'Higher Education as a Filter', *Journal of Public Economics* **2**: 193–216.

Arulampalam, W., Booth, A. and Elias, P. (1995), *Count Data Models of Work-Related Training: A Study of Young Men in Britain*, Working papers of the ESRC Research Centre on Micro-social Change, Paper 95–14, Colchester, University of Essex.

Ashton, D.N. (1986), *Unemployment Under Capitalism: The Sociology of*

*British and American Labour Markets*, Brighton, Wheatsheaf.

Ashton, D.N. (1991), 'All my Relations: The Affinity Between Education and Training', Inaugural lecture delivered at the University of Leicester, mimeo, Centre for Labour Market Studies.

Ashton, D.N. and Field, D. (1976), *Young Workers: From School to Work*, Hutchinson, London.

Ashton, D.N., Green, F. and Lowe, G. (1993), 'The Linkages Between Education and Employment: a Comparative Study of Britain and Canada', *Comparative Education* **29** (2): 125–43.

Ashton, D.N. and Maguire, M.J. (1986), *Young Adults in the Labour Market*, Research Paper No. 55, Department of Employment, London.

Ashton, D.N., Maguire, M.J. and Spilsbury, M. (1990), *Restructuring the Labour Market: The Implications for Youth*, London, Macmillan.

Ashton, D.N., Maguire, M.J. and Sung, J. (1991), 'Institutional Structures and the Provision of Intermediate Level Skills: Lessons from Canada and Hong Kong', in P. Ryan (ed.), *International Comparisons of Vocational Education and Training*, Lewes, Falmer.

Ashton, D.N. and Sung, J. (1994), *The State, Economic Development and Skill Formation: A New East Asian Model*, Working Paper No. 3, University of Leicester, Centre for Labour Market Studies.

Asplund, R. (1993), *Essays on Human Capital and Earnings in Finland*, Helsinki, ETLA, The Research Institute of the Finnish Economy.

Atkinson, A.B. (1993), *What is Happening to the Distribution of Income in the UK?*, Discussion Paper, STICERD, London School of Economics.

Auer, P. (1992), *Further Education and Training for the Employed (FETE): European Diversity*, Report Prepared for the Commission of the European Communities, Brussels.

Auerbach, P. (1988), *Competition*, Oxford, Basil Blackwell.

Auerbach, P. (1992), 'On Socialist Optimism', *New Left Review* **192** (March/April): 5–36.

Baker, M. (1994), 'Training Down Under: An Overview of the Australian Experience', in R. McNabb and K. Whitfield (eds), *The Market for Training*, Aldershot, Avebury.

Baker, M. and Wooden, M. (1992), 'Training in the Australian Labour Market: Evidence from the How Workers Get Their Training Survey', *Australian Bulletin of Labour* **18** (1, March): 25–45.

Baran, B. (1988), 'Office Automation and Women's Work: the Technological Transformation of the Insurance Industry', in R.E. Pahl (ed.), *On Work: Historical, Comparative and Theoretical Perspectives*, Oxford, Basil Blackwell.

Barro, R.J. (1991), 'Economic Growth in a Cross Section of Countries', *Quarterly Journal of Economics* **CVI** (2): 407–43.

Barron, J., Black, D.A. and Loewenstein, M.A. (1993), 'Gender Differences in Training, Capital, and Wages', *Journal of Human Resources* **28** (2): 343–64.

Bassi, L.J. (1995), 'Upgrading the U.S. workplace: do reorganization, education help?', *Monthly Labour Review* (May): 37–47.

Batt, R. and Osterman, P. (1993), 'Workplace Training Policy: Case Studies of State and Local Experiments' Case Studies for *A National Policy for Workplace Training*, Washington, DC, Economic Policy Institute.

Baumol, W.J. (1986), 'Productivity Growth, Convergence, and Welfare: What the Long-Run Data Show', *American Economic Review* **75** (5): 1073–85.

Baumol, W.J. and Wolff, E.N. (1988), 'Productivity, Growth, Convergence, and Welfare: Reply', *American Economic Review* **78** (5, December): 1155–9.

Becker, G.S. (1964), *Human Capital*, New York, National Bureau of Economic Research.

Berggren, C. (1995), 'Japan as Number Two: Competitive Problems and the Future of Alliance Capitalism after the Burst of the Bubble', *Work, Employment and Society* **9** (1): 53–95.

Berman, E., Bound, J. and Griliches, Z. (1994), 'Changes in the Demand for Skilled Labor Within US Manufacturing: Evidence from the Annual Survey of Manufactures', *The Quarterly Journal of Economics* **CIX** (2, May): 367–97.

Berman, E., Machin, S. and Bound, J. (1994), 'Implications of Skill Biased Technological Change: International Evidence', London School of Economics.

Bertrand, O. and Noyelle, T. (1988), *Human Resources and Corporate Strategy. Technological Change in Banks and Insurance Companies: France, Germany, Japan, Sweden, United States*, Paris, OECD.

Billett, S. (1992), 'Towards a Theory of Workplace Learning,' *Studies in Continuing Education*, **14** (2): 143–55.

Bishop, J.H. (1993), 'Impacts of School Organization and Signalling on Incentives to Learn in France, Holland, England, Scotland and the United States', paper presented to conference, International Conference on Human Capital Investments and Economic Performance, Santa Barbara.

Bishop, J.H. (1994), 'The impact of Previous Training on Productivity and Wages', in L.M. Lynch (ed.), *Training and the Private Sector: International Comparisons*, Chicago, University of Chicago Press.

Bjorklund, A. (1991), 'Evaluations of Labour Market Policy in Sweden', paper presented to conference, International Conference on the

Economics of Training, Cardiff Business School.

Blanchflower, D. and Freeman, R. (1990), *Going Different Ways: Unionism in the US and Other Advanced OECD Countries*, Discussion Paper No. 5, Centre for Economic Performance, London School of Economics.

Blanchflower, D.G. and Lynch, L.M. (1994), 'Training at Work: A Comparison of U.S. and British Youths', in LLM (ed.), *Training and the Private Sector: International Comparisons*, Chicago, University of Chicago Press.

Blossfeld, H.P. (1994), 'Different Systems of Vocational Training and Transition from School to Career, the German Dual System in Cross-national Comparison', in CEDEFOP (ed.), *The Determinants of Transitions in Youth*, papers from the conference organised by the ESF Network on Transitions in Youth and GRET, Berlin, CEDEFOP.

Blundell, R., Dearden, L. and Meghir, C. (1994), 'The Determinants and Effects of Work-Related Training in Britain', mimeo, paper presented to EMRU Labour Economics Workshop, Department of Employment, 18 November.

Bonnal, L., Fougére, D. and Sévandon, A. (1995), 'Une Modélisation du Processes de Recherche d'Emploi en Pre'sence de Meunes Publiques pour les Jeunes', *Revue Economique* **46** (3).

Booth, A. (1991), 'Job-Related Formal Training: Who Receives It and What Is It Worth?', *Oxford Bulletin of Economics and Statistics* **53** : 281–94.

Booth, A.L. and Satchell, S.E. (1993), 'On Apprenticeship Qualifications and Labour Mobility', paper presented to conference, The Skills Gap and Economic Activity, Centre For Economic Policy Research, London.

Bowles, S. and Gintis, H. (1976), *Schooling in Capitalist America*, London, Routledge & Kegan Paul.

Bowles, S. and Gintis, H. (1988), 'Schooling in Capitalist America: Reply to our Critics', in M. Cole (ed.), *Bowles and Gintis Revisited*, London, Falmer Press, 235–45.

Bowman, R.S. (1990), 'Smith, Mill and Marshall on Human Capital Formation', *History of Political Economy* **22**: 239–59.

Bracey, G.W. (1992), 'The Condition of Public Education', *Phi Delta Kappan* (October): 104–17.

Braverman, H. (1974), *Labor and Monopoly Capital*, New York, Monthly Review Press.

Breen, R. (1991), 'Assessing the Effectiveness of Training and Temporary Employment Schemes: Some Results from the Youth Labour Market', *The Economic and Social Review* **22** (3, April): 177–98.

Brooks, G., Foxman, D. and Gorman, T. (1995), *NCE Briefing. New Series*

*7. Standards in Literacy and Numeracy: 1948-1994*, London, National Commission on Education.

Brown, C., Reich, M. and Stern, D. (1990), *Skills and Security in Evolving Employment Systems: Observations from Case Studies*, Berkeley, University of California at Berkeley.

Brown, C., Reich, M. and Stern, D. (1993), 'Becoming a High-performance Work Organization: the Role of Security, Employee involvement and training', *The International Journal of Human Resource Management* **4** (2 May): 247–75.

Brown, C., Reich, M. and Stern, D. (1994), 'Training Structures, Skill Formation, and Wage Profiles in Japan and the U.S.', paper presented to conference, Meetings of the Industrial Relations Research Association, Boston, US.

Brown, P. (1990), 'The Third Wave: Education and the Ideology of Parentocracy', *British Journal of Sociology of Education*, **11** (1): 65–82.

Brunello, G. and Ariga, K. (1994), *Earnings and Seniority in Japan. A Re-appraisal of the Existing Evidence and a Comparison With the UK*, CEPR, Discussion Paper No. 974.

Burchell, B., Elliot, B., Rubery, J. and Wilkinson, F. (1994), 'Job Content and Skill: Managers' and Employees' Perspectives', in R. Penn, M. Rose and J. Rubery (eds), *Skill and Occupational Change*, Oxford, Oxford University Press.

Bushnell, D. (1990), 'Input, Process, Output: A Model for Evaluating Training', *Training and Development Journal* (March).

Bynner, J. and Roberts, K. (eds), (1991), *Youth and Work: Transition to Employment in England and Germany*, London, Anglo-German Foundation.

Caillods, F. (1994), 'Converging Trends Amidst Diversity in Vocational Training Systems', *International Labour Review* **133** (2): 241–57.

Cameron, S.V. and Heckman, J.J. (1994), 'Determinants of Young Males' Schooling and Training Choices', in L.M. Lynch (ed.), *Training and the Private Sector. International Comparisons*, Chicago, University of Chicago Press.

Campbell, D. (1994), 'Foreign Investment, Labour Immobility and the Quality of Employment', *International Labour Review* **133** (2): 185–204.

Campbell, R. (1747), *The London Tradesman*, reprinted by David & Charles, Newton Abbot, 1969.

Campinos-Dubernet, M. and Grando, J.-M. (1988), 'Formation Professionelle Ouvrière: Ivois Modèles Européenes', *Formation/Emploi* **22** : 5–29.

Cantor, L. (1989), *Vocational Education and Training in the Developed*

*World: A Comparative Study*, London, Routledge.

Cappelli, P. (1993), 'Are Skill Requirements Rising? Evidence from Production and Clerical Jobs', *Industrial and Labor Relations Review* **46** (3): 515–30.

Cappelli, P. and Rogovsky, N. (1994), 'New Work Systems and Skill Requirements', *International Labour Review* **133** (2): 205–20.

Card, D. and Krueger, A.B. (1992a), 'Does School Quality Matter? Returns to Education and the Characteristics of Public-Schools in the United States', *Journal of Political Economy* **100** (1): 1–40.

Card, D. and Krueger, A.B. (1992b), 'Returns to Schooling', paper presented to conference, EMRU, University of Wales at Bangor,

Casey, B. (1991), 'Recent Developments in the German Apprenticeship System', *British Journal of Industrial Relations* **29** (2): 205–21.

Castells, M. (1989) 'High Technology and the New International Division of Labour', *Labour and Society* **14** (Special Issue): 7–20.

Castells, M. (1992), 'Four Asian Tigers With a Dragon Head: A Comparative Analysis of the State, Economy and Society in the Asian Pacific Rim', in R.P. Appelbaum and J. Henderson (eds), *States and Development in the Asia Pacific Rim*, London, Sage.

Cavestro, W. (1989), 'Automation, New Technology and Work Content', in S. Wood (ed.), *The Transformation of Work?: Skill, Flexibility and the Labour Process*, London, Unwin Hyman.

CEDEFOP (1984), *Vocational Training Systems in the Member States of the European Community*, Luxemburg, Office for Official Publication of the European Communities.

CEDEFOP (1987a), *The Role of the Social Partners in Vocational Training and Further Training in the Federal Republic of Germany*, Berlin, CEDEFOP.

CEDEFOP (1987b), *The Role of Unions and Management in Vocational Training in France*, Berlin, CEDEFOP.

Centre for Educational Research and Innovation (1992), *Adult Illiteracy and Economic Performance*, Paris, OECD.

Chan, S. (ed.) (1991), *East Asian Dynamism: Growth, Order, and Security in the Pacific Region*, Boulder, Colo., Westview Press.

Chandler, Jr, A. D. (1977), *The Visible Hand: The Managerial Revolution in American Business*, Cambridge, Mass., Harvard University Press.

Chandler, Jr, A.D. (1990), *Scale and Scope: The Dynamics of Industrial Capitalism*, Cambridge, Mass., Harvard University Press.

Chee Soon Juan (1994), *Dare to Change: An Alternative Vision for Singapore*, Singapore, The Singapore Democratic Party.

Claydon, T. and Green, F. (1994), 'Can Trade Unions Improve Training in Britain?', *Personnel Review* **23** (1): 37–51.

Cockburn, C. (1983), *Brothers: Male Dominance and Social Change*, London, Pluto Press.

Cole, M. (1988), 'Correspondence Theory in Education: Impact, Critique and Re-evaluation', in M. Cole (ed.), *Bowles and Gintis Revisited*, London, Falmer Press, 7–15.

Commission on the Skills of the American Workforce (1990), *America's Choice: High Skills or Low Wages*, Rochester, NY, National Center on Education and the Economy.

Coyle, A. (1982), 'Sex and Skill in the Organisation of the Clothing Industry', in J. West (ed.), *Work, Women and the Labour Market*, London, Routledge & Kegan Paul.

Cummings, W.K. (1995), 'The Asian Human Resource Approach in Global Perspective', *Oxford Review of Education* 21 (1): 67–81.

Curran, M.M. (1988), 'Gender and Recruitment: People and Places in the Labour Market', *Work, Employment and Society* (2): 335–51.

Cusumano, M. (1985), *The Japanese Automobile Industry*, Cambridge, Mass., Harvard University Press.

Cutler, T. (1992), 'Vocational Training and British Economic Performance: A Further Instalment of the "British Labour Problem"', *Work, Employment and Society* 6 (2): 161–83.

Daly, A., Hitchens, D. and Wagner, K. (1985), 'Productivity, Machinery and Skills in a Sample of British and German Manufacturing Plants', *National Institute Economic Review* (11, February): 48–61.

Dandeker, C. (1978), 'Patronage and Bureaucratic Control : The Case of the Naval Officer in British Society 1780-1850', *British Journal of Sociology*, (September), 300–20.

de Koning, J. (1994), 'Evaluating Training at the Company Level', in R. McNabb and K. Whitfield (eds), *The Market for Training*, Aldershot, Avebury.

DeLong, B. (1988), 'Productivity, Growth, Convergence, and Welfare: Comment', *American Economic Review* 78 (5, December): 1138–54.

Denison, E. (1979), *Accounting for Slower Economic Growth: The United States in the 1970s*, Washington, Brookings Institution.

Dertouzos, M.L., Lester, R.K., Solow, R.M. and the MIT Commission on Industrial Productivity (1989), *Made in America. Regaining the Productive Edge*, Cambridge, Mass., MIT Press.

Devlin, B. and Jewson, N. (1995), *The Development of Public Education and Training in the State of Qatar*, Working Paper 8, Centre for Labour Market Studies, Leicester University.

Deyo, F.C. (ed.) (1989), 'Beneath the Miracle: Labor Subordination in the New Asian Industrialism', California, University of California Press.

Dickens, W.T. and Lang, K. (1985), 'A Test of Dual Labor Market

Theory', *American Economic Review* **75** : 792–805.

Dolton, P. J. (1993), The Econometric Assessment of Training Schemes: A Critical Review, mimeo, University of Newcastle-upon-Tyne, Department of Economics.

Dolton, P.J., Makepeace, G.H. and Treble, J.G. (1992), Evaluation of Training Schemes: Lessons From Britain, mimeo, Labour Economics Unit, Department of Economics, University of Hull.

Dore, R. (1973), *British Factory–Japanese Factory: The Origins of National Diversity in Industrial Relations*, London, George Allen & Unwin.

Dore, R. (1974), 'The Future of Japan's Meritocracy', mimeo, Sussex, Institute of Development Studies.

Dore, R. (1993), 'Japan: Institutional and Regulatory Framework', paper presented to conference, Human Capital Investments and Economic Performance, RAND/EAC/IET, Santa Barbara.

Dore, R. and Sako, M. (1989), *How the Japanese Learn to Work*, London, Routledge.

Dowrick, S. and Nguyen, D.T. (1989), 'OECD Comparative Economic Growth 1950–85: Catch-Up and Convergence', *The American Economic Review* **79** (5): 1010–30.

Ducci, M. (1988), 'Equity and Productivity of Vocational Training – The Latin American Experience', *Journal of Educational Development* **8** (3): 175–87.

Eaglesham, E.J.R. (1967), of *The Foundations of Twentieth-Century Education in England*, London, Routledge & Kegan Paul.

Edwards, R.C. (1979), *Contested Terrain*, New York, Basic Books.

Edwards, R.C. and Garonna, P. (1991), 'Patterns of Public Intervention in Training and the Labour Accords in Italy and the United States', in P. Ryan, P. Garonna and R.C. Edwards (eds), *The Problem of Youth: The Regulation of Youth Employment and Training in Advanced Economies*, London, Macmillan.

Edwards, R.C., Gordon, D.M. and Reich, M. (1982), *Segmented Work, Divided Workers: The Historical Transformation of Labor in the United States*, Cambridge, Cambridge University Press.

Elbaum, B. and Wilkinson, F. (1979), 'Industrial Relations and Uneven Development: a Comparative Study of the American and British Steel Industries', *Cambridge Journal of Economics* **3** (September): 275–303.

Elias, N. (1982), *The Civilising Process. Vol. II: State Formation and Civilisation*, Oxford, Blackwell.

Elias, P. (1994), 'Job-related Training, Trade Union Membership, and Labour Mobility: A Longitudinal Study', *Oxford Economic Papers* **46** (4): 563–78.

Elias, P., Hernaes, E. and Baker, M. (1992), 'Vocational Education and Training in Britain and Norway', paper presented to conference, Vocational Training in Britain and Europe, Oxford Institute of Economics and Statistics.

Elias, P., Hernaes, E. and Baker, M. (1994), Vocational Education and Training in Britain and Norway, in L.M. Lynch (ed.), *Training and the Private Sector. International Comparisons*, Chicago, University of Chicago Press.

Elley, W.B. and Schleicher, A. (1994), 'International Differences in Achievement Levels', in W.B. Elley (ed.), *The IEA Study of Reading Literacy: Achievement and Instruction in Thirty-Two School Systems*, Oxford, Pergamon.

Elsas, M. (ed.) (1960), 'Iron in the Making: Dowlais Iron Company Letters 1782–1860', Cardiff.

Employment Department (1990), *Labour Market and Skill Trends 1991/92*, Sheffield, Employment Department.

Felstead, A. (1994), 'Funding Government Training Schemes: Mechanisms and Consequences', Leicester University, Centre for Labour Market Studies, Working Paper No. 2.

Felstead, A., Ashton, D., Green, F. and Sung, J. (1994), *International Study of Vocational Education and Training in the Federal Republic of Germany, France, Japan, Singapore and the United States*, Leicester, Centre for Labour Market Studies, University of Leicester.

Felstead, A. and Green, F. (1994) 'Training During the Recession' *Work Employment and Society* **8** (2) 199–219.

Felstead, A. and Green, F. (1995), 'Cycles of Training? Evidence from the British Recession of the Early 1990s', in A. Booth and D. Snower (eds.), *The Skills Gap and Economic Activity*, Cambridge, Cambridge University Press.

Ferleger, L. and Lazonick, W. (1993) 'The Managerial Revolution and the Developmental State: The Case of U.S. Agriculture', *Business and Economic History* **22** (2).

Finegold, D. (1991), 'Institutional Incentives and Skill Creation: Understanding the Decisions that Lead to a High Skill Equilibrium', in P. Ryan (ed.), *International Comparisons of Vocational Education and Training for Intermediate Skills*, London, Falmer Press. 93–116.

Finegold, D. (1992a), 'The Changing International Economy and its Impact on Education and Training', *Oxford Studies in Comparative Education* **2** (2): 57–82.

Finegold, D. (1992b), 'The Low-skill Equilibrium: An Institutional Analysis of Britain's Education and Training Failure', University of Oxford, D.Phil. thesis.

Finegold, D. and Soskice, D. (1988), 'The Failure of British Training: Analysis and Prescription', *Oxford Review of Economic Policy* **4** (3): 21–53.

Finn, D. (1987), *Training Without Jobs*, London, Macmillan.

Fong, P.E. and Lim, L.Y.C. (1989), 'High Tech and Labour in the Asian NICs', *Labour and Society* **14** (Special issue on high tech and labour in Asia): 43–58.

Ford, B. (1987), 'A Learning Society: Japan through Australian Eyes', in J. Twining, S. Nisbet and J. Megarry (eds), *Vocational Education*, World Yearbook of Education.

Frazis, H.J., Herz, D.E. and Horrigan, M.W. (1995), 'Employer-Provided Training: Results from a New Survey', *Monthly Labor Review* (May): 3–17.

Freeman, C. (1987), *Technology, Policy and Economic Performance: Lessons from Japan*, London, Pinter.

Freeman, R.B. (1986), 'Demand for Education', in O. Ashenfelter and R. Layard (eds), *Handbook of Labor Economics*, Amsterdam, North-Holland, 357–86.

Froebel, F., Hendricks, J. and Kreye, O. (1980), *The New International Division of Labour*, Cambridge, Cambridge University Press.

Fuller, A., Maguire, M., Jones, L. and Pugh, V. (1994), *Disseminating for Change: Dissemination of Best Practice with Regard to Effective Learning*, University of Leicester, Centre for Labour Market Studies, Report to the Department of Employment.

Furlong, A. and Biggart, A. (1995), 'Social Reproduction in an Urban Context: Neighbourhoods, Labour Markets and Discouraged Workers', paper presented to The 1995 Conference of the British Sociological Society, Leicester.

Furth, D. (1985) 'Patterns of Provision', in OECD, *Education and Training after Basic Schooling*, Paris, OECD, Ch. 2.

Galbraith, J.K. (1967), *The New Industrial State*, London, Hamish Hamilton.

Gallie, D. (1991), 'Patterns of Skill Change: Upskilling, Deskilling or the Polarization of Skills?', *Work, Employment and Society* **5** (3, September): 319–51.

Gallie, D. and White, M. (1993), *Employee Commitment and the Skills Revolution*, London, PSI Publishing.

Gardiner, K. (1993), 'A Survey of Income Inequality Over the Last Twenty Years – How Does the UK Compare?', paper presented to conference, The Distribution of Well-being in the 1980s – An International Perspective, Sweden, (June) 21–23.

Gardner, P. (1984), *The Lost Elementary Schools of Victorian England*,

London, Croom Helm.

Gemmell, N. (1994), 'Human Capital, Education and Economic Growth', mimeo, Centre for Research in Economic Development and International Trade, University of Nottingham.

Gispen, K. (1989), *New Profession, Old Order: Engineers and German Society*, 1815–1914, Cambridge, Cambridge University Press.

Gleeson, D. and Wardle, G. (1980), *Further Education or Training?*, London, Routledge & Kegan Paul.

Goh-Tan, E. (1995) 'The Role of Trade Unions in Skill Formation in a Developmental State: the Singapore Case', dissertation submitted for the degree of Master of Science, CLMS, University of Leicester.

Gordon, D.M., Edwards, R. and Reich, M. (1982), *Segmented Work, Divided Workers: The Historical Transformation of Labor in the United States*, London, Cambridge University Press.

Government of Singapore (1991), 'The Next Lap', Singapore, Times Editions Pte Ltd.

Granvetter, M. (1985), 'Economic Action and Social Structure: the Problem of Embeddedness', *American Journal of Sociology* 91 (3): 481–510.

Green, A. (1990), *Education and State Formation: The Rise of Education Systems in England, France and the USA*, London, Macmillan.

Green, A. (1991), 'The Reform of Post–16 Education and Training and the Lessons from Europe', *Journal of Education Policy* 6 (3 July–September): 327–35.

Green, F. (1992), 'On the Political Economy of Skill in the Advanced Industrial Nations', *Review of Political Economy* 4 (4): 413–35.

Green, F. (1993a), 'The Determinants of Training of Male and Female Employees in Britain', *Oxford Bulletin of Economics and Statistics* 55 (1, February): 103–22.

Green, F. (1993b), 'The Impact of Trade Union Membership on Training in Britain', *Applied Economics* 25: 1033–43.

Green, F. (1994), 'The Determinants of Training of Male and Female Employees, and Some Measures of Discrimination', in R. McNabb and K. Whitfield (eds), *The Market for Training*, Aldershot, Avebury.

Green, F. and Ashton, D. (1992), 'Skill Shortage and Skill Deficiency: A Critique', *Work, Employment and Society* 6 (2): 287–301.

Green, F., Henley, A. and Tsakalotos, E. (1994), 'Income Inequality in Corporatist and Liberal Economies: a Comparison of Trends Within OECD Countries', *International Review of Applied Economics* 8 (3): 303–31.

Green, F., Hoskins, M. and Montgomery, S. (1994), *The Effects of Training, Further Education and YTS on the Earnings of Young*

*Employees*, Discussion Papers in Economics No. 94/10, University of Leicester.

Green, F., Machin, S. and Wilkinson, D. (1995), *Unions and Training: An Analysis of Training Practices in Unionised and Non-Unionised Workplaces*, Working Paper, Centre for Economic Performance, London School of Economics.

Green, F., Sung, J., Lu, K. and Huang, Q. (1994), *The Skill Formation System in China: Outline and Issues for Research*, Working Paper 4, Centre for Labour Market Studies, Leicester University.

Greenhalgh, C. and Mavrotas, G. (1993), 'Workforce Training in the Thatcher Era – Market Forces and Market Failures', *International Journal of Manpower* **14** (2/3): 17–32.

Greenhalgh, C. and Mavrotas, G. (1994), 'The Role of Career Aspirations and Financial Constraints in Individual Access to Vocational Training', *Oxford Economic Papers* **46** (4): 579–604.

Greenhalgh, C. and Stewart, M. (1987), 'The Effects and Determinants of Training', *Oxford Bulletin of Economics and Statistics* **49**: 171–90.

Groot, W., Hartog, J. and Oosterbeek, H. (1994), 'Returns to Within-Company Schooling of Employees: The Case of the Netherlands', in L.M. Lynch (ed.), *Training and the Private Sector. International Comparisons*, Chicago, University of Chicago Press.

Grubb, W.N. (1992), 'Postsecondary Vocational Education and the Sub-Baccalaureate Labor Market: New Evidence on Economic Returns', *Economics of Education Review* **11** (3): 225–48.

Grubb, W.N. (1994), 'Postsecondary Education and the Sub-Baccalaureate Labor Market: Corrections and Extensions', mimeo, University of California, Berkeley.

Guttsman, W.L. (1968), *The British Political Elite*, London, Mcgibbon & Kee.

Ham, J. and Lalonde, R.J. (1994), 'Looking into the Black Box: Using Experimental Data to Find Out How Training Works', in R. McNabb and K. Whitfield (eds), *The Market for Training*, Aldershot, Avebury.

Hampden-Turner, C. and Trompenaars, F. (1994), *The Seven Cultures of Capitalism*, London, Judy Piatkus.

Hannah, L. (1983), *The Rise of the Corporate Economy*, Second Edition, London, Methuen.

Hargreaves Heap, S. (1989), *Rationality in Economics*, Oxford, Blackwell.

Hashimoto, M. (1991), 'Employment-Based Training in Japanese Firms in Japan and in the United States: Experiences of Automobile Manufactures' paper presented to conference, International Comparisons of Private Sector Training, London School of Economics.

Hashimoto, M. (1993), 'Education, Training and Economic Performance:

Postwar Japanese Experience', paper presented to conference, Human Capital Investments and Economic Performance, RAND/EAC/IET, Santa Barbara.

Haskell, J. and Kersley, B. (1995), 'Skills and Profitability: Evidence from UK Establishments', paper presented to EMRU Labour Economics Conference, Dundee University, Dundee, 3–5 July.

Hawkins, J. and Steedman, H. (1993), 'Mathematics in Vocational Youth Training for the Building Trades in Britain, France and Germany', paper presented to conference, The Skills Gap and Economic Activity, Centre for Economic Policy Research, London.

Heckman, J.J. (1993), *Assessing Clinton's Program on Job Training, Workfare, and Education in the Workplace*, Working Paper Series, No. 4428, National Bureau of Economic Research, Inc., Cambridge, Mass.

Heckman, J.J., Roselius, R.L. and Smith, J.A. (1994), *U.S. Education and Training Policy: A Re-evaluation of the Underlying Assumptions Behind the 'New Consensus'*, Working Paper No. CSPE94–1, Centre For Social Program Evaluation, University of Chicago.

Heinz, W. (1991), 'Youth and Labour Markets: Promises of Comparative Research on Transition Processes', in D.N. Ashton and G.S. Lowe (eds), *Making Their Way: Education, Training and the Labour Market in Canada and Britain*, Milton Keynes, Open University Press.

Higgins, J. (1993), 'Beyond the Ideology of Upskilling: The Theory and Practice of Skill Trends Analysis', University of Otago, New Zealand, D.Phil. Thesis.

Higgins, J. (1994), 'Employment Trends and Training Schemes in a New Zealand Labour Market: Policy or Skills Mismatch?', 16th Conference of the International Working Party on Labour Market Segmentation, Strasbourg, 15–19 July.

Hill, S. (1981), *Competition and Control at Work*, London, Heinemann.

Hirschhorn, L. (1984), *Beyond Mechanisation: Work and Technology in a Post Industrial Age*, Cambridge, Mass., The MIT Press.

Hirst, P. and Thompson, G. (1992), 'The Problem of "Globalization": International Economic Relations, National Economic Management and the Formation of Trading Blocs', *Economy and Society* 21 (4): 357–96.

Hobsbawm, E.J. (1968), *Industry and Empire*, Harmondsworth, Penguin.

Hodgson, G.M. (1988), *Economics and Institutions*, Cambridge, Polity Press.

Hodkinson, P. (1991), 'NCVQ and the 16–19 Curriculum', *British Journal of Education and Work* 4 (3): 25–38.

Hodkinson, P. and Sparkes, A. (1994), 'Training Credits in Action: Action Planning in Training Credits as Innovation: An Ethnography of Stakeholder Interactions', Swindon, Economic and Social Research

Council, June.

Hollway, W. (1991), *Work Psychology and Organisational Behaviour: Managing the Individual at Work*, London, Sage.

Horrell, S., Rubery, J. and Burchell, B. (1990), 'Gender and skills', *Work, Employment and Society* (4): 189–216.

Hotchkiss, L. (1993), 'Effects of Training, Occupation, and Training – Occupation Match On Wage', *Journal of Human Resources* **28** (3): 482–96.

Hounshell, D.A. (1984), *From the American System to Mass Production, 1800–1932*, Baltimore, Johns Hopkins University Press.

Howell, D. and Wolff, E. (1991), 'Trends in the Growth and Distribution of Skill in the U.S. Workplace, 1960–1985', *Industrial and Labor Relations Review* **44** (3): 481–501.

Huam, Chak Khoon and Jewson, N. (1995), *Changing Hearts and Minds: Training Programmes for 'Mid-Career' Workers in Singapore*, Working Paper No. 7, University of Leicester, Centre for Labour Market Studies.

Institute of Technical Education (ITE) (1993), *Annual Report 1992/3*, Singapore, Institute of Technical Education.

International Association for the Evaluation of Educational Achievement (1988), *Science Achievement in Seventeen Countries*, Oxford, Pergamon Press.

IRDAC (1991), *Skills Shortages in Europe*, Brussels, Industrial Research and Development Advisory Committee of the Commission of the European Communities.

Ishikawa, T. (1991), *Vocational Training*, Japanese Industrial Relations Series, Tokyo, The Japan Institute of Labour.

Jessop, R. (1977), 'Recent Theories of the Capitalist State', *Cambridge Journal of Economics* (1): 353–73.

Joffe, A. (1993), 'Human resource development and governance processes for industrial restructuring', mimeo, Industrial Strategy Project.

Johnson, C. (1982), *MITI and the Japanese Miracle: The Growth of Industrial Policy 1925–1975*, Stanford, Ca., Stanford University Press.

Johnston, W.B. and Packer, A.E. (1987), *Workforce 2000: Work and Workers for the 21st Century*, Indianapolis, IN, Hudson Institute.

Jomo, K.S. (1994), *U-turn? Malaysian Economic Development Policies after 1990*, James Cook University of North Queensland.

Jones, R.S., King, R.E. and Klein, M. (1993), 'Economic Integration Between Hong Kong, Taiwan and the Coastal Provinces of China', *OECD Economic Studies* **20** (Spring): 115–44.

Katz, L.F. and Murphy, K.M. (1992), 'Changes in Relative Wages, 1963–1987: Supply and Demand Factors', *The Quarterly Journal of Economics* **107** (February): 35–78.

Katz, E. and Ziderman, A. (1990), 'Investment in General Training: the Role of Information and Labour Mobility', *The Economic Journal* **100** (September): 1147–58.

Keep, E. and Mayhew, K (1995a) 'Training Policy For Competitiveness – Time for a Fresh Perspective?', mimeo, Pembroke College, Oxford.

Keep, E. and Mayhew, K. (1995b), 'UK Training Policy – Assumptions and Reality', in A. Booth and D. Snower (eds), *The Skills Gap and Economic Activity*, Cambridge, Cambridge University Press.

Kelley, M.E. (1989), 'Unionization and Job Design Under Programmable Automation', *Industrial Relations* **28** (Spring): 174–87.

Kelly, M.R. (1989), 'Alternative Forms of Work Organisation under Programmable Automation', in S. Wood (ed.), (1989), *The Transformation of Work?: Skill, Flexibility and the Labour Process*, London, Unwin Hyman.

Kennedy, S., Drago, R. and Sloan, J. (1994), 'The Effect of Trade Unions on the Provision of Training: Australian Evidence', *British Journal of Industrial Relations* **32** (4, December): 565–80.

Kerr, C., Dunlop, J.T., Harbison, F.H. and Myers, C.A. (1962), *Industrialism and Industrial Man: the Problems of Labor and Management in Economic Growth*, London, Heinemann.

Kerr, C., Dunlop, J.T., Harbison, F.H. and Myers, C.A. (1971), 'Postscript to Industrialism and Industrial Man', *International Labour Review* **103**: 519–40.

Knell, J. (1993), 'Transnational Corporations and the Dynamics of Human Capital Formation: Evidence from West Yorkshire', *Human Resource Management Journal* **3** (4): 48–59.

Koike, K., Chan, C.P. and Woon, S.H. (1987 – approximate date), *Report on On-the-Job Training*, Singapore, National Productivity Board.

Koike, K. and Inoki, T. (eds) (1990), *Skill Formation in Japan and Southeast Asia*, Tokyo, University of Tokyo Press.

Kolb, D.A. (1988), 'The Process of Experiential Learning' in D.A. Kolb (ed.), *Experience as a Source of Learning and Development*, London, Prentice Hall International.

Krahn, H. and Lowe, G.S. (1991) 'Transitions to Work: Findings from a Longitudinal Study of High-School and University Graduates in Three Canadian Cities', in D.N. Ashton and G.S. Lowe, *Making their Way: Education, Training and the Labour Market in Canada and Britain*, Open Univeristy Press, Milton Keynes.

Landesmann, M. and Vartiainen, J. (1992), 'Social Corporatism and Long-Term Economic Performance', in J. Pekkarinen et al. (eds), *Social Corporatism: A Superior Economic System?*, Oxford, Clarendon Press.

Lane, C. (1991), 'Industrial Reorganization in Europe: Patterns of

Convergence and Divergence in Germany, France and Britain', *Work, Employment and Society* 5 (4): 515–39.

Lane, C. (1992), 'European Business Systems: Britain and Germany Compared', in R. Whitely (ed.), *European Business Systems: Firms and Markets in their National Context*, London, Sage.

Lash, S. and Urry, J. (1987), *The End of Organized Capitalism*, Oxford, Polity Press.

Laulhe, P. (1990), 'La Formation Continue: un Avantage pour les Promotions et un Accès Privilégié pour les Jeunes et les Techniciens', *Economie et Statistique* (January): 3–8.

Laxer, J. (1989), *Decline of the Super Powers*, Toronto, Lorimer.

Lazonick, W. (1990), *Competitive Advantage on the Shop Floor*, Cambridge, Mass., Harvard University Press.

Lazonick, W. and O'Sullivan, M. (1994), 'Skill Formation in Wealthy Nations: Organisational Evolution and Economic Consequences,' Paper presented to The Colloquium on Skills and Training, Centre for History and Economics, Kings College, Cambridge.

Leborgne, D. and Lipietz, A. (1990), 'How to Avoid a Two-tier Europe', *Labour and Society* (15): 177–200.

Lee, D. (1994), 'Sociological Approaches to Skill and Training: a review and critique,' Paper presented to The Colloquium on Skills and Training, Centre for History and Economics, Kings College, Cambridge.

Lee, D.J. (1968), 'Class Differentials in Educational Opportunity and Promotion from the Ranks', *Sociology* 2 (3): 293–312.

Lee, D.J., Marsden, D., Rickman, P. and Duncombe, J. (1989), *Scheming for Youth: A Study of the YTS in the Enterprise Culture*, Open University Press, Milton Keynes.

Lever-Tracy, C. and Tracy, N. (1992), 'The Dragon and the Rising Sun: Market Integration and Economic Rivalry in East and Southeast Asia' paper presented to the International Working Party on Labour Market Segmentation, Cambridge, UK.

Levine, S.B. and Kawada, H. (1980), 'Industrial Training in Japan: An Overview', in S.B. Levine and H. Kawada (eds), *Human Resources in Japanese Industrial Development*, Princeton, Princeton University Press.

Lillard, L.A. and Tan, H.W. (1986), *Private Sector Training: Who Gets It and What Are Its Effects?*, Santa Monica, The Rand Corporation.

Lipset, S.M. (1986), 'Historical Traditions and National Characteristics: a Comparative Analysis of Canada and the United States', *Canadian Journal of Sociology,* 11 (2): 113–55.

Littler, C.R. (1982), *The Development of the Labour Process in Capitalist Societies*, London, Heinemann.

Locke, R.R. (1984), *The End of the Practical Man: Entrepreneurship and*

*Higher Education in Germany, France and Great Britain, 1880-1940*, Jai Press.

Locke, R.R. (1989), *Management and Higher Education since 1940: The Influence of America and Japan on West Germany, Great Britain and France*, Cambridge, Cambridge University Press.

Low, L. (1993), 'From Entrepot to a Newly Industrialising Economy', in L. Low, T. M.H.Heng, T.W. Wong, T.K. Yam and H. Hughes (eds), *Challenge and Response: Thirty Years of the Economic Development Board*, Singapore, Times Academic Press.

Low, L. (1994), 'Report on the Singaporian Education and Training System', submitted for the Centre for Labour Studies Study of International VET systems, in A. Felstead et al., *International Study of Vocational Education and Training in the Federal Republic of Germany, France, Japan, Singapore and the United States*, Leicester, Centre for Labour Market Studies, University of Leicester.

Lucas, R.E.J. (1988), 'On the Mechanics of Economic Development', *Journal of Monetary Economics* **22**: 3–42.

Lucas, R.E.J. (1990), 'Why Doesn't Capital Flow from Rich to Poor Countries?', *American Economic Review* **80** (2): 92–6.

Lynch, L.M. (1991), 'Private Sector Training and the Mobility of Young Workers in the United States', paper presented to conference, International Conference on the Economics of Training, Cardiff Business School,

Lynch, L.M. (1992), 'Private Sector Training and the Earnings of Young Workers', *American Economic Review* **82** (1): 299–312.

Lynch, L.M. and Black, S.E. (1995), 'Beyond the Incidence of Training: Evidence from a National Employers Survey', *National Bureau of Economic Research*, Working Paper No. 5231.

Macduffie, J. P. and Kochan, T.A. (1995), 'Do U.S. Firms Invest Less in Human Resources? Training in the World Auto Industry', *Industrial Relations* **34** (2): 147–68.

MacEwan, A. (1991), 'Whats "New" About the "New International Economy"?', *Socialist Review* **21** (July–December): 111–31.

Machin, S. (1995), *Changes in the Relative Demand for Skills in the Labour Market*, Discussion Paper No. 221, LSE, Centre for Economic Performance.

Maglen, L.R. (1990), 'Challenging the Human Capital Orthodoxy: The Education–Productivity Link Re-examined', *The Economic Record* **66** (195, December): 281–94.

Maguire, M., Maguire, S. and Ashton, D.N. (1992), 'Education After Basic Schooling', in P. Brown and H. Lauder, (eds), *Education for Economic Survival*, London, Routledge.

Mahnkopf, B. (1992), 'The "Skill-oriented" Strategies of German Trade Unions: Their Impact on Efficiency and Equality Objectives', *British Journal of Industrial Relations* **30** (1): 61–81.

Makepeace, G.H. (1994), 'Lifetime Earnings and the Training Decisions of Young Men in Britain', mimeo, University of Hull.

Marginson, P., Armstrong, P., Edwards, P.K. and Purcell, J. (1995), 'Extending Beyond Borders: Multinational Companies and the International Management of Labour', Washington, DC, paper presented to the International Industrial Relations Association 10th World Congress, 31 May – 4 June.

Marquand, J. (1989), *Autonomy and Change: The Sources of Economic Growth*, London, Harvester Wheatsheaf.

Marsden, D. (1986), *The End of Economic Man? Custom and Competition in Labour Markets*, Brighton, Wheatsheaf.

Marsden, D. (1993), 'Skills and the Single European Market', *Skills Focus* **2** (Summer): 1–3.

Marshall, R. (1990), 'The Impact of Elementary and Secondary Education on State Economic Development', in J. Schmandt and R. Wilson (eds), *Growth Policy in the Age of High Technology*, Boston, Unwin Hyman, 211–53.

Marshall, R. and Tucker, M. (1992), *Thinking for a Living*, New York, Basic Books.

Marswick, V.J. (1987), 'New Paradigms for Learning in the Workplace', in V.J. Marswick (ed.), *Learning in the Workplace*, New York, Croom Helm.

Mason, G. (1993), 'Workforce Skills and Productivity Performance in Western Europe: Recent Matched–Plant Comparisons', paper presented to The International Conference on Human Capital Investments and Economic Performance, Santa Barbara, 17–19 November.

Mason, G. and van Ark, B. (1993), 'Productivity, Machinery and Skills in Engineering: an Anglo-Dutch Comparison', *National Institute of Economic and Social Research Discussion Paper* (New Series 36).

Mason, G., van Ark, B. and Wagner, K. (1994), 'Productivity, Product Quality and Workforce Skills: Food Processing in Four European Countries', *National Institute Economic Review* (February): 62–82.

Maurice, M., Sellier, F. and Silvester, J.J. (1986), *The Social Foundations of Industrial Power*, Cambridge, Mass., MIT Press.

Maynard, R.A. (1994), 'Methods for Evaluating Employment and Training Programs: Lessons from the US Experience', in R. McNabb and K. Whitfield (eds), *The Market for Training*, Aldershot, Avebury.

McCormick, K. (1988). 'Vocationalism and the Japanese Educational System', *Comparative Education*, **24** (1): 37–50.

Mennell, S. (1989), *Norbert Elias: An Introduction*, Oxford, Blackwell.

Middleton, J. (1988), 'Changing Patterns in World Bank Investments in Vocational Education and Training: Implications for Secondary Vocational Schools', *International Journal of Educational Development* **8** (3): 213–25.

Middleton, J., Ziderman, A. and van Adams, A. (1993), *Skills for Productivity. Vocational Education and Training in Developing Countries*, New York, Oxford University Press for the World Bank.

Mills, C. W. (1956), *The Power Elite*, New York, Galaxy.

Mincer, J. (1974), *Schooling, Experience and Earnings*, New York, NBER.

Ministry of Trade and Industry (1991), 'The Strategic Economic Plan: Towards a Developed Nation, Singapore: The Economic Planning Committee.

Mishel, L. and Bernstein, J. (1992), *The State of Working America*, Washington, DC, Economic Policy Institute.

Mishel, L. and Teixeira, R.A. (1991), *The Myth of the Coming Labor Shortage: Jobs, Skills and Incomes of America's Workforce 2000*, Washington, DC, Economic Policy Institute.

Mishel, L. and Voos, P.B. (eds) (1992), *Unions and Economic Competitiveness*, Armonk, New York, M.E. Sharpe, Inc.

Mitter, S. (1986), *Common Fate, Common Bond: Women in the Global Economy*, London, Pluto Press.

Mohun, S. (1979), 'Ideology, Knowledge and Neoclassical Economics: Some Elements of a Marxist Account', in F. Green and P. Nore (eds), *Issues in Political Economy*, London, Macmillan, 231–72.

Muller, W. (1993), 'Does Education Matter? – Evidence from cross-national comparisons?' mimeo, University of Mannheim.

Myles, J. (1988), 'The Expanding Middle: Some Canadian Evidence on the Deskilling Debate', *Canadian Review of Sociology and Anthropology* **25** (3, August): 335–64.

National Productivity Board (NPB) (1992), *Productivity Digest*, Singapore, NPB.

National Productivity Board (NPB) (1993), *Productivity Statement*, Singapore, NPB.

Nelson, R.R. and Wright, G. (1992), 'The Rise and Fall of American Technological Leadership: The Postwar Era in Historical Perspective', *Journal of Economic Literature* **XXX** (December): 1931–64.

Neumann, S. and Ziderman, A. (1986), 'Testing the Dual Labor Market Hypothesis: Evidence from the Israel Labor Mobility Survey', *Journal of Human Resources* (Spring).

Noble, D. (1977), *America by Design: Science, Technology, and the Rise of Corporate Capitalism*, Oxford, Oxford University Press.

Nohara, H. (1987), 'Technological Innovation, Industrial Dynamics and the Transformation of Work: the Case of the Japanese Machine-Tool Industry', cited in U. Jurgens, 'The Transference of Japanese Concepts in the International Automobile Industry', in S. Wood (ed.) (1989), *The Transformation of Work?: Skill, Flexibility and the Labour Process*, London, Unwin Hyman.

Nolan, P.J. (1989), 'The Productivity Miracle?', in F. Green (ed.), *The Restructuring of the UK Economy*, Hemel Hempstead, Harvester Wheatsheaf.

Odagiri, H. and Akira, G. (1993), 'The Japanese System of Innovation: Past, Present and Future', in R.R. Nelson (ed.), *National Systems of Innovation*, Oxford, Oxford University Press.

OECD (1985), *Education and Training after Basic Schooling*, Paris, OECD.

OECD (1989), *Education and the Economy in a Changing Society*, Paris, OECD.

OECD (1991a), *Employment Outlook*, Paris, OECD.

OECD (1991b), 'Further Education and Training of the Labour Force. A Comparative Analysis of National Strategies for Industry Training: Australia, Sweden and the United States', mimeo, Organisation for Economic Cooperation and Development.

OECD (1993), *Employment Outlook*, Paris, OECD.

OECD (1994), *Employment Outlook*, Paris, OECD.

Oliver, J.M. and Turton, J.R. (1982), 'Is There a Shortage of Skilled Labour?', *British Journal of Industrial Relations* (20): 195–200.

O'Mahoney, M. (1992), 'Productivity Levels in British and German Manufacturing Industry', *National Institute Economic Review* **139**: 46–63.

Osterman, P. (1995), 'Skill, Training, and Work Organization in American Establishments', *Industrial Relations* **34** (2): 125–46.

Payne, J. (1991), *Women Training and Skills Shortage: The Case for Public Investment*, London, Policy Studies Institute.

Pencavel, J. (1991), 'Higher Education, Productivity, and Earnings: A Review', *Journal of Economic Education* **22** (4, Fall): 331–59.

Penn, R. (1994), 'Technical Change and Skilled Manual Work in Contemporary Rochdale', in R. Penn, M. Rose and J. Rubery (eds), *Skill and Occupational Change*, Oxford, Oxford University Press.

Pohjola, M. (1992), 'Corporatism and Wage Bargaining', in J. Pekkarinen, M. Pohjola and R. Rowthorn (eds), *Social Corporation: A Superior Economic System?*, Oxford, Clarendon Press.

Pollard, S. (1965), *The Genesis of Modern Management*, London, Edward

Arnold.

Prais, S.J. (1987), 'Education for Productivity: Comparisons of Japanese and English Schooling and Vocational Preparation', *National Institute Economic Review* (February): 40–56.

Prais, S.J. (1993), 'Economic Performance and Education: The Nature of Britain's Deficiencies', paper presented to conference, Proceedings of the British Academy.

Prais, S.J., Jarvis, V. and Wagner, K. (1989), 'Productivity and Vocational Skills in Services in Britain and Germany: Hotels', *National Institute Economic Review* (November).

Psacharopoulos, G. (1983), 'The Contribution of Education to Economic Growth: International Comparisons', in J. Kendrick (ed.), *International Productivity Comparisons*, Washington, DC, American Enterprise Institute.

Raffe, D. (1992a), 'The Changing Scottish Scene: Implications for South of the Border', mimeo, Centre for Educational Sociology, University of Edinburgh.

Raffe, D. (1992b), 'Participation of 16–18 Year Olds in Education and Training', National Commission on Education, Briefing Paper No. 3.

Rainbird, H. (1990), *Training Matters. Trade Union Perspectives on Industrial Restructuring and Training*, Oxford, Basil Blackwell.

Rainbird, H. (1994a), 'The European Dimension on Training', in M. Gold (ed.), *Europe: The Social Dimension*, London, Macmillan.

Rainbird, H. (1994b), 'Comparative Perspectives on Training: Britain, France and Germany', in M. Gold (ed.), *Europe: The Social Dimension*, London, Macmillan.

Ray, G.F. (1990), 'International Labour Costs in Manufacturing, 1960–88', *National Institute Economic Review* (132): 67–70.

Redding, A.G. and Richardson, S. (1986), 'Participative Management and its Varying Relevance in Hong Kong and Singapore', *Asia Pacific Journal of Management* **3** (2): 76–98.

Reich, R.B. (1988), *Education and the Next Economy*, Washington, DC, National Education Association.

Report of the Schools Inquiry Commission (1868) i, 20, London.

Robinson, P. (1995), '*The British Disease Overcome? Living Standards, Productivity and Education Attainment, 1979–94*', LSE, Centre for Economic Performance, Discussion Paper No. 260.

Robitaille, D.F. and Garde, R.A. (eds) (1989), *The IEA Study of Mathematics II: Contexts and Outcomes of School Mathematics*, Oxford, Pergamon Press.

Romer, P.M. (1990a), 'Are Nonconvexities Important for Understanding Growth?', *American Economic Review* **80** (2): 97–103.

Romer, P.M. (1990b), 'Endogenous Technological Change', *Journal of Political Economy* **98** (5, pt 2): S71–S102.

Rosenberg, S. (1989), 'The Restructuring of the Labor Market, the Labor Force, and the Nature of Employment Relations in the United States in the 1980s', in S. Rosenberg (ed.), *The State and the Labor Market*, New York, Plenum Press.

Rosenfeld, S.A. and Atkinson, R.D. (1990), 'Engineering Regional Growth', in J. Schmandt and R. Wilson (eds), *Growth Policy in the Age of High Technology*, Boston, Unwin Hyman.

Rubery, J. (1994), 'Gender and Skills', in R. Penn, M. Rose and J. Rubery (eds), *Skill and Occupational Change*, Oxford, Oxford University Press.

Ryan, P.(ed.) (1991), *International Comparisons of Vocational Education and Training for Intermediate Skills*, London, Falmer Press.

Ryan, P. (1993a), 'Information Costs, Training Quality and Trainee Exploitation', mimeo, Cambridge University.

Ryan, P. (1993b), 'The Institutional Setting of Investment in Human Resources in the UK: in Search of Mass Industrial Education', paper presented to conference, Human Capital Investments and Economic Performance, RAND/EAC/IET, Santa Barbara.

Ryoshin, M. (1986), *The Economic Development of Japan: A Quantitative Study*, London, Macmillan.

Saint-Paul, G. (1994), *Unemployment and Increasing Returns to Human Capital*, Discussion Paper No. 921, Centre for Policy Research.

Samuels, A. (1995) 'The Birth and Evolution of the Training System on Cyprus: in the Service of Growth', paper presented to the Second Annual CLMS Conference, University of Leicester, September.

Sanderson, M. (1994), *The Missing Stratum: Technical School Education in England*, London, Athlone.

Scase, R. and Goffee, R. (1989), *Reluctant Managers: Their Work and Lifestyle*, London, Unwin Hyman.

Schoenberger, E. (1989), 'Multinational Corporations and the New International Division of Labour: a Critical Appraisal', in S. Wood (ed.), *The Transformation Of Work?*, London, Unwin Hyman.

Schoppa, L.J. (1990), 'Education Reform in Great Britain and Japan: Contrasting Policies and Processes', paper presented to conference, US and UK Education and Training Policy in Comparative Perspective, Warwick University.

SDF (1992), *The Skills Development Fund Annual Report*, 1991/2, S. 126 of 1992, 11 November, Singapore.

Selvaratnam, V. (1989), 'Vocational Education and Training: Singapore and Other Third World Initiatives', *Singapore Journal of Education* **10** (2): 11–23.

Senker, P. (1992), *Industrial Training in a Cold Climate: An Assessment of Britain's Training Policies*, Aldershot, Avebury Gower.

Sentier, P. (1995), 'Training Levies in Four Countries: Implications for British Industrial Training Policy', Watford, Entra Publications.

Setterfield, M. (1993), 'Change or Permanence? Growth and Development in Capitalist Economies', *Review of Income and Wealth* 39 (2): 217–23.

Sheldrake, J. and Vickerstaff, S. (1987), *The History of Industrial Training in Britain*, Aldershot, Avebury Gower.

Singh, A. (1994), 'Global Economic Changes, Skills and International Competitiveness', *International Labour Review* 133 (2): 167–83.

Skott, P. and Auerbach, P. (1993), *Cumulative Causation and the 'New' Theories of Economic Growth*, Institute of Economics, University of Aarhus, Denmark.

Smith, A. (1888), *An Inquiry into the Nature and Causes of the Wealth of Nations*, London, Longman & Co.

Smith, A. (1976), *An Inquiry into the Nature and Causes of the Wealth of Nations*, Oxford, Clarendon Press.

Smith, A.J. and Piper, J.A. (1990), 'The Tailor-made Training Maze: A Practitioner's Guide to Evaluation', *Journal of European Industrial Training* 14 (8).

Smithers, A. (1993), *Dispatches: All Our Futures: Britain's Education Revolution*, London, Channel 4 Television.

Snell, K.D.M. (1994), 'The Apprenticeship System in British History: a Framework for Analysis', paper presented at Skills and Training: A Colloquium in History and Economics, Centre for History and Economics, Kings College, Cambridge.

Soete, L. and Verspagen, B. (1993), 'Technology and Growth: The Complex Dynamics of Catching Up, Falling Behind and Taking Over', in A. Szirmai, B.V.Ark and D. Pilat (eds), *Explaining Economic Growth*, Amsterdam, North-Holland, 214, ed. 101–27.

Solow, R.M. (1956), 'A Contribution to the Theory of Economic Growth', *Quarterly Journal of Economics* LXX (February): 65–94.

Sorge, A. and Streeck, W. (1988), 'Industrial Relations and Technical Change: the Case for an Extended Perspective', in R. Hyman and W. Streeck (eds), *New Technology and Industrial Relations*, Oxford, Blackwell.

Soskice, D. (1993), 'Social Skills from Mass Higher Education: Rethinking the Company-based Initial Training Paradigm', *Oxford Review of Economic Policy* 9 (3, Autumn): 101–13.

Soskice, D. (1994), 'Reconciling Markets and Institutions: The German Apprenticeship System', in L.M. Lynch (ed.), *Training and the Private Sector: International Comparisons*, Chicago, University of Chicago

Press.

Steedman, H. and Wagner, K. (1987), 'A Second Look at Productivity, Machinery and Skills in Britain and Germany', *National Institute Economic Review* **122** (May): 84–95.

Steedman, H. and Wagner, K. (1989), 'Productivity, Machinery and Skills: Clothing Manufacturing in Britain and Germany', *National Institute Economic Review* **128** (May): 40–57.

Stevens, M. (1993), 'Transferable Training and Market Failure', paper presented to conference, The Skills Gap and Economic Activity, Centre For Economic Policy Research, London.

Stevens, M. (1994), 'A Theoretical Model of On-the-job Training with Imperfect Competition', *Oxford Economic Papers* **46** (4): 537–62.

Streeck, W. (1989), 'Skills and the Limits of Neoliberalism: the Enterprise of the Future as a Place of Learning', *Work, Employment and Society* **3** (1): 89–104.

Streeck, W. (1991), 'On the Institutional Conditions of Diversified Quality Production', in E. Matzner and W. Streeck (eds), *Beyond Keynesianism. The Socio-Economics of Production and Full Employment*, Cheltenham, Edward Elgar.

Swaim, P. (1993), 'Are American Workers Undertrained?', paper presented to conference, Annual Meeting of the Eastern Economic Association, Washington, DC.

Tan, H.W. and Peterson, C. (1992), 'Post-School Training of British and American Youth', *Oxford Studies in Comparative Education* **2** (2): 83–106.

Tansey, P. (1990), 'Graduating to Jobs Abroad: The Economic Cost of Rising Graduate Emigration', *Labour Market Review*, (1, June), FAS: The Irish Training and Employment Authority.

Teixeira, R.A. and Greenberg, E.J. (1993), 'Once Again on the Skills Mismatch Question', paper presented to conference, Annual Meeting of the Eastern Economic Association, Washington, DC.

Thurow, L. (1993), *Head To Head*, London, Nicholas Brealey.

Townley, B. (1991), 'Selection and Appraisal: Reconstituting "Social Relations"', in J. Storey (ed.), *New Perspectives on Human Resource Management*, London, Routledge.

Turner, H.A. (1962), *Trade Union Growth, Structure and Policy: A Comparative Study of the Cotton Unions*, London, George Allen & Unwin.

Tylecote, A. (1992), 'Core-Periphery Inequalities in European Integration, East and West', in W. Blaas and J. Foster (eds), *Mixed Economies in Europe*, Cheltenham, Edward Elgar, 237–71.

UNESCO (1993a), *World Education Report 1993*, Paris, UNESCO.

UNESCO (1993b), *Statistical Yearbook 1993*, Paris, UNESCO.

US General Accounting Office (1990), *Training Strategies: Preparing Noncollege Youth for Employment in the U.S. and Foreign Countries*, May, USGPO, Washington DC.

van Ark, B. (1990a), 'Comparative Levels of Labour Productivity in Dutch and British Manufacturing', *National Institute Economic Review* (131): 71–85.

van Ark, B. (1990b), 'Manufacturing Productivity Levels in France and the United Kingdom', *National Institute Economic Review* (133): 62–77.

Verdier, E. (1994), 'Training and Enterprise in France', in R. McNabb and K. Whitfield (eds), *The Market for Training*, Aldershot, Avebury.

Weale, M. (1993), 'A Critical Evaluation of Rate of Return Analysis', *The Economic Journal* **103** (May): 729–37.

Weber, M. (1947), *The Theory of Social and Economic Organisation*, Translated by A.M. Henderson and Talcott Parsons, London, Collier-Macmillan.

Whitley, R. (1992a), 'Societies, Firms and Markets: The Social Structuring of Business Systems', in R. Whitley (ed.), *European Business Systems: Firms and Markets in their National Context*, London, Sage.

Whitley, R. (ed.) (1992b), *Business Systems in East Asia: Firms, Markets and Societies*, London, Sage.

Wilkinson, F. (1983), 'Productive Systems', *Cambridge Journal of Economics* **7** (September–December), 413–29.

Willis, P. (1977), *Learning To Labour*, Farnborough, Saxon House.

Willis, R.J. (1986), 'Wage Determinants: a Survey and Reinterpretation of Human Capital Earnings Functions', in O. Ashenfelter and R. Layard (eds), *Handbook of Labor Economics*, Amsterdam, North-Holland, 525–602.

Wolff, E.N. (1993), 'Human Capital Investment and Economic Growth: Macro-Economic Perspectives and Evidence for Industrialized Countries', paper presented to conference, Human Capital Investments and Economic Performance, Santa Barbara.

Wolff, E.N. and Gittleman, M. (1993), 'The Role of Education in Productivity Convergence: Does Higher Education Matter?', in A. Szirmai, B.V. Ark and D. Pilat (eds.), *Explaining Economic Growth*, Amsterdam,North-Holland, 214, ed. 147–67.

Womack, J.P., Jones, D.T. and Roos, D. (1986), *Human Resource Practices for Implementing Advanced Manufacturing Technology*, Washington, DC, National Academy Press.

Womack, J.P., Jones, D.T. and Roos, D. (1990), *The Machine that Changed the World*, New York, Rawson Associates.

Wong, S.T. (1993), 'Education and Human Resource Development', in L.

Low, T.M.H. Heng, T.W. Wong, T.K. Yam and H. Hughes (eds), *Challenge and Response: Thirty Years of the Economic Development Board*, Singapore, Times Academic Press.

Wood, A. (1994), '*North-South Trade, Employment and Inequality*', Oxford, Clarendon Press.

Wood, S. (ed.) (1983), *The Degradation of Labour?*, London, Hutchinson.

Wood, S., (ed.) (1989), *The Transformation of Work?: Skill, Flexibility and the Labour Process*, London, Unwin Hyman.

World Bank (1991), *World Development Report 1991*, Oxford, Oxford University Press.

World Bank (1993), *The East Asian Miracle: Economic Growth and Public Policy*, Oxford, Oxford University Press.

World Bank (1995), *World Development Report 1995: Workers in an Integrating World*, New York, Oxford University Press.

Wright, G. (1990), 'The Origins of American Industrial Succcess 1879–1940', *American Economic Review* **80** (4): 651–68.

Yip, S.K.J. and Sim, W.K. (1994), 'Evolution of Educational Excellence: 25 Years of Education in the Republic of Singapore, Singapore, Longman Singapore Press.

Yun, Huing Ai (1995), 'Automation and New Work Patterns: Cases from Singapore's Electronics Industry', *Work, Employment and Society* **9** (2): 309–27.

Zweimuller, J. and Winter-Ebmer, R. (1991), *Manpower Training Programs and Employment Stability*, Arbeitspaper No. 9105, University of Linz.

# Name index

# Subject index